Palgrave Studies in European Union Politics

Series Editors
Michelle Egan, American University, Washington, DC, USA
Neill Nugent, Manchester Metropolitan University, Manchester, UK
William E. Paterson, Aston University, Birmingham, UK

Following on the sustained success of the acclaimed European Union Series, which essentially publishes research-based textbooks, Palgrave Studies in European Union Politics publishes cutting edge research-driven monographs. The remit of the series is broadly defined, both in terms of subject and academic discipline. All topics of significance concerning the nature and operation of the European Union potentially fall within the scope of the series. The series is multidisciplinary to reflect the growing importance of the EU as a political, economic and social phenomenon. To submit a proposal, please contact Senior Editor Ambra Finotello ambra.finotello@palgrave.com. This series is indexed by Scopus.

Editorial Board

Laurie Buonanno (SUNY Buffalo State, USA)
Kenneth Dyson (Cardiff University, UK)
Brigid Laffan (European University Institute, Italy)
Claudio Radaelli (University College London, UK)
Mark Rhinard (Stockholm University, Sweden)
Ariadna Ripoll Servent (University of Bamberg, Germany)
Frank Schimmelfennig (ETH Zurich, Switzerland)
Claudia Sternberg (University College London, UK)
Nathalie Tocci (Istituto Affari Internazionali, Italy)

Frank Wendler

Framing Climate Change in the EU and US After the Paris Agreement

palgrave macmillan

Frank Wendler
University of Hamburg
Hamburg, Germany

ISSN 2662-5873   ISSN 2662-5881 (electronic)
Palgrave Studies in European Union Politics
ISBN 978-3-031-04058-0   ISBN 978-3-031-04059-7 (eBook)
https://doi.org/10.1007/978-3-031-04059-7

© The Editor(s) (if applicable) and The Author(s), under exclusive license to Springer Nature Switzerland AG 2022
This work is subject to copyright. All rights are solely and exclusively licensed by the Publisher, whether the whole or part of the material is concerned, specifically the rights of translation, reprinting, reuse of illustrations, recitation, broadcasting, reproduction on microfilms or in any other physical way, and transmission or information storage and retrieval, electronic adaptation, computer software, or by similar or dissimilar methodology now known or hereafter developed.
The use of general descriptive names, registered names, trademarks, service marks, etc. in this publication does not imply, even in the absence of a specific statement, that such names are exempt from the relevant protective laws and regulations and therefore free for general use.
The publisher, the authors, and the editors are safe to assume that the advice and information in this book are believed to be true and accurate at the date of publication. Neither the publisher nor the authors or the editors give a warranty, expressed or implied, with respect to the material contained herein or for any errors or omissions that may have been made. The publisher remains neutral with regard to jurisdictional claims in published maps and institutional affiliations.

Cover illustration: Magic Lens/Shutterstock

This Palgrave Macmillan imprint is published by the registered company Springer Nature Switzerland AG
The registered company address is: Gewerbestrasse 11, 6330 Cham, Switzerland

Acknowledgments

Research for this book was funded by an individual, 36-month research grant by the German Science Foundation (DFG) with the title: "How Ideas Frame the Politics of Climate Change" (project number: WE 5071/4-1). This support is gratefully acknowledged.

Praise for *Framing Climate Change in the EU and US After the Paris Agreement*

"This comparative analysis of contemporary climate change discourse in the EU and the US impresses through its sound theoretical grounding and systematic empirical investigation. It makes an outstanding contribution to understanding the critical role of ideas and their framing in climate politics. It also provides new insights into the deep-rooted transatlantic differences in this policy field. Recommended reading!"
—Sebastian Oberthür, *Vrije Universiteit Brussel and University of Eastern Finland, Finland*

"This book provides the first comprehensive comparison of climate action in the EU and the US after the Paris Agreement. Contrasting policy development in both cases, it shows the power of ideas in explaining different approaches to tackling climate change. While recognizing the role of institutions and actor interest, Frank Wendler offers a solid empirical study of how discourse employed by key actors within both systems shapes their climate politics. Recommended reading!"
—Jon Birger Skjærseth, *the Fridtjof Nansens Institute, Norway*

"This book makes a novel contribution to our understanding of different discourses in climate change policy-making on the EU level and in the US. It offers a nuanced analysis. The book makes an important and very timely contribution to the literature. It breaks new ground and provides a comprehensive assessment of core ideas and discourses which shape EU and American climate policy-making."

—Rüdiger Wurzel, *University of Hull, UK*

Contents

1 Introduction: How Ideas and Discourse Frame the Politics of Climate Change — 1

2 Theoretical Framework: Framing, Issue Dimensions and Political Space — 35

3 Climate Change Policy in the EU: From the Paris Agreement to the European Green Deal — 65

4 US Climate Politics Since the Paris Agreement — 119

5 Comparative Analysis: Framing Climate Change Discourse in the EU and the US — 187

6 Conclusion: Framing Climate Change in the EU and US After the Paris Agreement — 217

Annex: List of Documents Coded for the Empirical Analysis — 233

Index — 251

About the Author

Frank Wendler is Senior Faculty Member (*Privatdozent*) at the Department of Social Sciences and Lead Researcher for the project 'How Ideas Frame the Politics of Climate Change', funded by the German Science Foundation (DFG) and based at the Center for Sustainable Society (CSS) of the University of Hamburg, Germany.

List of Figures

Fig. 5.1	Paradigmatic salience of frames in climate policy discourse of the EU	202
Fig. 5.2	Paradigmatic salience of frames in climate policy discourse of the US	203
Fig. 5.3	Variation of the similarity indicator of keyword rank orders as an indicator for political contestation of climate policy discourse in the EU	210
Fig. 5.4	Variation of the similarity indicator of keyword rank orders as an indicator for political contestation of climate policy discourse in the US	211
Graph 1.1	Survey of countries concerning their vulnerability towards and readiness to deal with climate change, based on the Global Adaptation Index and data set established by the University of Notre Dame, Indiana (ND-Gain)	14
Graph 3.1	Structure of climate change frames in EU policy discourse (EP Pty Grps = European Parliament Party Groups)	96
Graph 3.2	Code map of frames in EU Council conclusions on climate change	100
Graph 3.3	Code map for EU Commission policy documents on climate change	101
Graph 3.4	Code map for EP plenary resolutions on climate change	102
Graph 3.5	Code map for EP party group motions for an EP resolution on the European Green Deal	104
Graph 4.1	Structure of frames in US climate policy discourse	163

Graph 4.2	Code map for climate change discourse by the Obama administration	168
Graph 4.3	Code map for discourse on climate change in speeches by President Obama	169
Graph 4.4	Code map for legislative proposals on climate change sponsored by Democrats	170
Graph 4.5	Code map of policy discourse on climate and energy policy by the Trump administration	171
Graph 4.6	Code map of legislative proposals on climate and energy policy sponsored by Republicans	173

LIST OF TABLES

Table 1.1	Overview of criteria for the evaluation of climate policy development in the EU and US since the adoption of the Paris Agreement (explanation of abbreviations used: GHG = greenhouse gases, NDC = Nationally Determined Contributions as required from signatories of the Paris Agreement)	10
Table 2.1	Typology of six approaches to framing climate change (CC) and climate change policy (CCP)	47
Table 2.2	Survey of analytical dimensions and comparative hypotheses	51
Table 2.3	Survey of comparative hypotheses on framing of climate change in the EU and US	53
Table 3.1	Overview of European Council conclusions on climate change; abbreviations in order of appearance: PL = Poland; COP = Conference of the Parties; NDC = Nationally Determined Contributions	75
Table 3.2	Rank order of frames in policy documents of the three main EU institutions	98
Table 3.3	Framing of motions for the EP resolution on the European Green Deal by EP party groups	105
Table 4.1	Rank orders and cumulative percentage of frames in US policy discourse on climate change	164
Table 5.1	Rank order of frames with cumulative percentages in EU policy discourse on climate change	191

Table 5.2	Rank order of frames with cumulative percentages in US policy discourse on climate change	192
Table 5.3	Issue categories in climate policy discourse in the EU	193
Table 5.4	Issue categories in climate policy discourse of the US	193
Table 5.5	Composition, scope and density of linkages between frames in policy discourse of the EU	196
Table 5.6	Composition, scope and density of linkages between frames in policy discourse of the US	196
Table 5.7	Keyword rankings for six climate frames in EU policy discourse; keywords were partly abbreviated for reasons of space; full list of keywords can be found in the annex	205
Table 5.8	Keyword rankings for six climate frames in US policy discourse; keywords were partly abbreviated for reasons of space; full list of keywords can be found in the annex	207
Table 5.9	Similarity of keyword rank orders in policy discourse of the EU	209
Table 5.10	Similarity of keyword rank orders in policy discourse of the US	209

CHAPTER 1

Introduction: How Ideas and Discourse Frame the Politics of Climate Change

This book approaches climate change as a problem of collective action whose solution depends to a significant degree on policy beliefs and their underlying ideas. We posit that ideas become critical for framing the political space of climate governance as they are adopted by political agents to provide justificatory reasons for policy-making through political discourse. Taking this approach does not mean to question that climate change exists as a material fact created by changes in atmospheric and natural cycles that will result in massive impacts on ecosystems and society (Haines and Frumkin 2021; Romm 2018; Schellnhuber 2015; Rosenzweig et al. 2017). It also does not deny that dealing with a changing climate will require substantial material efforts from society involving the use of considerable economic, technological and financial resources, both in terms of the mitigation of and adaptation to climate change and including loss and damage (Keskitalo et al. 2019; Mechler et al. 2018; Bäckstrand and Lövbrand 2015; Dryzek et al. 2011). Focusing on ideas about climate policy, however, follows the assumption that a major challenge of dealing with global warming is political and more specifically, discursive: namely, to establish a justification for collective action that adopts a commonly accepted definition of climate change and proposes mutually acceptable principles, approaches and timelines of action to mitigate its causes and effects in a sufficiently specified political and institutional framework. In this context, three main reasons can be given for why climate change is a field of policy-making where ideas and discourse can be assumed to matter substantially, and probably more than in other fields of environmental or economic policy-making.

First, when raising global warming as a problem for society, a major challenge for political agents is the fact that it cannot be identified as a visible, evident, or easily quantifiable material phenomenon such as pollution levels or species depletion. Instead, it is a problem that is identified and evaluated through ideational concepts and perspectives. This is rooted in the fact that the very concept of climate is an abstraction from specific everyday experience to longer-term observation whose evaluation varies with regard to its temporal (i.e., shorter- or longer-term) and spatial (i.e., local, regional or global) framework of reference. Addressing climate change as a problem in political discourse, moreover, has to engage with the fact that it proceeds through largely intangible atmospheric processes and is evaluated with regard to effects on ecosystems and human society that are probable or likely, but also uncertain with regard to their specific manifestation in terms of time, space and scope. Therefore, climate change is inevitably an ideational concept by involving a generalization from single events to systemic processes and cause–effect relationships with slow, diffuse and uncertain effects. Even recent advances in climate attribution scholarship remain hesitant to directly relate specific events such as extreme weather to climate change beyond the discussion of probabilities (Otto 2020; Stott et al. 2016; NASEM 2016). As a consequence, climate change evokes a variety of different futures for society when raised as a problem in political discourse, based on different perceptions and values as well as their contestation.

Second, concerning the development of policy, possible solutions to the climate crisis are neither evident nor reducible to technical fixes. Instead, recognizing the reality of a changing climate prompts a range of questions about what normative principles should be applied to devise approaches and instruments to either mitigate or adapt to global warming. Against this background, climate change has been described as a 'wicked' or 'diabolical' problem involving multiple intractable ethical and moral dilemmas (Incoprera 2016; Jamieson 2014; 2012; Sun and Yang 2016; Dryzek et al. 2013; Levin et al. 2012; Steffen 2011). This implies that global warming emerges as a challenge for society that defies unequivocal, purely efficiency-based solutions and involves deeply political questions about trade-offs between competing normative goals of society. The scope and structure of ensuing controversy can be seen to depend in large part on what aspect of society is brought in relation with impacts of global warming. Normative dilemmas arising from climate change as a source of conflict for political decision-making emerge most drastically from questions of climate equity and justice, both between generations and social groups but also on a global scale between industrialized countries and those most vulnerable to global warming (Okereke 2011, 2018; Okereke/Coventry 2016). In this vein, climate change has been considered as a transformative challenge arising from the failure of a capitalist model of growth (Klein 2014) and as sign of a transition to the Anthropocene as a new stage in Earth history resulting from the exploitation of fossil fuels (Pickering and Dryzek 2019; Latour 2018). Approached in this way, climate change has the potential to raise questions about fundamental ethical values of society including attitudes towards growth, consumption and individual lifestyles in political debate. In this context, only passing mention can be made of scholarly accounts covering epistemic, ethical and cultural perspectives on climate change (Leichenko and O'Brien 2019; Hulme 2009; Dryzek et al. 2011; Breakey et al. 2015; O'Brien et al. 2010).

Finally, a major question to be addressed at the level of ideas and discourse by policy-makers is how to define the political and institutional framework for action against climate change. At a programmatic level, this involves the question whether climate action is conceptualized just as a subset of environmental policy, or whether it must be addressed in a broader framework that includes energy and economic policy, social, employment and agricultural policies or fields of external action such as trade, foreign and security or migration policy. In its broadest definition, action against climate change is defined as a challenge involving the entity of all departments of government as a cross-cutting question, requiring leadership at the highest executive level and an adjustment of virtually every field of policy-making. Beyond this task of defining the horizontal cooperation of various departments within a given political system, a related question is how to identify and relate levels of action within a vertical dimension, reaching from the local to the national, regional and global levels. Concepts of action against climate change envisaged through political ideas and discourse vary widely in this regard—from suggestions for changes in individual behavior at the local level to debates about global governance. This aspect is further emphasized through the fact that the architecture of global climate governance after the Paris Agreement is a complex combination of legally binding rules and provisions of 'soft law', based on a polycentric dispersion of authority, and still in a process of evolution (Gupta 2014; Popovski 2019; Oberthür 2016). An essential question in this context is whether climate change is a challenge that re-defines the boundaries and sovereignty of the nation-state as the central framework of democratic legitimacy and representation (Dryzek et al. 2019). Combining these three points, ideas and their promotion through discourse matter for action against climate change in relation to three questions: namely, why it is a problem, what policy change it requires and what political framework is suitable to take collective action. This point is brilliantly reflected in an introductory chapter of a widely recognized handbook of global climate and environment policy (Falkner 2013):

> Even scientific consensus cannot tell us what kind of a problem climate change is: scientific understanding translates uneasily into policy-making at the global or indeed other levels because it does not make political, economic, technological, and social definitions of the problem obvious (…). In fact, scientific uncertainties … pale in comparison to the obstacles and uncertainties that come with understanding what kind of problem climate is from a social-economic-political perspective. (Hoffmann 2013: 6)

How does political discourse and controversy that arises from the advocacy of competing ideas about climate change affect policy-making in empirical cases? This question invokes a research agenda exploring the political space of climate governance: namely, the thematic scope and institutional venues of policy debates, prevalent issue dimensions as well as ideological foundations of positions, and forms of resulting contestation between political agents. This book seeks to advance research in this field by comparing two political systems with far-reaching institutional and economic similarities but diverging forms of discourse and policy on climate change: namely, the European Union (EU) and United States (US), focusing on how political discourse affects their respective policy-making on climate change since the conclusion of the Paris Agreement (COP21) in December 2015.

While this volume cannot present a comprehensive theoretical explanation of policy developments in these two cases, it presents the first detailed comparative survey of climate change discourse and contestation in the EU and US. More specifically, it provides insights about how the political space of climate politics in both cases, as derived from the salience structure, linkages and contestation of frames used to advocate positions towards climate change, can be linked to the divergence of their policy development. Its foundation is a typology of discursive frames derived from the distinction of three levels of controversy about climate change discussed above: its definition as a problem for society, the evaluation of policies and controversy on levels and forms of collective action. From this point of departure, the study compares the evolution of policy discourse leading up to and resulting from the European Green Deal in the EU case with the more fragmented and polarized debate on carbon pricing, the energy transition and the Green New Deal agenda in the US case. This comparison will demonstrate that policy debates in both cases are not distinguished adequately through a simplistic dichotomy between positions associated with environmentalism and climate denial; it also questions that the US case differs from its EU counterpart simply through more intense polarization between two ideologically coherent camps of advocates and opponents of climate action. Instead, the present study demonstrates that in a highly dynamic policy debate about appropriate political responses to the climate crisis, the volatility and fragmentation of discursive justifications for climate policy are key to understanding the divergence of both systems in terms of their policy-making output.

The subsequent sections go on to explain the approach and rationale of this study by reviewing the state of research and discussing a range of approaches that can be used to explain policy divergence, including material, institutional and ideational factors. The concluding section of this chapter once more specifies the main question of this study and provides an overview of the structure of this book.

1.1 Rationales for Comparing the EU and US in Climate Change Policy

Comparing the European Union and United States as actors of global climate governance is compelling for two main reasons. First, in terms of their political and economic clout, both jurisdictions represent the most significant part of the economically developed world, covering 12.6 (US) and 7.3 (EU) percent of global greenhouse gas (GHG) emissions according to current figures compiled by the Emissions Database for

Global Atmospheric Research of the EU Joint Research Center (Crippa et al. 2021). While the involvement of both is considered politically critical, the EU and US have taken different positions towards the establishment of a global climate regime during its first phase under the 1997 Kyoto Protocol; the latter was agreed by the Clinton administration but never submitted to ratification and rejected by the subsequent Bush administration. Both jurisdictions became members of a comprehensive global agreement on climate change only with the conclusion of the Paris Accord in December 2015. After the expression of intent by President Trump to withdraw the US from the agreement in June 2017, and the proclamation of a European Green Deal by the new EU Commission President von der Leyen to achieve carbon neutrality until 2050 in December 2019, the position of 'the rich world' towards climate change continues to be characterized by the sharp contrast between European and US positions. Evaluating and explaining the positions of both jurisdictions therefore seems of utmost importance to predict future developments of global climate policy agreements, even after the US has rejoined the Paris Agreement following the election of President Biden in November 2020.

Second, in a context of comparative research, studying the EU and US is an intriguing case of two contrasting cases of globalized multi-level governance (cp. Zürn 2012, 2018). Both political systems are constituted as (quasi-)federal multi-level systems with a comparable state of economic development and far-reaching institutional similarities involving an independent executive and bicameral legislature (Fabbrini 2019; Kreppel 2018). In this sense, both systems have subscribed to the same international agreement whose implementation, however, requires cooperation between different branches of government and with constituent states that enjoy far-reaching autonomy from the federal or supranational level. An evident difference between both systems, however, is the degree of political polarization of positions and discourse concerning the issue of climate change, established as a clear marker of party-political orientation in the US and involving a strong current of climate change skepticism and denial across the Republican party. In this sense, a comparative study of controversy and policy-making on this issue in both systems is relevant not just for research specifically interested in climate policy, but also the broader research debate on political responses to global governance and its contestation in different political and institutional settings.

Against this background, it is surprising that within the extended research literature on climate governance, only few direct comparisons exist between the EU and US, and none that directly compares policy-making developments within both jurisdictions since the Paris Agreement. There is no shortage of surveys of EU and US climate policy independently of each other, starting with compact surveys of both systems in several of the main research handbooks on climate change policy (Bäckstrand and Lövbrand 2015; Simonis 2017; Carlarne et al. 2016). In addition, one of the most comprehensive edited volumes on the EU in its role as a leader of global climate governance contains chapters on EU Member States and institutions, but also on the United States (Wurzel et al. 2021, 2017). Several other monographs include detailed surveys of EU climate policy and its specific instruments and legislation in all relevant areas, but no comparison to other jurisdictions such as the US (Delbeke and Vis 2015, 2019; Boasson and Wettestad 2013; Oberthür and Dupont 2015). A commonality of these surveys is that they focus on aspects of policy, while focusing less on party politics, contestation and public controversy.

Unsurprisingly, this emphasis on policy in the literature on the EU is reversed in existing studies of US climate governance, where the politics of climate change—namely, questions of advocacy, controversy and polarization—generally move to the foreground in relation to analyzing the content and instruments of specific policies (Sussman and Daynes 2013; Vezirgiannidou 2013; Bailey 2015; Atkinson 2018; Mildenberger 2020). The fact that the US climate policy remains fragmented, however, does not imply that there is a shortage of detailed research about its development and explanation. In this context, the two case studies on the US by Brewer (2015) and particularly Karapin (2016) engage in a substantial review and scrutiny of theoretical explanations for policy development. In this context, both studies also take into consideration the development of contrasting policies at the federal and state level, particularly in California and several states on the East Coast, particularly New York state (Karapin 2016: 112–191). More recent analyses have focused on executive action by the presidential administration (Thompson et al. 2020) and discussed the patchwork of carbon pricing across subnational jurisdictions across Northern America (Rabe 2018).

Against the background of this rich and theoretically sophisticated literature, it is surprising how few direct comparisons exist between EU and US climate change policy: so far, mostly one major reconstruction of developments since the adoption of the Kyoto Protocol written from a legal perspective (Carlarne 2010), a collection of analyses on energy law (Heffron and Little 2016) and a brief research article concentrating on institutional features of both systems (Skjaerseth et al. 2013). In addition, several case studies covering the emergence of emissions trading as a concept originally established in the US for sulfur dioxide and later adopted by the EU for carbon emission regulation involve insights from both systems (Meckling 2011; Neuhoff 2011; Biedenkopf et al. 2017). Finally, some general surveys of climate policy at a global level include the EU and US without engaging in a specific comparison between them (Harrison et al. 2010; Luterbacher and Sprinz 2018, Kalantzakos 2017). Finally, both the EU and US are covered in a broad, theory-oriented explanation of environmental policy performance in 21 OECD countries based on a model of agenda-setting and veto power of involved political actors (Jahn 2016). Especially this latter study provides relevant insights for the subsequent discussion about how institutional features of political systems shape conditions for the advocacy of climate policy. However, aside from conceptual difficulties of subsuming action against climate change as a part of environmental policy, this account remains relatively unspecific for explaining the striking divergence of advances in climate action between the EU and US.

Focusing on this question, the following sections discuss several broad approaches for explaining this variance, and thereby to embed the subsequent analysis of ideas and discourse in the context of other analytical perspectives. In this vein, the discussion in this chapter starts by identifying the explanandum of comparison: namely, the diverging development of climate policy in the EU and US since the adoption of the Paris Agreement in 2015. From this point of departure, we review three broad approaches to the explanation of this divergence: first, material factors arising from the exposure of countries to the impacts of climate change and key economic interests; second, institutional factors potentially affecting policy development in a comparison of the EU and US as two multi-level systems; and finally, ideas and beliefs as expressed through attitudes towards and discourse about the issue of climate change.

1.2 Climate Policy in the EU and US Since the Paris Agreement

The Paris Agreement sets a suitable framework for the comparison between EU and US climate policy, as it is the first comprehensive international agreement on action against climate change to which both systems have subscribed. While the main commitment of signatories to the Agreement is to make efforts to keep global warming well below 2 degrees Celsius relative to pre-industrial values, the agreement prescribes no explicit targets for the reduction of GHG emissions, and also leaves the choice of specific policies for mitigating the causes of climate change to its signatories. Against this background, there is no straightforward, linear measurement for the stringency of climate action goals set by the signatories of the Paris Agreement. In order to capture the climate policy development of the EU and US, however, we can apply the following three criteria: (1) the overall ambition of action aiming at climate change mitigation, as measured by the percentage of GHG emission reduction in the mid-term until 2030, and longer-term until 2050; (2) the scope of climate policies concerning the reach and synergy of regulatory instruments covering sources of GHG emissions such as energy, transport, buildings and industry; and finally, (3) the interrelation of institutions responsible for adopting and implementing climate policy decisions within the vertical and horizontal separation of powers (i.e., between the executive and legislative branches, and between the federal/supranational level and constituent states). A survey of these indicators is shown in Table 1.1.

Accordingly, climate policy development of EU and US can be summarized as follows.

First, concerning ambitions of climate governance, the EU has adopted the goal of net-zero carbon emissions until 2050 and a corresponding mid-term target of 55 percent emission reductions by 2030 through the proclamation of its European Green Deal agenda. In the US, mid-term carbon emission reductions of 26–28% by 2025 relative to 2005 values have been pledged in the National Determined Contribution (NDC) by the Obama administration; however, this commitment was rescinded through the complete refusal to commit to any GHG reduction pledges by the subsequent Trump administration. After committing to the goal

Table 1.1 Overview of criteria for the evaluation of climate policy development in the EU and US since the adoption of the Paris Agreement (explanation of abbreviations used: GHG = greenhouse gases, NDC = Nationally Determined Contributions as required from signatories of the Paris Agreement)

	The European Union (EU)	The United States (US)
Ambition of GHG emission reduction	Achievement of carbon neutrality until 2050; agreed 2030 mid-term targets	Controversial; mid-term targets for 2030 specified in NDC
Scope of policies for mitigation of climate change	Comprehensive, including emissions trading, energy sector, vehicle standards and effort sharing	Fragmentary, with stay on energy framework and dispute on vehicle standards
Relation between institutional levels (horizontal/vertical)	Cooperative, with regulation adopted through legislative procedure and workable compliance of Member States	Adversarial, with regulation issued through executive and contestation of policies between state and federal level
Summary	Stable and progressive policy development	Fragmentary and contested policy development

of net-zero economy-wide emissions by 2050 as a candidate,[1] President Biden has proclaimed climate change as the second of seven major priorities of his presidency and made the pledge to "put the United States on a path to achieve net-zero emissions, economy-wide, by no later than 2050" (White House 2021a). This commitment has been complemented by the pledge to achieve a 50–52% reduction of greenhouse gas (GHG) emissions by 2030 relative to 2005 levels (White House 2021b).

Second, the EU has developed a comprehensive policy framework to achieve decarbonization covering CO_2 emissions trading (ETS) from industry and the energy sector, effort sharing for sectors outside the ETS and vehicle and product standards; in the US, policies remain fragmentary, as the main set of regulations governing the energy sector remains stayed, vehicle standards have remained controversial, fragmented and partially dependent on voluntary industry pledges, and no emissions

---

[1] The website of the Biden/Harris presidential campaign contains the pledge to 'build a more resilient, sustainable economy – one that will put the United States on an irreversible path to achieve net-zero emissions, economy-wide, by no later than 2050' (https://joebiden.com/clean-energy/.

trading exists at the federal but only at the state and regional level (in California and through the Regional Greenhouse Gas Initiative).

Finally, relations between institutional levels can be described as relatively cooperative in the EU, as regulation has been adopted through legislative procedures following initiatives by the executive, and Member State support and compliance has remained at a level not obstructing further decision-making. By contrast, inter-institutional relations in the political system of the US are highly adversarial as climate regulation has been adopted (and repealed) almost exclusively through executive action against opposition from the legislature; relations between states and the federal government are characterized by confrontation and an often highly publicized role of litigation through the courts, particularly concerning regulation covering energy production and vehicles.

Taken together, these points establish the point of departure for our comparison of the EU and US concerning their policy-making development: For the EU, it can be characterized as generally stable and progressive in the sense of advancing steadily towards more stringent and comprehensive regulation; by contrast, the climate policy framework for the US remains fragmentary by being based on a narrow and not fully enforced set of standards particularly in energy policy, and intensely contested between institutional levels, both between the legislative and executive branches and through controversy between US states and the federal government.

1.3 Material factors: Vulnerability and economic interests

A first possible approach for explaining the diverging policy responses of the EU and US to climate change could be based on material factors and interests: namely, that actual and anticipated material impacts of climate change, and of policies proposed for its mitigation, determine policy responses. Starting by focusing on the expected impacts of climate change as an explanatory factor, we could expect that the exposure to threats posed by global warming—such as floods, heat periods and extreme weather—prompt policy-makers to take more stringent action against climate change.

A usable measure for the material threat posed by climate change is provided through the Global Adaptation Index and data set,[2] developed by the University of Notre Dame in Indiana (ND-GAIN, cp. Chen et al. 2015). This index combines two aspects of the material efforts required for an adaptation to the consequences of climate change: first, a vulnerability score that combines indicators of the exposure of a given country to climate change from a biophysical perspective, its sensitivity in terms of dependence on sectors negatively affected by climate hazards, and the adaptive capacity in terms of available social resources for sector-specific adaptation. This score is operationalized as a value that can vary between 0 and 1, with higher values indicating a greater degree of exposure to climate hazards (Chen et al. 2015). Second, the index considers a readiness score, defined as a measure of a country's ability to mobilize investments for an adaptation to climate change, including an economic (business investment), governance (factors for adaptation investment) and social aspect (including factors of social equality, education and capacity for innovation). This score can equally range between 0 and 1, and is combined with the vulnerability index to result in the overall adaptability score with a value between 0 and 100 (with increasing values indicating higher readiness and adaptive capacity). We would assume that lower degrees of vulnerability and greater readiness scores might work as a limiting factor for a country's support of climate action.

However, comparing the 2017 data for the Member States of the EU and the United States leads to no substantial comparative insight other than that both jurisdictions belong to a group of upper-income countries with relatively low vulnerability and high readiness scores. The vulnerability index for the US (0.339) is almost identical with the average value for the EU-28 (0.340), indicating a slightly higher exposure to climate change than Germany, France, Italy and the UK, but a lower one than other EU Member States with a higher degree of exposure such as Hungary, Croatia, Latvia or Romania.[3] The readiness score of the US (0.697) is somewhat above the average of the EU-28, but on a similar

---

[2] The country index, explanation of methodology, technical document and full data set are available from the website of the University of Notre Dame, Inidiana, URL: https://gain.nd.edu/our-work/country-index/ (last retrieved 26 February 2020).

[3] The exact vulnerability scores for the countries mentioned are as follows: Germany .292, France .296, the UK .299, Italy .320, Hungary .365, Croatia .387, Latvia .393 and Romania .411. Source: https://gain.nd.edu/our-work/country-index/rankings/.

or lower level as major EU countries supporting climate policy such as Germany, the UK during its membership in the EU or the Scandinavian countries, where the highest readiness scores can be found within the EU.[4] Considering the overall adaptation index, the value for the US (67.9) is again somewhat higher than the average of the EU-28 (63.1), but close to values for key EU states such as Germany (69.3), the UK before Brexit (69.1) and France (66.6). Within this comparison, the highest values are found in the Scandinavian countries, and the lowest in some states of Southern Europe, the Baltic states and particularly the South East European Member States.[5] Considering the global ranking of countries, the US is in 22nd place globally in its vulnerability score, and therefore well within the range of EU countries whose positions rank between third and 85th places. In the overall adaptive index, the US is ranked in 15th place globally, well within the range of EU countries whose position in this ranking varies between 3rd and 65th positions.

A limitation of this data is that the US is included only as a single entity, without considering the substantial variation in climate exposure between regions and states. More detailed insights about anticipated economic effects of climate change within the US are provided by Climate Impact Lab, a cooperation between scientists and policy experts from several institutions including Berkeley and Rutgers University (Hsiang et al. 2017). While restrictions of space make it impossible to go into very much detail, an impact map published by the project demonstrates that both the current and anticipated effects of climate change are strongest in the Southern regions of the US, particularly covering states such as Arizona, Texas, Louisiana, Alabama and Florida[6]. This observation stands in notable contrast with the political support and progress of US States in relation to climate policy, where the states mentioned score low in

---

[4] The respective scores for the countries mentioned are as follows: Germany .678, the UK .681, Sweden .728, Finland .747 and Denmark .756. *Source* https://gain.nd.edu/our-work/country-index/rankings/.

[5] In Southern European Member States, values range between 62.6 (Spain) and 56.9 (Malta), with intermediate values for Portugal (61.6), Italy (60.7) and Greece (58.6); the values for the three Baltic states are 62.4 (Estonia), 61.1 (Lithuania) and 60.8 (Latvia); the lowest values for all EU Member States are found in the case of Bulgaria (56.8), Croatia (56.0) and Romania (52.8). Source: https://gain.nd.edu/our-work/country-index/rankings/.

[6] Retrieved online from the project website: http://www.impactlab.org/, last access: 26 February 2020.

the evaluation of their respective energy and climate policies (as documented, inter alia, by Karapin 2016: 31–42, using an aggregated Climate Policy Index). The two US states identified in this latter study as the most progressive—namely, California and New York State—display relatively low levels of exposure to impacts of climate change in this ranking, both currently and in the medium-term future (Hsiang et al. 2017: 1364–1367). Similar observations could be made about the Member States of the EU, where vulnerability is lowest in the Scandinavian countries and higher particularly in Eastern and South Eastern Member States, where skepticism towards climate action is stronger (Wurzel et al. 2017).

In short, the survey demonstrates more similarities than differences between the EU and the US, a finding that is further strengthened when set in global perspective: Here, both systems are close to each other but contrast with countries facing more substantial threats through climate change such as Indonesia, Bangladesh, Vietnam and major African countries such as Congo, Nigeria or Zimbabwe (see Graph 1.1).

To summarize this review, it is striking how little the most immediate material impact of climate change—namely, the degree of vulnerability

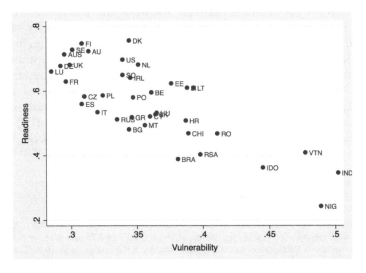

Graph 1.1 Survey of countries concerning their vulnerability towards and readiness to deal with climate change, based on the Global Adaptation Index and data set established by the University of Notre Dame, Indiana (ND-Gain)

of societies and their readiness to adapt—seems to affect the readiness of countries and regions to act against it. A limitation of this argument is, arguably, that it focuses on the probable effects of climate change in the longer-term future, and much less on more short-term material effects of mitigation policies on economic and material interests, particularly through cuts in carbon emissions that may affect industries based on fossil fuels or carmakers. Some contributions to the literature have demonstrated how the regional concentration of these industries particularly in the southern, south-eastern and some of the Midwest states of the US are correlated with their rejection of further action against climate change (Brewer 2015: 28ff.; Karapin 2016: 75ff. and 92ff.). However, it is evident that similar disparities in the dependence on fossil fuels and carbon-intensive industries exist in a comparison of EU Member States, as manifested particularly in objections to more stringent climate policy particularly from Central and Eastern Member States and addressed, inter alia, through the differentiation of GHG reduction targets through EU effort-sharing rules. More research is required to investigate these factors affecting the political economy of climate regulation in a comparative perspective including the EU and US. However, taking these regional disparities into account, it seems difficult to explain how the wide degree of policy divergence comes about in both systems at the aggregate level, as described in the previous section.

1.4 Institutional Variables: Comparing the EU and US as Multi-Level Systems

A second approach towards explaining divergent climate policies of the EU and US is to recur to institutional features of their respective political systems. Approaching the comparison of both systems from an institutional lens is intriguing particularly through the combination of some far-reaching similarities and specific sharp differences. On a very general level, a major similarity is that both jurisdictions operate as multi-level systems and have frequently been included in comparative analyses of federal and multi-level systems (cp. Benz/Sonnicksen 2021; Sonnicksen 2021; Fabbrini 2005, 2007, 2017; Verdun 2016; Hueglin and Fenna 2015; Sbragia 2008; Gehler 2005; Börzel and Hosli 2003). More specifically, and zooming in particularly on the vertical and horizontal division of powers and interaction between levels and branches of government, three major institutional similarities between both systems can be identified.

First, both systems have a high degree of vertical division of powers as (quasi-)federal systems. This implies that policies aiming at the reduction of carbon emissions evolve or are envisaged through the establishment of framework regulation setting general targets or establishing a mechanism of emission trading at the federal/supranational level, leaving some flexibility in the choice of specific policies, such as the promotion of renewable energy or the choice of energy mixes, for implementation at the EU member/US state level. In this context, a remarkable detail is that one of the centerpieces of EU climate policy—namely, emissions trading covering CO_2 emissions from the energy and some industry sectors—originally emerged as a regulatory approach promoted by the US as a better alternative to a carbon tax, and proposed for cap-and-trade of carbon emissions at the federal level in the failed 2009 Markey/Waxman bill (Brewer 2015: 157).

Second, both systems feature a strong division of powers between the executive and legislative branches of government that interact based on a principle of independence from each other. Most importantly, this implies that the legislative branch features no stable majority coalition aligned with the executive with control over agenda-setting and access to veto points as typical for parliamentary systems (cp. Jahn 2016: 71–89). In this regard, drawing parallels between both systems has limitations primarily concerning the structure and legitimation of the central executive. This branch of government is led by a directly elected President in the US but established in the EU case through cooperation between the European Council and Commission, whose College of Commissioners is elected by and accountable to the European Parliament (cp. Dawson 2019). A critical difference is therefore the capacity for political leadership of the relatively hierarchical central executive of the US in comparison to the more non-hierarchical, network-like set of executive institutions in the EU. However, an important commonality with considerable relevance for legislative decision-making is that legislative institutions emerge as independent veto players in relation to acts of agenda-setting by the executive: Whereas the US is commonly considered an ideal typical case of a presidential system in this regard (for critical discussion of this point, see Jahn 2016: 72), the EU is close to the presidential model in its everyday legislative decision-making by operating through a legislative branch that is not dominated by a government majority; the latter would be necessary to maintain trust in the incumbent government and to ensure the passage of legislation according to the operating logic of parliamentary systems (Hix et al. 2007: 12–21).

Finally, legislative decision-making has similarities in the EU[7] and US as it requires the cooperation of two legislative chambers for proposed acts to become law: namely, between a larger, directly elected lower chamber primarily representing party-political interests (European Parliament/House of Representatives), and a smaller, but equally influential upper chamber leaning towards the representation of territorial constituencies and interests (Council of the EU/US Senate). In both cases, these two chambers interact as equal partners through several readings in the legislative procedure and have to adopt a joint text approved by both chambers, granting a potential veto right for both sides. Reaching an agreement between both chambers features a strong role of specialized committees in both cases and is embedded in some sort of institutionalized conciliation procedure; consensus requirements are stringent in both cases as agreement in the 'upper chamber' (Council/US Senate) requires an oversized majority of more than 50 percent (namely, a qualified majority vote in the Council of the EU, and a three-fifth majority usually requiring 60 Senators to move to cloture in the US Senate).

Summarizing these aspects as features of a strong horizontal and vertical division of power, and adding the shared feature of a relatively strong role of judicial review by the courts as a corrective restraint on legislative decision-making, both the EU and US qualify as multi-level systems with strong elements of a consensus democracy in the terminology of Arend Lijphart (2012: 30–46), at least in terms of its institutional criteria and leaving aside more actor-based, particularly party-political ones. This would suggest that large and relatively stable coalitions of political actors are required to overcome possible veto points in decision-making and to adopt legislation. Identifying these broad institutional similarities helps to bring into sharp focus a set of pronounced

---

[7] The institutional similarities between the EU and US legislative procedures discussed in this paragraph apply only for those acts of decision-making in the EU where the Ordinary Legislative Procedure (OLP) as specified through the provisions of the Lisbon Treaty adopted in 2009 is applied; however, being assigned the status of a standard procedure for legislative decision-making on EU regulation applicable to almost all fields of policy-making, this procedure is the one relevant for the subsequent discussion of EU Regulations and Directives relevant for climate policy-making.

differences concerning the institutional context and operation of legislative politics in the EU and US. These can also be summarized in three main points.

First, a difference of major relevance lies in the form of legislative agenda-setting in both political systems (Jahn 2016: 71ff., Skjaerseth et al. 2013: 63ff.). Whereas legislative proposals can only be launched by the European Commission in the EU following on political guidelines adopted by the European Council, agenda-setting in the form of specific legislative proposals is the privilege of Members of Congress in the US. While any House Member or Senator is entitled to make legislative proposals, in political reality agenda-setting is effectively controlled in most cases by the political majority in the House of Representatives and the Senate. With the House being re-elected every two years (and frequently forming majorities opposing the incumbent US President), legislative agenda-setting is therefore more dispersed, volatile and competitive than in the political system of the EU. Here, the Commission controls the timing of proposals and usually works in close consultation with other EU institutions and based on the proposals of multi-annual work programs and a five-year political mandate (for more detailed discussion, cp. Laloux/Delreux 2021). Based on these differences, it is plausible to expect a more instable and contested process of policy-making in the US in comparison to the EU.

A second, less openly visible but relevant difference of both systems in the specific field of climate policy is what could be called their respective institutional infrastructure: particularly, the existence of institutional arrangements providing relevant expertise and allowing for negotiations involving issue linkages and coalition-building between groups and agents with competing interests (cp. Skjaerseth 2013: 64). Concerning the drafting and advocacy for legislative proposals, the EU Commission emerges as a relatively well-resourced policy entrepreneur, with a Directorate General in charge of climate policy and more recently, a Vice President tasked with overseeing the move towards carbon neutrality. This is not mirrored in any stable arrangements within the US Presidential Administration and federal executive, where policies relevant for climate change are dispersed between the President, the Environmental Protection Agency and the Departments of Energy, the Interior and Commerce. Within the White House, special envoys and policy directors have been established to coordinate initiatives in climate policy (including senior policy-makers such as Gina McCarthy or John Kerry), but their position and mandates depend on the respective presidency and have less stability than the network of climate policy-makers in the EU institutions.

Moving to the legislative branch, an additional difference is that bargaining on specific policy proposals is more fragmented and embedded in a less stable and well-resourced set of institutions in the US than the EU system. In the European Parliament, the two committees in charge of industry, research and energy (ITRE) and the environment (ENVI) are two influential committees regularly tasked with the negotiation of climate policy proposals. Research on decision-making in the EP has demonstrated the relevance of committees and particularly specialized agents (rapporteurs and shadow rapporteurs) for negotiating compromise both between EP party groups and the Council (Finke 2017; Rosen 2016; Bressanelli et al. 2016; Roederer-Rynning and Greenwood 2015; Ringe 2010). By comparison, legislative negotiation about energy and climate policy proposals in the US Congress is dispersed between several (politically less influential) subcommittees of the House and Senate. Most relevant among these are the House Subcommittee for Environment and Climate Change, affiliated to the Energy and Commerce Committee, and the Senate Subcommittee on Energy, affiliated to the Energy and Natural Resources Committee. In addition, committees are created and dissolved more flexibly and depending on party-political majorities, such as the House Select Committee on the Climate Crisis[8]. Furthermore, some of the most widely recognized proposals such as the Green New Deal are not launched from a committee but rather a group of politically aligned legislators. Again, these aspects are a potential source of volatility and contestation of climate policy proposals in the US case.

Finally, a rather evident point is that the interaction of the executive and legislative branches differs between a primarily cooperative form in the EU as most law-making proposals by the Commission are ultimately adopted by the Council and EP, and a more competitive interaction in the US, where legislative proposals backed by the central executive are more frequently blocked by the legislature. In this sense, exchanges between representatives of the two chambers of Congress and the Presidential administration are usually more adversarial than between members of the EU Commission, Council and European Parliament. Mainly two factors are relevant for this different form of interaction. First, the degree

---

[8] This point is explained in more detail in Chapter 4 on the development of US climate change policy.

of publicity and public visibility of legislative proposals is considerably higher in US politics, compared to the relatively remote and less strongly politicized process of legislative negotiation in the EU. A related aspect of this point is that sponsorship for specific bills is usually attributed to particular Members of the House or Senate and their respective party-political identity, whereas legislative proposals negotiated in the EU are less directly identified with a particular person or party (even considering the frequently high-profile role of EP rapporteurs).

Second, legislative negotiations are more directly related to party-political competition and electoral accountability in the US system, where major elections take place every two years, and particularly House Representatives are easily singled out as supporting or opposing a particular bill. By comparison, policy negotiations between the Council of Ministers and EP are less directly connected to elections, with EP elections taking place only every five years and being less strongly politicized. In short, the publicity and party-political capture of legislative institutions differs between both cases. Taken together, these observations about institutional similarities and differences between both political systems provide some first avenues towards explaining policy divergence between the EU and US.

1.5 Ideas and Discourse About Climate Change: The Missing Link?

Finally, we turn to the role of ideas for the development of policy-making on climate change. The extensive literature in this field has approached this topic mainly from four angles: as a structure of concepts underlying political discourse; as the ideological foundation of individual attitudes and party positions towards climate change; through studies focused on the role of expertise and political advocacy for specific policy instruments; and finally, as an element of deliberation considered in a perspective towards a democratization of global climate governance. These four strands of research inform the present study in the following ways.

First, contributions based on concepts of discourse analysis have evaluated how certain interpretations of climate change become dominant in a given setting, often from a hermeneutic and critical perspective. Some contributions to this debate focus on a particular type of discourse, such as studies on the 'securitization' of climate change (Oels 2012; Rothe 2016;

Gilman et al. 2011), but also focusing on other variants such as 'economization' and 'technocratization' (Methmann et al. 2013). A reverse perspective of this approach—namely, one evaluating how aspects of multilateral cooperation adopt institutional venues, agents and discursive frames associated with the global climate regime—is established through literature on 'climatisation' of global governance, including detailed case studies on the role of wording and terms in global climate negotiations (Aykut et al. 2017, 2021). Concerning more specific studies of discourse, the literature contains attempts to discuss the emergence of different variants of discursive advocacy on climate change, including a case study on Sweden (Anshelm and Hultman 2015) and reviewing debates in separate but interrelated stakeholder forums in the context of global climate change negotiations (Stevenson and Dryzek 2014). On a broader scale, debates on the concept of Anthropocene have addressed the question how concepts and narratives of human development and society need to be rethought and subjected to reflexive forms of innovation through the onset of climate change (Kelly 2019; Latour 2018; Pickering and Dryzek 2019; Biermann and Lövbrand 2019). While all of these contributions emphasize the relevance of ideas for the recognition, appraisal and treatment of climate change, most are not directly suitable for the comparative explanation of policy development but focus on critical and conceptual questions and perspectives.

Second, the politics of climate change is highlighted in approaches investigating attitudes at the individual level and positions of political parties. Taking up the concept of frames as cognitive heuristics to perceive political problems, particularly research by US-based scholars has investigated how language and specific choices of terminology and their underlying ideas (such as global warming vs. climate change) shape the way individuals perceive and assess this problem (Benjamin et al. 2016; Flusberg et al. 2017). In addition to the empirical mapping of attitudes, this discussion involves a debate on the mechanisms through which individuals make sense of complex problems such as climate change. In this context, a prominent contribution written by climate activist George Marshall links the perception of climate change to the activation of cognitive shortcuts familiar from social psychology, such as the use of an availability, confirmation and selection bias (Marshall 2014, cp. also Hoggett 2019). Beyond the discussion of individual attitudes, considerable research exists on media reporting about climate change and the way the topic is framed through concepts, stories, narratives and images (Boykoff 2011; Engesser and Brüggemann 2016; Bowe et al. 2014; Rebich-Hespanha et al. 2015; Weathers and Kendall 2016; Schäfer and O'Neill 2017). By comparison, research on party-political positions towards climate change is still relatively sparse, although first surveys based on a systematic comparative mapping of manifestos have been published (Carter et al. 2018; Batstrand 2015). Finally, a considerable amount of literature has been published on climate denial and its underlying ideas and arguments (Almiron and Xifra 2019), including contributions specifically focusing on nationalist right parties (Lockwood 2018; Schaller and Carius 2019) and in the particular case of the United States (Collomb 2014; Cann and Raymond 2018; Fisher et al. 2013; Dunlap/McCright 2011). While this research is relevant for mapping attitudes and positions towards climate change at the individual level, it is still in the early stages concerning relevant issue dimensions, party competition and subsequent effects on policy-making in comparative perspective.

Third, the introduction of innovative policy instruments for climate governance, and particularly the development of emissions trading has invited research to investigate how ideas shape policy through the dissemination of expertise and policy beliefs (Meckling 2011, Dreger 2014; Biedenkopf et al. 2017). In fact, emissions trading originated in the US where it was first applied to reduce the emission of sulfur dioxides and only then adopted by the EU to achieve reductions in carbon dioxides, establishing the most prominent example for a diffusion of policy instruments between both systems (Neuhoff 2011). Case studies like these resonate with a broader turn of the literature about global climate governance towards the concept of polycentricity: a term used to capture the emergence of multiple and intertwined, but often incongruent governance networks involving multiple constellations of state, civil society and private actors in the climate regime after the Paris Agreement (Jordan et al. 2018; Popovski 2019; Dorsch and Flachsland 2017; Bulkeley 2014; Ostrom 2009; Obertühr 2016). In this context, many contributions anticipate or emphasize dynamics of policy change based on the exchange of ideas such as learning, mutual adjustment, experimentation and deliberation as increasingly important for advances in climate policy (Turnheim et al. 2018); in a similar vein, recent developments of the global climate regime have been characterized as a turn towards 'incantatory governance' (Aykut et al. 2021). This research debate provides an important background for the present study of climate debates since the Paris Agreement; however, polycentric governance is still more of a broad concept than a set of explicit theoretical explanations, requiring further specification for given empirical cases.

Finally, the consideration of ideas matters for climate governance in a normative perspective. In this vein, a polycentric account provides the point of departure for a model of democratization of global climate governance, based on a network of deliberative settings within the framework of UN institutions (Dryzek et al. 2019; Stevenson and Dryzek 2014). An empirically based counterpart for this proposal is a case study on the forms and deliberative quality of debate on climate change in the European Parliament (Roald and Sangolt 2012). Furthermore, the discussion of normative concepts underlying the design of the current and future climate regime, particularly the discussion relating to climate equity and justice, engage with ideas and their contested interpretation (Okereke 2011, 2018; Okereke and Coventry 2016; Meyer and Sanklecha 2017; Gardiner 2011). This literature provides a relevant background for the conceptualization of discursive frames and their underlying ideas, particularly concerning normative questions.

While many of the existing contributions are primarily critical or normative in their intention, a question that remains underexplored is the explanatory value of ideas for climate policy in comparative perspective: We have very few systematic accounts of how the clash of competing ideas about climate change in public controversy (*politics*) affects decision-making about steps to reduce GHG emissions (*policy*) in given empirical cases. More specifically, a gap in existing research is to answer how the strategic use of ideas as a foundation of discourse by political agents in specified institutional settings shapes the political contestation of climate change and its subsequent effect on policy-making. This point leads us to specifying the research question for this present volume.

1.6 Rationale and Structure of the Book

The argument developed in this chapter can be summarized in two main points. First, we posit that ideas are a critical, yet underexplored factor for understanding the relation between the politics and policy of climate change: namely, how the promotion of ideas about climate shapes the space and issue dimensions of political debate, and how resulting political contestation feeds into policy-making processes. Second, we argue that the EU and US are globally relevant cases of multi-level governance whose direct comparison is both understudied and particularly interesting with an empirical focus on the interaction between executive and legislative institutions, as these create a suitable framework of comparison based on their broad similarity and distinctive differences.

From this point of departure, the main rationale of this book is to develop and apply a framework for evaluating ideas about climate change policy in both systems and how they shape their respective political space of climate change politics; the latter term is used as a summary term for relevant institutional venues, issue categories, ideological foundations for proposed positions and emerging forms of polarization. The main research question pursued in the book is: How can the divergence of climate policy-making of the EU and US be linked to the promotion and contestation of ideas through political discourse in both cases? As the following chapters will explain, ideas are captured as the foundation of discursive frames—or sets of justificatory arguments that are raised to advocate or reject climate change policy. Based on this approach, the subsequent case studies and comparative analysis will move towards the scrutiny of hypotheses between observed policy development and the expected structure, linkages and contestation of relevant climate frames.

The following chapter presents the theoretical approach of this study, followed by two detailed case studies of our two cases, presented in the subsequent Chapters 3 and 4. The following Chapter 5 presents the comparative analysis of the EU and US based on the concept of political space. The final chapter summarizes key findings and identifies questions and topics for a future research agenda engaging with the role of ideas and discourse for political action against climate change.

References

Almiron, Núria, and Jordi Xifra i Triadú. 2019. *Climate Change Denial and Public Relations: Strategic Communication and Interest Groups in Climate Inaction*. Routledge New Directions in Public Relations and Communication Research. Abingdon, Oxon and New York, NY: Routledge.

Anshelm, Jonas, and Martin Hultman. 2015. *Discourses of Global Climate Change: Apocalyptic Framing and Political Antagonisms*. Routledge Studies in Environmental Communication and Media. Abingdon, Oxon: Routledge.

Atkinson, Hugh. 2018. *The Politics of Climate Change under President Obama*. London and New York: Routledge.

Aykut, Stefan C., Jean Foyer, and Edouard Morena. 2017. *Globalising the Climate: COP21 and the Climatisation of Global Debates*. Abingdon: Routledge.

Aykut, Stefan C., Edouard Morena, and Jean Foyer. 2021. "'Incantatory' Governance: Global Climate Politics' Performative Turn and Its Wider Significance for Global Politics." *International Politics* 58 (4): 519–540. https://doi.org/10.1057/s41311-020-00250-8.

Bäckstrand, Karin, and Eva Lövbrand, eds. 2015. *Research Handbook on Climate Governance*. Cheltenham, UK: Edward Elgar Publishing Limited.

Bailey, Christopher J. 2015. *US Climate Change Policy*. Transforming Environmental Politics and Policy. Farnham, Surrey Burlington, VT: Ashgate.

Båtstrand, Sondre. 2015. More Than Markets: A Comparative Study of Nine Conservative Parties on Climate Change. *Politics & Policy* 43 (4): 538–561. https://doi.org/10.1111/polp.12122.

Benjamin, Daniel, Han-Hui. Por, and David Budescu. 2016. Climate Change Versus Global Warming: Who Is Susceptible to the Framing of Climate Change? *Environment and Behavior*. https://doi.org/10.1177/0013916516664382.

Benz, Arthur, and Jared Sonnicksen, eds. 2021. *Federal Democracies at Work. Varieties of Complex Government*. Toronto: University of Toronto Press.

Biedenkopf, Katja, Patrick Müller, Peter Slominski, and Jørgen. Wettestad. 2017. A Global Turn to Greenhouse Gas Emissions Trading? Experiments, Actors, and Diffusion. *Global Environmental Politics* 17 (3): 1–11. https://doi.org/10.1162/GLEP_e_00412.

Biermann, Frank, and Eva Lövbrand. 2019. *Anthropocene Encounters: New Directions in Green Political Thinking*. Earth System Governance series. Cambridge: Cambridge University Press.

Boasson, Elin Lerum, and Jørgen Wettestad. 2013. *EU Climate Policy: Industry, Policy Interaction and External Environment*. Farnham: Ashgate.

Börzel, Tanja, and Madeleine Hosli. 2003. Comparative Federalism Meets the European Union. *Governance* 16 (2): 179–202.

Bowe, Brian J., Tsuyoshi Oshita, Carol Terracina-Hartman, and Wen-Chi. Chao. 2014. Framing of Climate Change in Newspaper Coverage of the East Anglia E-Mail Scandal. *Public Understanding of Science* 23 (2): 157–169. https://doi.org/10.1177/0963662512449949.

Boykoff, Maxwell T. 2011. *Who Speaks for the Climate?: Making Sense of Media Reporting on Climate Change*. Cambridge: Cambridge University Press.

Breakey, Hugh, Vesselin Popovski, and Rowena Maguire, eds. 2015. *Ethical Values and the Integrity of the Climate Change Regime. Law, Ethics and Governance*. Farnham, Surrey, UK: Ashgate.

Bressanelli, Edoardo, Christel Koop, and Christine Reh. 2016. The Impact of Informalisation: Early Agreements and Voting Cohesion in the European Parliament. *European Union Politics* 17 (1): 91–113. https://doi.org/10.1177/1465116515608704.

Brewer, Thomas L. 2015. *The United States in a Warming World: The Political Economy of Government, Business, and Public Responses to Climate Change*. Cambridge: Cambridge University Press.

Bulkeley, Harriet, ed. 2014. *Transnational Climate Change Governance*. Cambridge: Cambridge University Press.

Cann, Heather W., and Leigh Raymond. 2018. Does Climate Denialism Still Matter? The Prevalence of Alternative Frames in Opposition to Climate Policy. *Environmental Politics* 27 (3): 433–454. https://doi.org/10.1080/09644016.2018.1439353.

Carlarne, Cinnamon Piñon. 2010. *Climate Change Law and Policy: EU and US Approaches*. Oxford [u.a.]: Oxford University Press.

Carlarne, Cinnamon Piñon, Kevin Gray, and Richard Tarasofsky, eds. 2016. *The Oxford Handbook of International Climate Change Law*. First edition. Oxford Handbooks in Law. Oxford, UK: Oxford University Press.

Carter, Neil, Robert Ladrech, Conor Little, and Vasiliki Tsagkroni. 2018. Political Parties and Climate Policy: A New Approach to Measuring Parties' Climate Policy Preferences. *Party Politics* 24 (6): 731–742. https://doi.org/10.1177/1354068817697630.

Chen, C, I Noble, J Hellmann, J Coffee, M Murillo, and M Chawla. 2015. "University of Notre Dame Global Adaptation Index: Country Index Technical Report." University of Notre Dame, Indiana. https://gain.nd.edu/assets/254377/nd_gain_technical_document_2015.pdf.

Collomb, Jean-Daniel. 2014. "The Ideology of Climate Change Denial in the United States." *European Journal of American studies* 9 (9–1). https://doi.org/10.4000/ejas.10305.

Crippa, Monica, Diego Guizzardi, Efisio Solazzo, Marilena Muntean, Edwin Schaaf, Fabio Montforti-Ferrario, Manola Banja, et al. 2021. "GHG Emissions of All World Countries." Publications Office of the European Union. https://publications.jrc.ec.europa.eu/repository/handle/JRC126363.

Dawson, Mark. 2019. The Lost Spitzenkandidaten and the Future of European Democracy. *Maastricht Journal of European and Comparative Law* 26 (6): 731–735.

Delbeke, Jos, and Peter Vis. 2015. *EU Climate Policy Explained*. Abingdon, OX [u.a.]: Routledge.

Delbeke, Jos, and Peter Vis. 2019. *Towards a Climate-Neutral Europe: Curbing the Trend*. London: Routledge.

Dorsch, Marcel J., and Christian Flachsland. 2017. A Polycentric Approach to Global Climate Governance. *Global Environmental Politics* 17 (2): 45–64. https://doi.org/10.1162/GLEP_a_00400.

Dreger, Jonas. 2014. *The European Commission's Energy and Climate Policy: A Climate for Expertise?* Energy, Climate and the Environment Series. Houndsmills [u.a.]: Palgrave Macmillan.

Dryzek, John S., Quinlan Bowman, Jonathan Kuyper, Jonathan Pickering, Jensen Sass, and Hayley Stevenson. 2019. *Deliberative Global Governance*. Cambridge Elements. Elements in Earth System Governance. Cambridge: Cambridge University Press.

Dryzek, John S., Richard B. Norgaard, and David Schlosberg, eds. 2011. *Oxford Handbook of Climate Change and Society*. Oxford: Oxford University Press.

Dryzek, John S., Richard B. Norgaard, and David Schlosberg. 2013. *Climate-Challenged Society*. Oxford: Oxford University Press.

Dunlap, Riley E., and Aaron M. McCright. 2011. "Organized Climate Change Denial." Edited by John S. Dryzek. *The Oxford Handbook of Climate Change and Society*, 144–60. https://doi.org/10.1093/oxfordhb/9780199566600.003.0010.

Engesser, Sven, and Michael Brüggemann. 2016. Mapping the Minds of the Mediators: The Cognitive Frames of Climate Journalists from Five Countries. *Public Understanding of Science* 25 (7): 825–841. https://doi.org/10.1177/0963662515583621.

Fabbrini, Sergio, ed. 2005. *Democracy and Federalism in the European Union and the United States. Exploring Post-National Governance*. Abingdon, OX [u.a.]: Routledge.

Fabbrini, Sergio. 2007. *Compound Democracies: Why the United States and Europe Are Becoming Similar*. Oxford: Oxford University Press. https://doi.org/10.1093/acprof:oso/9780199235612.001.0001.

Fabbrini, Sergio. 2017. Intergovernmentalism in the European Union. A Comparative Federalism Perspective. *Journal of European Public Policy* 24 (4): 580–597. https://doi.org/10.1080/13501763.2016.1273375.

Fabbrini, Sergio. 2019. Between Power and Influence: The European Parliament in a Dual Constitutional Regime. *Journal of European Integration* 41 (3): 417–428. https://doi.org/10.1080/07036337.2019.1599370.

Falkner, Robert, ed. 2013. *The Handbook of Global Climate and Environment Policy*. Handbooks of Global Policy Series. Chichester [u.a.]: Wiley-Blackwell.

Finke, Daniel. 2017. Bicameralism in the European Union: Parliamentary Scrutiny as a Tool for Reinforcing Party Unity. *West European Politics* 40 (2): 275–294. https://doi.org/10.1080/01402382.2016.1188549.

Fisher, Dana R., Philip Leifeld, and Yoko Iwaki. 2013. Mapping the Ideological Networks of American Climate Politics. *Climatic Change* 116 (3): 523–545. https://doi.org/10.1007/s10584-012-0512-7.

Flusberg, Stephen J., Teenie Matlock, and Paul H. Thibodeau. 2017. Metaphors for the War (or Race) Against Climate Change. *Environmental Communication* 11 (6): 769–783. https://doi.org/10.1080/17524032.2017.1289111.

Gardiner, Stephen M. 2011. Climate Justice. In *The Oxford Handbook of Climate Change and Society*, ed. John S. Dryzek, Richard B. Norgaard, and David Schlosberg, 309–320. Oxford: Oxford University Press.

Gehler, Michael, ed. 2005. *Towards a European Constitution: A Historical and Political Comparison with the United States.*, vol. 3. Wien: Böhlau.

Gilman, Nils, Doug Randall, and Peter Schwartz. 2011. "Climate Change and 'Security.'" Edited by John S. Dryzek. *The Oxford Handbook of Climate Change and Society*, 251–66. https://doi.org/10.1093/oxfordhb/9780199566600.003.0017.

Gupta, Joyeeta. 2014. *The History of Global Climate Governance*. Cambridge: Cambridge University Press.

Haines, Andy, and Howard Frumkin. 2021. *Planetary Helath. Safeguarding Human Helath and the Environment in the Anthropocene*. Cambridge: Cambridge University Press.

Harrison, Kathryn, and Lisa McIntosh Sundstrom, eds. 2010. *Global Commons, Domestic Decisions: The Comparative Politics of Climate Change*. American and Comparative Environmental Policy. Cambridge, MA [u.a.]: MIT Press.

Heffron, Raphael J, and Gavin F. M. Little, eds. 2016. *Delivering Energy Law and Policy in the EU and the US: A Reader*. Edinburgh: Edinburgh University Press.

Hix, Simon, Abdul Noury, and Gérard Roland. 2007. *Democratic Politics in the European Parliament*. 1. publ. Themes in European Governance. Cambridge [u.a.]: Cambridge University Press.

Hoffmann, Matthew. 2013. "Global Climate Change." In *The Handbook of Global Climate and Environment Policy*, edited by Robert Falkner, 3–18. Malden, MA: Wiley-Blackwell.

Hoggett, Paul. 2019. *Climate Psychology*. New York, NY: Springer Berlin Heidelberg.

Hsiang, S, R.E. Kopp, A. Jina, J. Rising, M. Delgado, S. Mohan, D.J. Rasmussen, et al. 2017. "Estimating Economic Damage from Climate Change in the United States." *Science*. https://doi.org/10.1126/science.aal4369.

Hueglin, Thomas, and Alan Fenna, eds. 2015. *Comparative Federalism: A Systematic Inquiry*, 2nd ed. Toronto: University of Toronto Press.

Hulme, Mike. 2009. *Why We Disagree About Climate Change: Understanding Controversy, Inaction and Opportunity*. Cambridge [u.a.]: Cambridge University Press.

Incropera, Frank. 2016. *Climate Change: A Wicked Problem. Complexity and Uncertainty at the Intersection of Science, Economics, Politics, and Human Behavior*. Cambridge: Cambridge University Press.

Jahn, Detlef. 2016. *The Politics of Environmental Performance: Institutions and Preferences in Industrialized Democracies*. Cambridge: Cambridge University Press.

Jamieson, Dale. 2012. The Nature of the Problem. In *Oxford Handbook of Climate Change and Society*, ed. John S. Dryzek, Richard B. Norgaard, and David Schlosberg, 38–54. Oxford: Oxford University Press.
Jamieson, Dale. 2014. *Reason in a Dark Time. Why the Struggle against Climate Change Failed—And What It Means for Our Future*. Oxford: Oxford University Press.
Jordan, Andrew, Dave Huitema, Harro van Asselt, and Johanna Forster, eds. 2018. *Governing Climate Change: Polycentricity in Action?* Cambridge: Cambridge University Press.
Kalantzakos, Sophia. 2017. *The EU, US and China Tackling Climate Change: Policies and Alliance for the Anthropocene*. Routledge Studies in Environmental Policy. London New York: Routledge.
Karapin, Roger. 2016. *Political Opportunities for Climate Policy: California, New York, and the Federal Government*. Cambridge: Cambridge University Press.
Kelly, Duncan. 2019. *Politics and the Anthropocene*. Cambridge, UK: Polity.
Keskitalo, E.C.H., and Benjamin L. Preston, eds. 2019. *Research Handbook on Climate Change Adaptation Policy*. Cheltenham, UK: Edward Elgar Publishing.
Klein, Naomi. 2014. *This Changes Everything: Capitalism vs. the Climate*, ed. Simon & Schuster hardcover. New York [u.a.]: Simon & Schuster.
Kreppel, Amie. 2018. Bicameralism and the Balance of Power in EU Legislative Politics. *The Journal of Legislative Studies* 24 (1): 11–33. https://doi.org/10.1080/13572334.2018.1444623.
Latour, Bruno. 2018. *Down to Earth: Politics in the New Climatic Regime*. Cambridge: Polity.
Leichenko, Robin M., and Karen O'Brien. 2019. *Climate and Society: Transforming the Future*. Cambridge, UK: Polity.
Levin, Kelly, Benjamin Cashore, Steven Bernstein, and Graeme Auld. 2012. Overcoming the Tragedy of Super Wicked Problems: Constraining Our Future Selves to Ameliorate Global Climate Change. *Policy Sciences* 45 (2): 123–152. https://doi.org/10.1007/s11077-012-9151-0.
Lijphart, Arend. 2012. *Patterns of Democracy: Government Forms and Performance in Thirty-Six Countries*. 2. updated and Expanded ed. New Haven, CT [u.a.]: Yale University Press.
Lockwood, Matthew. 2018. Right-Wing Populism and the Climate Change Agenda: Exploring the Linkages. *Environmental Politics* 27 (4): 712–732. https://doi.org/10.1080/09644016.2018.1458411.
Luterbacher, Urs, and Detlef F. Sprinz, eds. 2018. *Global Climate Policy: Actors, Concepts, and Enduring Challenges*. Cambridge, MA: MIT Press.
Marshall, George. 2014. *Don't Even Think About It. WHy Our Brains Are Wired to Ignore Climate Change*. London: Bloomsbury.

Mechler, Jonas, Laurens Bouwer, Thomas Schinko, Sonja Surminski, and JoAnne Linnerooth-Bayer. 2018. *Loss and Damage from Climate Change*. New York, NY: Springer Berlin Heidelberg.

Meckling, Jonas. 2011. *Carbon Coalitions: Business, Climate Politics, and the Rise of Emissions Trading*. Cambridge, MA [u.a.]: MIT Press.

Methmann, Chris, Delf Rothe, and Benjamin Stephan, eds. 2013. *Interpretive Approaches to Global Climate Governance: (De)constructing the Greenhouse*. Interventions. London [u.a.]: Routledge.

Meyer, Lukas, and Pranay Sanklecha, eds. 2017. *Climate Justice and Historical Emissions*. Cambridge: Cambridge University Press.

Mildenberger, Matto. 2020. *Carbon Captured: How Business and Labor Control Climate Politics*. Cambridge, MA: The MIT Press.

NASEM (National Academies of Sciences, Engineering, and Medicine). 2016. "Attribution of Extreme Weather Events in the Context of Climate Change." National Academies Press. https://doi.org/10.17226/21852.

Neuhoff, Karsten. 2011. *Climate Policy after Copenhagen: The Role of Carbon Pricing*. Cambridge: Cambridge University Press.

Oberthür, Sebastian. 2016. Reflections on Global Climate Politics Post Paris: Power, Interests and Polycentricity. *The International Spectator* 51 (4): 80–94.

Oberthür, Sebastian, and Claire Dupont. 2015. *Decarbonization in the European Union: Internal Policies and External Strategies*. Basingstoke: Palgrave Macmillan.

O'Brien, Karen, Asuncion Lera St, and Clair, and Berit Kristoffersen, eds. 2010. *Climate Change, Ethics and Human Security*. Cambridge: Cambridge University Press.

Oels, Angela. 2012. "From 'Securitization' of Climate Change to 'Climatization' of the Security Field: Comparing Three Theoretical Perspectives." In *Climate Change, Human Security and Violent Conflict. Challenges for Societal Stability*, edited by Jürgen Scheffran, Michael Brzoska, Hans Günter Brauch, Peter MIchael Link, and Janpeter Schilling, 185–205. Hexagon Series on Human and Environmental Security and Peace. Berlin: Springer.

Okereke, Chukwumerije. 2011. Moral Foundations for Global Environmental and Climate Justice. *Royal Institute of Philosophy Supplements* 69: 117–135. https://doi.org/10.1017/S1358246111000245.

Okereke, Chukwumerije. 2018. Equity and Justice in Polycentric Climate Governance. In *Governing Climate Change: Polycentricity in Action?*, ed. Andrew Jordan, Dave Huitema, Harro van Asselt, and Johanna Forster, 320–337. Cambridge: Cambridge University Press.

Okereke, Chukwumerije, and Philip Coventry. 2016. Climate Justice and the International Regime: Before, during, and after Paris. *Wiley Interdisciplinary Reviews: Climate Change* 7 (6): 834–851. https://doi.org/10.1002/wcc.419.

Ostrom, Elinor. 2009. *A Polycentric Approach for Coping with Climate Change*. Washington, DC: World Bank.
Otto, Friederike. 2020. *Angry Weather: Heat Waves, Floods, Storms, and the New Science of Climate Change*. Vancouveer and Berkeley: Greystone Books.
Pickering, Jonathan, and John S. Dryzek. 2019. *The Politics of the Anthropocene*. Oxford Scholarship Online. New York, NY: Oxford University Press.
Popovski, Vesselin. 2019. *The Implementation of the Paris Agreement on Climate Change*. Law, Ethics and Governance Series. London: Routledge.
Rabe, Barry. 2018. *Can We Price Carbon?* Cambridge, MA: MIT Press.
Rebich-Hespanha, Stacy, Ronald E. Rice, Daniel R. Montello, Sean Retzloff, Sandrine Tien, and João. P. Hespanha. 2015. Image Themes and Frames in US Print News Stories About Climate Change. *Environmental Communication* 9 (4): 491–519. https://doi.org/10.1080/17524032.2014.983534.
Ringe, Nils. 2010. *Who Decides, and How?: Preferences, Uncertainty, and Policy Choice in the European Parliament*. Oxford [u.a.]: Oxford University Press.
Roald, Vebjorn, and Linda Sangolt. 2012. *Deliberation, Rhetoric, and Emotion in the Discourse on Climate Change in the European Parliament*. Eburon Academic Publishers.
Roederer-Rynning, Christilla, and Justin Greenwood. 2015. The Culture of Trilogues. *Journal of European Public Policy* 22 (8): 1148–1165. https://doi.org/10.1080/13501763.2014.992934.
Romm, Joseph. 2018. *Climate Change: What Everyone Needs to Know*, 2nd ed. What Everyone Needs to Know. New York, NY: Oxford University Press.
Rosén, Guri. 2016. A Match Made in Heaven? Explaining Patterns of Cooperation Between the Commission and the European Parliament. *Journal of European Integration* 38 (4): 409–424. https://doi.org/10.1080/07036337.2016.1141903.
Rosenzweig, Cynthia, David Rind, Andrew A. Lacis, and Danielle Peters, eds. 2017. *Our Warming Planet: Topics in Climate Dynamics*. New Jersey: World Scientific.
Rothe, Delf. 2016. *Securitizing Global Warming: A Climate of Complexity*. Routledge Studies in Resilience. London: Routledge.
Sbragia, Alberta M. 2008. "American Federalism and Intergovernmental Relations." In *The Oxford Handbook of Political Institutions*, ed. Sarah Binder, R.A.W. Rhodes, and Bert Rockman.
Schäfer, Mike, and Saffron O'Neill. 2017. Frame Analysis in Climate Change Communication. *In Oxford Research Encyclopedia*. New York: Oxford University Press. https://doi.org/10.1093/acrefore/9780190228620.001.0001/acrefore-9780190228620-e-487.
Schaller, Stella, and Alexander Carius. 2019. "Convenient Truths: MApping Climate Agendas of Right-Wing Populist Parties in Europe." Berlin: adelphi. https://www.adelphi.de/de/publikation/convenient-truths.

Schellnhuber, Hans-Joachim. 2015. *Selbstverbrennung : Die Fatale Dreiecksbeziehung Zwischen Klima, Mensch Und Kohlenstoff*, 2nd ed. München: C. Bertelsmann.

Simonis, Georg, ed. 2017. *Handbuch Globale Klimapolitik*. Uni-Taschenbücher, UTB-Band-Br. 8672. Paderborn: Ferdinand Schöningh.

Skjærseth, Jon Birger, Guri Bang, and Miranda A. Schreurs. 2013. Explaining Growing Climate Policy Differences Between the European Union and the United States. *Global Environmental Politics* 13 (4): 61–80. https://doi.org/10.1162/GLEP_a_00198.

Sonnicksen, Jared. 2021. Can the EU Be a Federal Democracy? Assessing the Horizontal and Vertical Dimension of the EU Government from Comparative Perspective. *Comparative European Politics*. https://doi.org/10.1057/s41295-021-00265-2.

Steffen, Will. 2011. "A Truly Complex and Diabolical Policy Problem." In *The Oxford Handbook of Climate Change and Society*, edited by John S. Dryzek, 21–37.

Stevenson, Hayley, and John S. Dryzek. 2014. *Democratizing Global Climate Governance*. Cambridge: Cambridge University Press.

Stott, Peter, Nikolaos Christidis, Friederike Otto, Ying Sun, Jean-Paul. Vanderlinden, Geert Jan, Robert van Oldenborgh, Vautard, et al. 2016. Attribution of Extreme Weather and Climate-Related Events. *Wires Climate Change*, 7: 23–41. https://doi.org/10.1002/wcc.380.

Sun, Jiazhe, and Kaizhong Yang. 2016. "The Wicked Problem of Climate Change: A New Approach Based on Social Mess and Fragmentation." *Sustainability* 8 (1312): 1–14. https://doi.org/10.3390/su8121312.

Sussman, Glen, and Byron W. Daynes. 2013. *US Politics and Climate Change: Science Confronts Policy*. Boulder, CO [u.a.]: Lynne Rienner Publ.

Thompson, Frank, Kenneth Wong, and Barry Rabe. 2020. *Trump, the Administrative Presidency, and Federalism*. Washington, DC: Brookings Institution Press.

Turnheim, Bruno, Paula Kivimaa, and Frans Berkhout, eds. 2018. *Innovating Climate Governance: Moving beyond Experiments*. Cambridge: Cambridge University Press.

Verdun, Amy. 2016. "The Federal Features of the EU: Lessons from Canada." *Politics and Governance* 4 (3): 100–110. https://doi.org/10.17645/pag.v4i3.598.

Vezirgiannidou, Sevasti-Eleni. 2013. Climate and Energy Policy in the United States: The Battle of Ideas. *Environmental Politics* 22 (4): 593–609. https://doi.org/10.1080/09644016.2013.806632.

Weathers, Melinda R., and Brenden E. Kendall. 2016. Developments in the Framing of Climate Change as a Public Health Issue in US Newspapers. *Environmental Communication* 10 (5): 593–611. https://doi.org/10.1080/175 24032.2015.1050436.

White House. 2021a. "The Biden-Harris Administration Immediate Priorities." Washington, DC. https://www.whitehouse.gov/priorities/.

White House. 2021b. "Fact Sheet: President Biden Sets 2030 Greenhouse Gas Pollution Reduction Target Aimed at Creating Good-Paying Union Jobs and Securing U.S. Leadership on Clean Energy Technologies." April 22, 2021b, Washington, DC. https://www.whitehouse.gov/briefing-room/sta tements-releases/2021b/04/22/fact-sheet-president-biden-sets-2030-greenh ouse-gas-pollution-reduction-target-aimed-at-creating-good-paying-union-jobs-and-securing-u-s-leadership-on-clean-energy-technologies/.

Wurzel, Rüdiger, Mikael Skou Andersen, and Paul Tobin, eds. 2021. *Climate Governance across the Globe. Pioneers, Leaders and Followers*. Abingdon, OX [u.a.]: Routledge.

Wurzel, Rüdiger, James Connelly, and Duncan Liefferink, eds. 2017. *The European Union in International Climate Change Politics: Still Taking a Lead?* Routledge Studies in European Foreign Policy. London: Routledge.

Zürn, Michael. 2012. "Global Governance as Multi-Level Governance." In *The Oxford Handbook of Governance*, edited by David Levi-Faur, 731–45. Oxford University Press.

Zürn, Michael. 2018. *A Theory of Global Governance: Authority, Legitimacy, and Contestation*, 1st ed. Oxford: Oxford University Press.

CHAPTER 2

Theoretical Framework: Framing, Issue Dimensions and Political Space

This chapter presents the theoretical framework for the comparative analysis of climate change policy in the EU and the US. Adopting an understanding of discourse that is based on political agency and advocacy, a key point of departure is that ideas matter for policy-making processes in their role as an intellectual foundation of justificatory arguments raised by political agents in specific institutional settings (Schmidt 2010: 15–20; Meckling 2011: 12–15). The main tool used to capture the role of ideas for promoting particular policies is the concept of discursive frames, and their comparative evaluation in the context of an evolving political space of climate change policy. The chapter develops this framework by presenting a typology of six climate frames derived from three key issue categories; the second half of the chapter then goes on to outline comparative hypotheses and to explain the data and method used for this study.

2.1 Framing: Linking Ideas, Discourse and Political Contestation

The concept of framing has been applied in many fields of the social sciences, including in political psychology (Lakoff 2014, Wehling 2016), media and communication studies (Engesser and Brüggemann 2016), practical political advocacy and political science (for overviews cp. Vliegenthart 2012; Atikcan 2015: 15–53, de Vreese 2012, Schön and Rein 1995) and particularly in research on political parties (Grande et al. 2016; Hoeglinger et al. 2012, Hoeglinger 2016: 100–124; Diez Medrano and Gray 2010, Helbling et al. 2010) as well as for climate change policy (Dirikx and Gelders 2010, Paterson 2021a, b: 14–18, McHugh et al. 2021, Newell et al. 2015, Schäfer and O'Neill 2017). The approach taken here adopts an understanding that defines framing as a rhetorical device used by political agents to select and emphasize particular aspects of complex policy issues for purposes of political advocacy and justification, and based on an underlying analytical or evaluative idea (cp. Daviter 2011: 33). This approach follows the definition of framing by Robert Entman that stresses the function of frames as a cognitive and normative heuristic used in political discourse:

> Framing essentially involves *selection* and *salience*. *To frame is to select some aspects of a perceived reality and make them more salient in a communicating text, in such a way as to promote a particular problem definition, causal interpretation, moral evaluation, and/or treatment recommendation.*
> (Entman 1993: 52, emphasis in the original)

Two specifications need to be added to this definition for the purposes of the present study. First, the approach used here assumes that the main criterion for distinguishing different frames is not at the object level (i.e., what thing or problem a political claim refers to), although some discussion will follow on different issue categories of climate change that are relevant in this regard. However, the main emphasis is laid here on the distinction of frames at the level of justification: what principles and criteria of reasoning are used to evaluate climate change and to endorse or object to specific courses of action. Second, the definition implies that the most plausible path towards a typologization of frames—defining what frames should be considered in empirical analysis and how they relate to each other—leads through the discussion of relevant *ideas* applied to the phenomenon of climate change. In this context, an idea is understood as an intellectual concept that provides an abstraction to relate individual observations to generalized assumptions (for example, the subsumption of threats caused by climate change such as floods, heat waves and drought as a public health or security issue). This point leads us to the discussion on how to identify and typologize relevant ideas on climate change.

2.2 Framing Climate Change: Issue Categories, Justificatory Principles and Scope of Ideas

The typology of frames that will be used for the subsequent analysis is developed in three steps. First, we identify three main issue categories—broad groups of issues raised in debates about climate change—as a point of departure for further typologization; second, we present six main frames to evaluate and justify action against climate change across the three issue categories based on a distinction between normative and instrumental forms of rationality; and finally, we introduce a differentiation between three different scopes applied to the empirical mapping and evaluation of justificatory ideas, reaching from paradigmatic to more technical, policy-specific ideas. The resulting typology will serve as the framework for the analysis of climate discourse in the empirical main part, providing specific distinctions about what aspect of climate change is addressed, at what level of generality or specificity, and what fundamental justificatory idea is applied to validate a claim.

The first step of this conceptualization starts by identifying relevant issue categories: namely, sets of political questions and challenges that refer to clusters of topics within the complex issue of climate change. This initial step therefore engages with the different objects of reference in political discourse, or general sets of challenges posed by global warming. As discussed in the introductory chapter, we assume that controversy about climate change involves three such categories: namely, sets of claims relating to its appraisal as a problem for society; subsequent controversy about the criteria applied to design and evaluate policy for its treatment; and finally, questions raised about the appropriate and most effective forms of collective action to adopt and implement envisaged policies. Spelled out in more detail, the distinction between these three issue categories can be defined in the following terms:

First, a *problem definition* category is defined as the entity of concepts and criteria used to evaluate the scope and quality of climate change as a problem, without directly prescribing a particular treatment or course of action. At a general level, climate change represents a problem whose definitions can be defined from various angles, reaching from relatively short-term concerns about damaging effects of extreme weather to more long-term and fundamental appraisals of global warming as a catalyst of transition to the Anthropocene as a new stage in Earth history (Pickering and Dryzek 2019). In this sense, political debates need to find answers to the question: Why is climate change a problem? Claims within this dimension refer to harmful impacts of a changing climate, either globally or in relation to a particular group or segment of society and set in a certain temporal framework of reference. The subsequent typology suggest that particularly two frames based on risk and ecological criteria relate to this dimension by proposing criteria to identify causal mechanisms through which global warming becomes a threat requiring political action: namely, either by posing a material threat for human security, or by compromising the intactness of ecosystems. In both cases, however, no specific policy treatment or regulatory approach is prescribed or recommended in more specific terms.

Second, a *policy evaluation* category is created by debates on what basic criteria are relevant to design and evaluate specific policy-making instruments and regulatory approaches to address climate change. This category creates a distinct dimension of debate in relation to discursive approaches to problem identification: Even a shared understanding of the urgency of climate change as a problem does not prescribe an evident or uncontested course of political action. This second issue dimension of climate politics therefore involves debates about the design of regulatory instruments; this particularly concerns the appropriate balance between state intervention, markets, and voluntary action by businesses, civil society groups and individuals. This issue category therefore turns to treatments of climate change, providing answers to the question: What policy change is required to act against climate change? Our subsequent typology suggests that particularly frames based on economic and justice criteria are relevant in this dimension, as these frames propose criteria for assessing the costs and benefits of policy-making. These include classical principles of economic rationality such as competitiveness, efficiency or effects of policies on economic growth, but also involve criteria for striking a balance between economic competition, state-led regulatory intervention and compensation based on ideas of social justice. A shared feature of these various approaches to framing are, however, that they primarily refer to the effects of policies proposed or enacted against climate change, but not the causal mechanisms or effects of the manifestations of atmospheric changes themselves.

Finally, a *collective action* category emerges through controversies about particular steps of action against climate change in terms of political decision-making, concerning its progress, degrees of support and practical consequences after implementation. Relevant issues involved in this dimension are how to identify appropriate political frameworks for action against climate change, but also questions assessing the determination of governing agents to act and their support at the level of society and ways of effective implementation. In this context, particularly controversies about the authority, support and legitimacy of institutions and governance at the supranational level in relation to local agents and authorities emerges as a key question. What moves to the foreground is therefore the shape, progress and support of political frameworks to enact policies against climate change, without specific attention to the content of policy and answering to the question: How can politics and society respond to climate change? The main issue of contention within this dimension, are ideas of political community and authority and how to negotiate them in relation to the problem of climate change. Subsequent claims in this field can reach from calls for individual or grassroot-level action to claims about the relevance and legitimacy of global governance to solve the problem of global warming. The subsequent typology considers two variants of frames, covering political and societal aspects of collective action against climate change, as relevant forms of justification in this dimension.

To summarize, the first step of distinguishing relevant issue categories seeks to systematize the multi-layered structure of discourse on climate change in relation to three major questions, asking if and why climate change is a problem, what policy change and development it requires and how and where the best framework can be found to act. Using this categorization as a point of departure, a second step towards creating a typology of frames turns from objects of reference to distinguishing the variants of justification used to raise a claim about the three issue categories. Here, we seek to specify the most relevant of myriad ways through which political agents justify or reject steps to act against global warming. A key distinction in this regard is between *instrumental ideas* as concepts entailing assumptions about causal relationships between aspects of reality (e.g., carbon emissions and global warming, or between the introduction of a carbon tax and losses in economic competitiveness) on the one hand; and *normative ideas* as generalized claims about appropriate orientations and forms of social action (e.g., the preservation of ecosystems for future generations, or distributive justice in the introduction of a carbon tax), on the other (cp. Schmidt 2008, 2010). The distinction between both is not just analytical: In the case of normative ideas, a priori principles are raised to confront the problem of climate change, mostly based on an appeal to ideological positions or cultural identifications that resonate with entrenched patterns of political polarization. Instrumental ideas, by contrast, follow a primarily consequentialist logic to present factual claims about the effects of certain pathways of action, and are therefore more secondary to the expression of ideologically founded principles.

The distinction between normative and instrumental ideas establishes only a general point of departure, requiring further specification of justificatory frames. Starting with normative forms of reasoning, discourse theory provides a productive secondary distinction between three modes of norms-based justification: first, moral reasoning as a category of arguments based on ideas of reciprocity, fairness and justice; second, ethical ideas as concepts expressing claims about intrinsically good or valuable orientations for a social group or community; and finally, cultural claims as expressions of symbols and values related to the identity of a particular group (Wendler 2016: 34–40; Niemi 2008; Sjursen 2006; Diez and Steans 2005; Rustin 1999). Based on this threefold distinction, we conceptualize the following three (ideal–typical) normative variants of justificatory arguments about political action on climate change:

First, an *ecological frame* is conceptualized as a form of justification that emerges primarily within the problem definition category of debate about climate change: Statements based on this frame raise global warming as a threat to the intactness of ecosystems while appraising their protection as something that is intrinsically valuable, even independently of its immediate effects on humans (O'Brien et al. 2010a; Hulme 2009: 109–42). This frame therefore engages most closely with an ethical form of reasoning: What is captured is the value that is ascribed to nature and biodiversity as an aspect of the good life—as something to be pursued independently from the material use of natural resources, or financial and material effects of a degrading of habitats and ecosystems for humans (O'Brien et al. 2010b: 6–8). Deploring the extinction of species, appealing to the preservation of national parks or natural monuments such as coral reefs or forests, but also depicting how ways of life will be affected negatively by climate change, for example in terms of staying outside or enjoying nature, fall in this category. A symbolic expression of this frame are public appearances of high-level politicians in natural habitats and environments to make statements about the urgency of climate action, such as visits by the US President in glacier regions or Yosemite National Park, but also visual forms of framing based on depictions of nature (Rebich-Hespanha 2015). An important addition is that this and the subsequent frames are conceptualized without prescribing evaluative tendencies of related statements, therefore capturing both progressive and critical stances towards climate action. In this sense, it is also used to capture a group of claims affirming human, rather than ecological needs and concerns and rejects the idea of acting towards a stabilization of climate as not worth pursuing or secondary to other, more important aims. An extreme form of this critical stance is the depiction of climate scientists and activists as members of a fanatical sect or quasi-religious movement, as observed particularly in nationalist right narratives (Wendler 2022). This negative version of ecological framing is often used in conjunction with terms describing arguments about climate change as alarmist or expressions of 'climate hysteria', or those making ironic use of religious terms such as guilt, sinners, redemption or indulgences to describe the ethical stance of the climate movement. What is identified by applying this first form of framing are claims expressing an ethical statement about the relationship between human society and nature, comprising both those advocating for more stringent action based on concerns for the environment, and those rejecting it as a secondary or unfounded ethical value of political action.

Second, our typology conceptualizes a *justice frame* as one capturing those claims and statements that are based on a normative principle of reciprocity and mutual obligation between social groups or individuals. We assume that this frame is relevant particularly within the policy evaluation dimension of debate about climate change: In this context, central demands subsumed in the discussion of climate justice, such as calls for immediate action because of a responsibility towards future generations, or calls for compensatory payments or mechanisms between those causing emissions and being affected by climate change stand out as particularly relevant (Okereke 2011, 2018; Okereke and Coventry 2016; Meyer and Sanklecha 2017; Gardiner 2011). Both the Fridays for Future Movement and many claims raised by supporters of a Green New Deal in the US debate take up arguments framed in these moral arguments to call for more stringent and immediate action against climate change. In addition to these progressive positions, however, this and the subsequent frames are not necessarily used to advocate for climate policy, but equally capture arguments expressing a critical stance against it. This aspect engages with the fact that claims based on justice are frequently applied to argue against further progress in global climate policy. Perhaps the most prominent example is the public announcement of US President Trump to withdraw from the Paris Agreement, based on the claim that the US is treated unfairly (Okereke 2018: 326). In a similar vein, positions rejecting climate change as a hoax or conspiracy, as upheld by parts of the US Republican right (Inhofe 2012) and some nationalist right parties in Europe (Lockwood 2018; Almiron and Xifra 2019), are often framed in moral terms: At its core, the claim rejecting climate change as a lie or manipulation aims at the honesty and integrity of its advocates. What such claims call into question are the motives of climate scientists and activists, suggesting that global warming is fabricated only to introduce new regulation or taxes for sinister or even hostile purposes. The underlying logic of this sort of argumentation aims at the delegitimization of agents, policies and institutions, and therefore involves a moral accusation, rather than a cognitive statement about the validity of scientific findings about climate change. Concerning more specific claims about policies, particularly aspects of financial transfers and compensation are included in this frame as distributive aspects of climate policy agendas, as these include appeals related to ideas of social justice and fairness of burden-sharing.

Third, a *society frame* captures arguments made about specific action against climate change based on references to forms of political community, tradition and identity (cp. Wittmayer et al. 2019; Hammack 2008). This frame arguably moves towards the issue category of collective action. As the previous frame, this form of justification resonates with ethical forms of reasoning by aiming at intrinsically valuable aspects of the good life. However, in contrast to an ecological framing, it is focused on human—individual and social—needs and aspirations, rather than appraising the relationship between humans and their natural environment. An essential concept for the expression of this frame is the idea of freedom, both on an individual level as the possibility to realize culturally defined ways of life, and on a political level as a right of self-determination and (national) sovereignty (cp. Kriesi et al. 2012: 16ff.). The specific aspect of controversies on climate policy captured by this frame is how global warming will and should affect our way of life: Arguments falling in this category are appeals to change forms of consumption and behavior in relation to food, clothing, individual mobility and travel. The flip side of such claims are critical counter-arguments insisting that climate change should be no reason to give up established ways of life and living standards, or that they should not be used to call for a restraint in consumption. In this sense, the (individual) freedom as a right to consume meat, enjoy unlimited mobility and consume a broad diversity of products from global sources is often held up as a priority even when faced with the challenge of climate change (Hulme 2009: 142–78). On a broader level, this societal frame focuses on institutional and political frameworks of action, confronting claims upholding the sovereignty of the nation-state with calls for a transnational or global community as the appropriate scale of political action. Concerning specific policies, the balance between state authority and individual freedom, as expressed in the choice between voluntary and legally sanctioned forms of regulation, is an important aspect highlighted by this frame.

To sum up, a commonality of the normative frames presented here is that their logic of justification is based on a priori values that are raised as principles to guide political action to deal with the challenge of climate change, including its minimization or denial. In this sense, concepts of justice as well as ethical or cultural ideas are emphasized as a normative heuristic to select and evaluate particular aspects of climate change as a problem for political debate. While reducing the number of frames distinguished within this normative perspective to three, this approach captures a wide variety of views within the climate debate, ranging from generational justice to the defense of established ways of life and the rejection of climate change as the belief of a fanatical sect of believers.

In addition to these types of normative framing, we consider three (ideal–typical) forms of instrumental or consequentialist reasoning about (in)action towards climate change. The point of departure for this distinction is that this type of claims refers to causal effects of global warming and climate policy measures on resources—i.e., material factors establishing incentives and constraints for social transactions and individual survival and welfare. Once again applying the distinction between the three issue categories discussed at the outset, our typology identifies three specific frames under this heading:

First, and primarily relating to problem definitions of climate change, a *risk frame* is conceptualized to capture statements relating to potentially harmful consequences of climate change for human security in its different facets (Gilman et al. 2011; Oels 2012). This includes references to impacts of extreme weather events, longer-term threats to the safety of cities and regions, and public health issues concerning infectious diseases and direct effects of increased heat on vulnerable persons (Haines and Frumkin 2021; Weathers and Kendall 2016). Arguably a strong current of reasoning in this frame is the reference to scientific models and predictions such as those published under the direction of institutions establishing the scientific foundation for the global climate regime such as the UNEP or IPCC, including claims discussing the veracity of their findings (cp. Hartman and Oshita 2013). The majority of science-based claims in this frame makes the case for stringent action against climate change. However, this category of frames also captures statements that relativize or even deny the gravity of the consequences based on (quasi- or pseudo-scientific) claims of risk and security. Statements claiming that a trend towards global warming is not measurable, that higher carbon dioxide levels and temperatures are beneficial for plants and ecosystems, that climate change is a result of natural cycles in sun activity or simply a repetition of previous warm periods in the Middle Ages are of course scientifically unsound. Nevertheless, on a political level these claims emerge as a subset of discourse that *claim to suggest* a scientific foundation for the evaluation of climate change in political debates. In this context, an interesting example is the publication 'The Greatest Hoax' by James Inhofe, one of the most prominent opponents of climate policy in the US Senate. While using numerous questionable or unfounded arguments such as those cited above, its main argument proposed to question the seriousness of climate change is that a scientifically based evaluation of climate change does not support a case for action and needs to be held up against the allegedly distorted, ideological view of climate policy advocates (Inhofe 2012). Claims raised by climate skeptics particularly from the nationalist right similarly make the case for a 'rational', 'un-ideological' or 'realistic' approach to make the case that science does not support the need to act; in the same vein, several of the climate skeptic think tanks in the US, to be covered in more detail in our case study, present their position with a framing purporting to present scientific facts rather than political positions. This observation seems important because it highlights the difficulties of establishing scientific claims about global warming that are not contested as lacking credibility by opponents of climate action.

Second, and primarily relating to the issue category of policy evaluation, our typology considers an *economic frame* as a perspective that evaluates policy solutions based on criteria of returns from market-based exchanges; this form of justification is arguably a highly relevant, but also a potentially very contentious form for evaluating policy-making against climate change. The costs of inaction against global warming have been raised as a widely recognized argument for progressive action; most prominently, this form of reasoning was established in the Stern Review and its strong emphasis on economic and financial arguments in favor of stringent action on climate change (Stern 2007). By contrast, the potentially negative effects of carbon emissions regulation on economic growth, its impact on losses of jobs and decline of industries are an equally relevant argument in controversies on climate change. An important difference between these two antagonistic perspectives is often the choice of time frames, distinguishing assessments of effects on shorter-term profit from longer-term perspectives on sustainable forms of economic activity. Taken together, this frame bundles arguments bringing to the fore a very fundamental question—namely, whether climate change calls into question the viability and sustainability of a capitalist form of economic management and consumption. In a mid-term perspective, the economic frame establishes action against climate change as a question of economic growth and efficiency, particularly in relation to energy production and consumption, but also trade, transport and infrastructure (Karplus and Valerie 2014; Schlichting 2013). At the policy level, the consideration of economic incentives and mechanisms is a frequent issue in the design of regulatory approaches, most prominently in the development of emissions trading (Neuhoff 2011); it also features as a prominent aspect in debates on costs and returns in the transition to renewable energies. Considering these aspects, this frame is probably the most controversial, inviting both passionate pleas in favor of stringent action against climate change and its rejection as economically damaging. Beyond political debates, controversy on this point is reflected in academic debate about the concept of 'climate capitalism', approaches of political economy (Paterson 2021a, b; Newell et al. 2021; Newell and Paterson 2010), and the concept of 'eco-modernization' in the context of debate on variants of a Green New Deal (Ajl 2021).

Finally, and covering the issue category of collective action, a *political frame* is defined as one covering those claims that evaluate climate change in terms of its perception by the general public and concerning the feasibility of action in terms of support, institutional access, majorities, electoral cycles and phases of the policy cycle. Here, the cost–benefit relations central to consequentialist reasoning are evaluated in terms of political, rather than economic or other material resources. A major aspect of this framing are criteria of political leadership in climate policy, in terms of political resources and support, available institutional frameworks for creating and managing processes of governance, and entrepreneurial skills and authority of particular agents (cp. Wurzel et al. 2017; Rayner and Jordan 2013; Luterbacher and Sprinz 2018). Beyond policy-makers, a political framing also covers references to degrees of support by electorates and ordinary citizens: In this sense, climate change may be referred to as something that is (not) recognized as an urgent problem by ordinary citizens and civil society organizations. The causal mechanism suggested by this frame as a relevant criterion for climate action is the interrelation between political decision-making and public support: In this sense, the mobilization of citizens protesting for more consequent action against global warming creates an argument for policy-makers to act. However, references to the (potentially) adverse reactions of citizens to burdens imposed by a carbon tax or similar measures are equally relevant for justifying a cautious and gradual approach to specific climate policy. Recent debates in Germany about the Federal Government's climate policy package ('Klimapaket') are a case in point: Conceding the criticism that the highly incremental approach taken towards the introduction of a carbon tax did not amount to a stringent course of action, Chancellor Merkel made the point in her public statements that reservations and sensitivities by citizens were the main reason for taking a cautious approach (FAZ 2019). This example illustrates how (in)action towards climate change is sometimes justified in purely political, rather than scientific or economic criteria.

To summarize this discussion, the typology of frames presented here distinguishes six forms of justification for the empirical analysis of public discourse on climate change: We consider a justice, ecological, and society frame as variants of normative discourse on climate change; in addition, a risk-based, political and economic frame are distinguished as three different forms of instrumental or consequentialist reasoning. Within this sixfold distinction, we assume that three pairs of frames are related to the main issue categories identified above: namely, that risk and ecology frames are primarily used within a problem identification dimension to describe the existence, severity and consequences of climate change; that forms of economic and justice-based framing are used to evaluate policies proposed to act against global warming; and that the political and society frames distinguished here engage with the collective action dimension of climate politics. The full typology of six climate frames and their relation to issue dimensions and underlying logics of justification is summarized once more below (Table 2.1).

Based on this typology, we include a third step of conceptualization to create a more fine-grained evaluation of arguments within each frame: While the distinction of six main climate frames creates an analytical grid

Table 2.1 Typology of six approaches to framing climate change (CC) and climate change policy (CCP)

	Instrumental/consequential rationality	*Normative/Ethical & moral rationality*
Problem definition: Why is climate change a problem?	**Risk:** CC as a threat to individual and collective security (e.g., extreme weather)	**Ecology:** CC as a threat to intrinsically valuable natural assets (e.g., biodiversity)
Policy evaluation: What policy change is required to act against climate change?	**Economy:** Efficiency and economic returns from measures of CCP (e.g., technological advantage)	**Justice:** Fairness in the assignment of burdens to enact CCP (e.g., climate finance)
Collective action: How can politics and society respond to climate change?	**Political:** Access to and support within processes of decision-making (e.g., veto points)	**Society:** Resonance with culture, tradition, forms of community (e.g., regional cultures)

to evaluate different forms of justification, a difficulty for applying it to concrete empirical material such as speeches or legislative text may be that a whole range of claims of very different specificity fall under each of the frames distinguished. For example, aspects of climate justice can be expressed in very broad, fundamental terms such as an emphasis of responsibility towards future generations, but also at a more specific and technical level by defining the operation of a just transition funding mechanism. Within the typology of frames, we therefore add a threefold distinction concerning the scope and specificity with which ideas are raised and expressed through discourse. Here, our approach borrows from the literature on policy paradigms and discursive institutionalism by distinguishing three different stages concerning the scope of policy ideas (Carson 2009; Surel 2000; Schmidt 2008, 2010):

First, *paradigmatic ideas* entail fundamental ontological and normative principles, such as ideas about foundations of social and political community or the embedding of human society in its natural environment. At this level, we capture ideas that are expressed in very general or fundamental terms, without any specification of their temporal, institutional or political limits (such as emphatic endorsements of economic growth or national sovereignty). Second, the term *programmatic ideas* is used to capture concepts describing the overall scope, rationale and framework of climate action, particularly in terms of time horizons, institutions and political levels of action. Finally, *policy ideas* are defined as those concepts that relate to specific approaches and instruments to realize the ambitions defined at the programmatic level. The distinction between these three levels will be taken up again in the comparative chapter, when it is used to describe the paradigmatic salience of positions, used as a term for how agents combine general emphases on frames with references to either highly fundamental or more specific terms.

As described above, each of the six frames distinguished here is used to capture both positive and skeptical statements about climate change policy. The typology therefore deliberately pulls together statements that are based on the same justification but reach different evaluative conclusions. The rationale behind this conceptualization is twofold: First, rather than subsuming all arguments rejecting climate action as denialist, the approach taken here allows a differentiation of the varieties of climate skepticism and related forms of contestation in terms of political, economic and cultural arguments. We posit that better insight into the controversy on climate action is gained by evaluating what kinds of frame emerge as contested focal points—namely, bases of justification that both advocates and opponents harness to argue for their case—than to assign all critical or rejectionist arguments to an own, distinctive frame. Second, the approach described here enables our analysis to distinguish two different types of contestation: namely, a form where claims about climate action are contested between arguments that are, however, based on the fundamentally same criteria of a single frame (e.g., such as economic efficiency); and one where different political agents address and dispute climate change based on entirely different and potentially disparate perspectives (e.g., a vision of ecological destruction versus claims about effects of climate policy on job losses). The implications of such distinctions are captured within the concept of political space, discussed in the subsequent section.

2.3 Research Hypotheses: Linking Frames, Issue Categories and Political Space

How are different approaches to framing climate change related to the emergence of political controversy and divergence in the policy development of the EU and US? In order to develop comparative hypotheses in this regard, our approach harnesses the concept of political space; more specifically, this concept is applied to evaluate the structure, linkages and contestation of climate frames in political discourse. While space is sometimes evoked in relation to aspects of territoriality in the literature on climate change (Latour 2018; Lövbrand and Stripple 2006), the term of political space is familiar particularly from the comparative literature on party systems (Benoit and Laver 2012, Gabel and Hix 2002; Pennings 2002). In this context, it is commonly used to capture the positions and interaction of political agents or parties along one or several issue dimensions. These, in turn, can be defined as relatively stable structuring logics of political conflict that result from the emergence of bundles of related political issues as salient questions of political contestation, and the emergence of a relatively stable spectrum of ideologically defined responses of competing agents towards these questions (Hutter et al. 2016: 3–33; Hooghe and Marks 2018; Kriesi et al. 2012: 96–108, Hoeglinger 2016: 23–29). The main value of using this concept for the present analysis is that it provides a holistic framework of analysis for evaluating three interrelated aspects of political controversy arising from discourse on climate change: namely, relevant issue categories[1] involving clusters of related issues that are addressed from competing ideological angles by involved political agents; linkages between those issue categories and underlying ideological positions; and patterns of political contestation. The application of this concept for the present analysis is primarily inductive: Rather than applying a pre-defined set of issues and criteria to map positions and polarization, the rationale of the present study is to explore what issues and ideological principles are relevant within the complex, expanding and relatively volatile field of climate politics. To explore these aspects, the subsequent empirical analysis proceeds in three steps:

First, an initial step of exploring political space is to identify relevant issue categories, defined as clusters of thematically related questions of

---

[1] The terms of issue category and issue dimension refer to different analytical concepts, as described in the relevant sections of this chapter: We introduce the term *issue category* to identify thematically related aspects of controversy about climate change and their respective objects of reference; the concept of *issue dimension*, however, is discussed to consider the emergence of a politically salient structuring logic of political discourse and contestation with identifiable ideological principles defining competing political positions. In this sense, an issue dimension can emerge within a single or in combination of various frames depending on their respective salience and linkages in political discourse, as elaborated in the subsequent discussion.

political choice that are addressed in political debate. By mapping the occurrence of the six climate frames discussed above, the present study seeks to explore what topical dimensions emerge as relevant in the climate debates of the EU and US, and what ideological criteria are promoted in the debate as defined by the respective frames. The primary question for this first step of analysis is: How salient are the issues of problem definition, policy evaluation and collective action, and what criteria are used to address them? The comparative survey therefore starts by mapping the structure of frames used in climate discourse of the EU and US debates, particularly with regard to their respective salience and comparing subsets of discourse involving executive and legislative agents.

Second, a subsequent step of analysis is to find out how issue categories and frames are linked with each other, and how linkages created between these frames differ in a comparison of various agents and subsets of discourse. By zooming in on particular combinations of frames and their variation across agents, this step creates an intermediate stage between the mapping of discourse in the policy debate on the one hand, and the evaluation of controversy between specific agents and positions, on the other. Linkages between the six main climate frames are measured by the degree to which arguments associated with different frames (such as economic and political claims) are used in combination with each other within the same segment of speech or policy document. A more specific rationale of this step is to evaluate and compare the degree of inclusiveness or selectiveness of framing within a particular subset of discourse: namely, to what degree agents frame their arguments in broad, inclusive terms by linking various forms of justification, or whether a more focused and selective form of reasoning is presented.

Finally, the third step of our analysis contrasts different strands of debate and actor-specific variants of discourse to evaluate their respective polarization in relation to each other. The framing approach applied here makes it possible to distinguish between two different forms of controversy: namely, contestation created between agents that address climate change from divergent angles, as expressed through the use of contrasting forms of framing and evaluated using the concept of paradigmatic polarization; and controversy emerging between agents that adopt competing positions within the same justificatory frame but promote contradictory evaluations and arguments within this frame, discussed subsequently as discursive contestation.

To summarize, the concept of political space is used here to draw inference from the approach of framing analysis to gain insights into three aspects of political conflict, namely: thematic issue categories as derived from the structure of framing; profiles of discourse promoted by particular agents as derived from linkages between frames; and finally, polarization and contestation as derived between contrasting uses and evaluations of the various frames. Applied to the two main cases compared in this book, the overall assumption to guide the establishment of more specific hypotheses is that the political space of climate politics is more coherently structured and stable in the EU case than in the US. This means that EU policy discourse is assumed to evolve through the interaction of relatively broad, coherent and stable forms of framing in comparison to the US, where the space of climate politics is assumed to be more fragmented and volatile. Based on this overall assumption, the comparative analysis evaluates three sets of hypotheses concerning the structure, linkages and contestation of climate frames, presented in the survey below and discussed in subsequent paragraphs (Table 2.2).

1. <u>Structure of framing</u>: In a first step, we evaluate the assumption that the more stable policy development in the EU case is rooted in a discursive framing that is focused on a more single-dimensional structure in terms of issue categories and related frames, and more

Table 2.2 Survey of analytical dimensions and comparative hypotheses

	The European Union (EU)	The United States (US)
Structure of framing: Issue categories (H1)	**Coherent**: More single-dimensional and coherent across levels	**Fragmented**: More multi-dimensional and divergent across levels
Linkages of frames: Actor positions (H2)	**Inclusive**: Broader and more widely shared linkages of frames	**Selective**: Focused and more distinct linkages of frames
Evaluation of frames: Polarization of actors (H3)	**Discursive**: Primarily contestation within frames	**Epistemic**: Primarily contestation between frames
Finding/conclusion: Format of political space	**Structured**: Stable, coherent and more single-dimensional	**Volatile**: Unstable, contested and multi-dimensional

coherently shared between involved political agents and across institutional venues. We therefore evaluate two assumptions linking policy divergence in the EU and US to the discursive framing of their respective policy debates: first, that the more stringent policy development in the EU is linked to fewer issue dimensions as created through more prominent master frames that are highly salient in policy discourse (H1a); and second, that this framing is more coherent across agents and institutional venues (H1b).

2. <u>Linkages between frames</u>: Second, we hypothesize that policymaking in the EU is based on a more inclusive form of framing, defined as one that includes broader and more widely shared linkages between frames. Considering the two related aspects of weight and density as empirical measurements of linkages, two more specific hypotheses result. First, we scrutinize the assumption that climate discourse in the EU is generally framed in broader and more inclusive terms than in the US by including linkages that are less concentrated on the most salient frames (weight) and less selective (density) than in the US case (H2a). Second, in comparison of different variants of discourse between institutional settings and party-political agents, we assume more coherent linkages of frames in the EU as compared to more diverse sets of frame linkages in the US (H2b).

3. <u>Contestation of frames and polarization</u>: This final pair of hypotheses focuses on two types of controversy on climate change, namely, one created through the promotion of different frames by competing political agents, and another through the promotion of different evaluations of climate change within the same frame. From this point of departure, the comparative discussion scrutinizes the following two hypotheses: First, we test the assumption that more continuous policy progress in the EU case is based in an overall lower intensity of polarization of climate discourse between involved political agents (H3a). Second, we scrutinize the assumption that climate discourse in the US case is more disparate in the sense of involving a clash between fundamentally different frames and issue categories; we therefore test the assumption that contestation in the US is expressed particularly through paradigmatic polarization (i.e., between frames) in comparison to stronger discursive contestation (i.e., within frames) in the EU (H3b).

Presented in this order, the three steps of comparative analysis follow an approach of zooming in to political debates about climate change, starting with a global survey of issue dimensions and proceeding towards more agent-specific discourse and polarization. An overview of our comparative hypotheses is shown once more below (Table 2.3).

Table 2.3 Survey of comparative hypotheses on framing of climate change in the EU and US

Level of comparison	Comparative hypotheses
Structure of frames/Issue dimensions	H1a: Fewer salient frames and issue dimensions in the EU than in the US H1b: Greater coherence across levels and agents in the EU than in the US
Linkages of frames/Discursive profiles	H2a: More inclusive framing/broader frame linkages in the EU H2b: More coherent frame linkages across agents and institutions in the EU
Contestation/Forms of polarization	H3a: Lower intensity of contestation in the EU than in the US H3b: Occurrence of paradigmatic polarization primarily in the US

2.4 Data and Method: Operationalization of Frames and Document Analysis

The empirical material for the present study consists of policy documents covering controversy on climate change following the Paris Agreement by and within key political institutions of the EU and US. This material includes public declarations and policy documents of executive agents, such as speeches and climate action programs issued by the US presidential administration and federal government, as well as European Council conclusions and policy documents of the EU Commission. Furthermore, it includes parliamentary resolutions, motions and legislative proposals, covering both chambers of US Congress and the European Parliament, as well as a set of party group motions on the European Green Deal from all party groups within the EP. Overall, the material selected for the present study consists of a body of 32 documents comprising text of about 132,000 words and 7,920 coded statements for the EU case; and a selection of 79 documents with an overall volume of about 108,000 words and overall 5.844 coded statements in the US case. A full list of the documents used for the subsequent analysis is provided in the annex, and a closer survey of documents chosen for the analysis is given in the two respective case studies on the EU and US.

It is evident that this empirical material primarily covers the public announcements of policy initiatives and their justification towards larger political audiences; what is largely excluded through this selection of material is more specific documentation of disagreement and policy debate within administrations and the details of intra-institutional negotiation of policy-making acts between party groups. This limitation, however, is deliberate as the present study seeks to elucidate the political space of climate policy debate within the realm of public political debate rather than intra-institutional coordination. Put in terms of Discursive Institutionalism, our analysis focuses on communicative discourse as the realm of public justification of policy, rather than on coordinative discourse as the realm of policy-specific negotiation on practical details of regulation within closed institutional settings (Schmidt 2008, 2010).

The subsequent empirical analysis applies a mixed method approach using content analysis software (MaxQDA) to identify, map and evaluate the use of frames in political discourse about climate policy. The approach of mapping statements about climate change and identifying them with one or several of the frames discussed above is primarily quantitative and conducted through dictionary-based automated coding, thereby excluding problems of inter- and intra-coder reliability. Compiling the dictionary used for coding the policy documents of both cases is, of course, of critical relevance. In the research process, this was conducted through a combination of quantitative screening and qualitative analysis and close reading. Following an initial screening of relevant keywords and their respective frequencies throughout the documents under analysis, rank orders of potentially relevant keywords were scrutinized and their use and context checked by reading through the lists of statements with hits for those keywords.[2] To arrive at keywords with a maximum degree

---

[2] The automatic coding function of the content analysis software was run several times using gradually refined versions of the dictionary to single out the use of discursive frames; each of these frames and their specification at the paradigmatic, program and policy level was coded when at least one keyword was identified by the software. Coded statements include the sentence containing the keyword and following sentence. This means that a statement can be coded with more than one frame if it contains keywords of several frames, as analyzed more closely in the subsequent discussion of linkages between frames.

of specificity for each frame, and to avoid including keywords with a highly generic or ambiguous meaning, efforts were made to include word combinations that are both frequent enough to return useable results and specific for a particular aspect of climate politics. For each of the frames discussed above, a dictionary of about 20 keywords was compiled across the three levels of paradigmatic, programmatic and policy-specific statements for both cases; different sets of keywords were compiled for the EU and US to account for different word usages and structures of both debates. These dictionaries will be presented in more detail within the two case study chapters on the EU and US; a full overview of the two dictionaries is presented in the annex of this book.

Several of the concepts used for the previous discussion of comparative hypotheses—particularly concerning observed linkages of frames and their contestation—require further explanation with regard to their operationalization and measurement.

First, a *linkage* between two frames is assumed to exist when the author of a public statement or policy document refers to two or several frames within the same statement (operationalized as the sentence in which a coding keyword occurs plus the following sentence). In practice, such links are quite frequent, as political actors advocating a specific approach to policy often tend to make the point that a proposed course of action meets the criteria of more than one, or even of opposing logics of action (e.g., by promoting an eco-friendly technology that at the same time, is also competitive and efficient). To evaluate these linkages in a systematic way, the subsequent analysis primarily proceeds through the identification of clusters: namely, by evaluating what pairs and subsequent three- and four-part combinations of frames are established most often within policy documents under analysis. A cluster of frames, in this sense, is a specific combination of frames a particular agent decides to use more frequently than other combinations.

From this point of departure, the mapping and evaluation of linkages involves the two related aspects of weight and density. The relative *weight* of clusters between frames is operationalized as the relative number of

---

As an additional check to confirm coding results and to eliminate inadequate assignments of frames as far as possible, several rounds of modification were conducted by reading through result lists of coded documents and adjusting keywords in the dictionary. A more specific survey of the most frequently coded keywords in comparison of both cases is provided in the comparative chapter.

statements absorbed by a particular combination of frames: put differently, what proportion of discourse is covered by this combination. Starting with the strongest 2-point cluster and gradually extending the analysis by one additional frame until a five-point cluster is reached, it is possible to identify how much an agent focuses a political discourse on very few selected frames, or extends it to a very broad combination of arguments. The empirical key to evaluating this aspect is to review the percentage of coded text segments comprised in the strongest cluster of two, three or four frames: Frequent combinations of two highly salient (i.e., frequently used) frames create a strong focus of discourse on this particular combination, whereas linkages between less generally emphasized frames can establish a more diversified form of discourse with several relatively salient combinations of frames. Furthermore, analyzing the relative *density* of linkages covers the focus of a specific discourse on a particular combination of frames, operationalized as the relative number of linkages within a cluster as compared to its external linkages. In simpler terms, the density of a framing cluster is an indicator for how close the connection is between two frames as compared to other combined references. For example, if the indicator for the density of linkages between an economic and risk-based framing in a given sample of text is very high, the association between these two frames is particularly strong in comparison to other possible linkages. In terms of practical empirical measurement, the indicator used to evaluate this density is the percentage of linkages between frames within a given cluster relative to the overall number of linkages identified by the text coding software. More details about this step of analysis are discussed in the comparative chapter (Chapter 5). On a theoretical level, the linkages evaluated through the two related indicators presented here is to proceed from a mapping of debate to the closer identification of actor-specific positions and, more specifically, to assess their distinctness in relation to each other. Furthermore, the evaluation of framing linkages also provides first insights into the significance of the various climate frames as a fault line of political controversy, particularly concerning the question whether emphases on particular frames are distinctive for particular positions, or whether frames are absorbed into combinations that occur across political divides.

Second, and building on the previous point, a conceptual and methodical challenge is to evaluate different forms of *contestation* and their empirical measurement. As discussed at the outset, a central tenet of the present study is that climate change appears as a complex, multi-dimensional policy problem that cannot be reduced a priori to a single, unidimensional political space and subsequent measurement of actor positions along a single axis. Rather than offering a quantifiable measurement of actor positions along pre-defined issue dimensions, therefore, the conceptual approach of framing is used here primarily to explore and compare the diverse perspectives and potential issue dimensions emerging within controversies on climate change. Based on this approach, we distinguish two different forms of controversy: namely, contestation resulting from the engagement of contrary arguments within the same perspective of rationalizing criteria (i.e., disputes between agents adopting the same framing of climate change); and polarization created as a result of more fundamentally diverging worldviews that adopt different cognitive and normative criteria to approach the topic of climate change.

This results in a distinction of two different forms of polarization: First, the concept of *paradigmatic polarization* is used when two or more agents apply divergent forms of framing to address the problem of climate change. In terms of empirical measurement, this form of polarization is operationalized through an indicator that combines data on the salience of a particular frame and the level of its specification in paradigmatic, programmatic or policy-specific terms, subsequently discussed as paradigmatic salience. This indicator is designed to reflect how often a frame is used in political discourse, and whether key terms used to define this frame are chosen at a very general, paradigmatic or a more specific policy level. In this sense, a form of discourse that keeps repeating fundamental criteria of a specific frame such as growth, justice or nature would achieve a high value in terms of its paradigmatic salience. Turning to controversy, two or more agents create paradigmatic polarization to the degree to which their respective discourse acquires high values of paradigmatic salience in two different frames and related issue categories.

Furthermore, the term *discursive contestation* is subsequently used as a concept to capture disputes between two or more agents adopting contrary or incompatible arguments within the same basic frame of justification: for example, by raising contrary views about the green energy transition as either creating or endangering economic growth and jobs. Here, we evaluate to what degree key terms of reference in discourse about climate policy—as identified through rank orders of keywords for politically salient frames—are shared across institutional settings and political agents with competing positions. Based on this approach, a high degree of divergence in the use of terms of reference—e.g., as in a case where one political camp frequently uses the term 'investment' while another keeps referring to 'growth'—is considered as an indicator for discursive polarization within a particular frame. To evaluate the degree to which compared sets of political agents use congruent or divergent sets of keywords, a specific similarity indicator will be introduced and evaluated in later stages of analysis, as discussed in more detail in the comparative chapter.

2.5 Conclusion: Framing and the Political Space of Climate Change Policy

To summarize, the theoretical approach of this study is based on three main components. First, we harness framing analysis to conceptualize six main approaches to the discursive justification of (in)action against climate change. This typology is based on the distinction of three issue categories related to the appraisal of climate change as a problem for society, the evaluation of policy proposed for its mitigation, and specific frameworks and decisions to achieve collective action. This typology serves as an analytical grid to map variants of climate discourse, but also creates a first systematization of salient topics and ideological positions proposed in the debate.

Second, the concept of political space is introduced with the rationale of embedding the comparative evaluation of frames and discourse in a framework allowing three related steps of analysis: namely, the identification of relevant issue dimensions emerging from the identification of the most salient frames and underlying ideological principles of justification; profiles of discourse held by involved agents as resulting from linkages between different frames; and finally, the intensity and form of polarization arising from the contestation of claims both within and between different frames.

Finally, three sets of comparative hypotheses are presented to evaluate the political space of climate change policy within the EU and US particularly in terms of their respective volatility and fragmentation. Beyond the comparison of the two cases, the rationale of scrutinizing these hypotheses is to explore the dimensionality of political conflict around issues of climate change in a comparative perspective, paving the way for further research into relevant issue dimensions and party-political polarization. The following empirical discussion takes a two-step approach, starting with case studies on the EU and US that provide a qualitative survey of key documents, positions and stages of decision-making. This is followed by a comparative chapter covering data from both cases in a quantitative analysis and test of comparative hypotheses. The following chapter starts with a survey of the EU case, focusing on how the European Green Deal emerged as a core agenda for climate action after the conclusion of the Paris Agreement.

REFERENCES

Ajl, Max. 2021. *A People's Green New Deal*. London: Pluto Press.
Almiron, Núria, and Jordi Xifra i Triadú. 2019. *Climate Change Denial and Public Relations: Strategic Communication and Interest Groups in Climate Inaction*. Routledge New Directions in Public Relations and Communication Research. Abingdon, Oxon; New York, NY: Routledge.
Atikcan, Ece Özlem. 2015. *Framing the European Union: The Power of Political Arguments in Shaping European Integration*. Cambridge: Cambridge University Press
Benoit, Kenneth, and Michael Laver. 2012. "The Dimensionality of Political Space: Epistemological and Methodological Considerations." *European Union Politics* 13 (2): 194–218. https://doi.org/10.1177/1465116511434618.
Carson, Marcus. 2009. *Paradigms in Public Policy: Theory and Practice of Paradigm Shifts in the EU*. Frankfurt am Main [u.a.]: Lang.
Daviter, Falk. 2011. *Policy Framing in the European Union*. Palgrave Studies in European Union Politics. Basingstoke [u.a.]: Palgrave Macmillan.
Diez Medrano, Juan, and Emily Gray. 2010. "Framing the European Union in National Public Spheres." In *The Making of a European Public Sphere. Media Discourse and Political Contention*, edited by Ruud Koopmans and Paul Statham, 195–219. Cambridge [u.a.]: Cambridge University Press.
Diez, Thomas, and Jill Steans. 2005. "A Useful Dialogue? Habermas and International Relations." *Review of International Studies* 31 (1): 127–40. https://doi.org/10.1017/S0260210505006339.
Dirikx, Astrid, and Dave Gelders. 2010. "To Frame Is to Explain: A Deductive Frame-Analysis of Dutch and French Climate Change Coverage during the Annual UN Conferences of the Parties." *Public Understanding of Science* 19 (6): 732–42. https://doi.org/10.1177/0963662509352044.
Engesser, Sven, and Michael Brüggemann. 2016. "Mapping the Minds of the Mediators: The Cognitive Frames of Climate Journalists from Five Countries." *Public Understanding of Science* 25 (7): 825–41. https://doi.org/10.1177/0963662515583621.

Entman, Robert M. 1993. "Framing: Toward Clarification of a Fractured Paradigm." *Journal of Communication* 43 (4): 51–58. https://doi.org/10.1111/j.1460-2466.1993.tb01304.x.

FAZ. 2019. "Merkel verteidigt Klimapaket: „Politik ist das, was möglich ist"." *FAZ.NET*, 2019. https://www.faz.net/1.6393990.

Gabel, Matthew, and Simon Hix. 2002. "Defining the EU Political Space: An Empirical Study of the European Elections Manifestos, 1979-1999." *Comparative Political Studies* 35 (8): 934–64. https://doi.org/10.1177/001041402236309.

Gardiner, Stephen M. 2011. "Climate Justice." In *The Oxford Handbook of Climate Change and Society*, edited by John S. Dryzek, Richard B. Norgaard, and David Schlosberg, 309–20. Oxford: Oxford University Press.

Gilman, Nils, Doug Randall, and Peter Schwartz. 2011. "Climate Change and 'Security.'" Edited by John S. Dryzek. *The Oxford Handbook of Climate Change and Society*, 251–66. https://doi.org/10.1093/oxfordhb/9780199566600.003.0017.

Grande, Edgar, Swen Hutter, Alena Kerscher, and Regina Becker. 2016. "Framing Europe: Are Cultural-Identitarian Frames Driving Politicisation?" In *Politicising Europe: Integration and Mass Politics*, 181–206. https://doi.org/10.1017/CBO9781316422991.009

Haines, Andy, and Howard Frumkin. 2021. *Planetary Helath. Safeguarding Human Helath and the Environment in the Anthropocene.* Cambridge: Cambridge University Press.

Hammack, Phillip L. 2008. "Narrative and the Cultural Psychology of Identity." *Personality and Social Psychology Review* 12 (3): 222–47. https://doi.org/10.1177/1088868308316892.

Hartman, Carol Terracina, and Tsuyoshi Oshita. 2013. "Climate Change on Trial: An Analysis of the Media Coverage of Climategate." *Journal of Climate Change ISSN 1865-7156* 4: 119–32.

Helbling, Marc, Dominic Hoeglinger, and Bruno Wüest. 2010. "How Political Parties Frame European Integration." *European Journal of Political Research* 49 (4): 495–521. https://doi.org/10.1111/j.1475-6765.2009.01908.x.

Hoeglinger, Dominic. 2016. *Politicizing European Integration: Struggling with the Awakening Giant.* Challenges to Democracy in the 21st Century. Basingstoke: Palgrave Macmillan.

Hoeglinger, Dominic, Bruno Wüest, and Marc Helbling. 2012. "Culture versus Economy: The Framing of Public Debates over Issues Related to Globalization." In *Political Conflict in Western Europe*, 229–53.

Hooghe, Liesbet, and Gary Marks. 2018. "Cleavage Theory Meets Europe's Crises: Lipset, Rokkan, and the Transnational Cleavage." *Journal of European Public Policy* 25 (1): 109–35. https://doi.org/10.1080/13501763.2017.1310279.

Hulme, Mike. 2009. *Why We Disagree about Climate Change: Understanding Controversy, Inaction and Opportunity*. Cambridge [u.a.]: Cambridge University Press.

Hutter, Swen, Edgar Grande, and Hanspeter Kriesi, eds. 2016. *Politicising Europe: Integration and Mass Politics*. Cambridge: Cambridge University Press.

Inhofe, James M. 2012. *The Greatest Hoax: How the Global Warming Conspiracy Threatens Your Future*, 1st ed. Washington, DC: WND Books.

Karplus, Sebastian Rausch and J. Valerie. 2014. "Markets versus Regulation: The Efficiency and Distributional Impacts of U.S. Climate Policy Proposals." *The Energy Journal* 35 (Special Issue). https://econpapers.repec.org/article/aenjournl/ej35-si1-11.htm.

Kriesi, Hanspeter, Edgar Grande, Martin Dolezal, Marc Helbling, Dominic Hoeglinger, Swen Hutter, and Bruno Wüest. 2012. *Political Conflict in Western Europe*. Cambridge: Cambridge University Press.

Lakoff, George. 2014. *Don't Think of an Elephant: Know Your Values and Frame the Debate*. White River Junction, VT: Chelsea Green.

Latour, Bruno. 2018. *Down to Earth. Politics in the New Climatic Regime*. Cambridge: Polity Press.

Lockwood, Matthew. 2018. "Right-Wing Populism and the Climate Change Agenda: Exploring the Linkages." *Environmental Politics* 27 (4): 712–32. https://doi.org/10.1080/09644016.2018.1458411.

Lövbrand, Eva, and Johannes Stripple. 2006. "The Climate as Political Space: On the Territorialisation of the Global Carbon Cycle." *Review of International Studies* 32 (2): 217–35. https://doi.org/10.1017/S0260210506006991.

Luterbacher, Urs, and Detlef F. Sprinz, eds. 2018. *Global Climate Policy: Actors, Concepts, and Enduring Challenges*. Cambridge, MA: The MIT Press.

McHugh, Lucy Holmes, Maria Carmen Lemos, and Tiffany Hope Morrison. 2021. "Risk? Crisis? Emergency? Implications of the New Climate Emergency Framing for Governance and Policy." *WIREs Climate Change* 12 (6): e736. https://doi.org/10.1002/wcc.736.

Meckling, Jonas. 2011. *Carbon Coalitions: Business, Climate Politics, and the Rise of Emissions Trading*. Cambridge, MA [u.a.]: MIT Press.

Medrano, Juan Díez, and Emily Gray. 2010. "Framing the European Union in National Public Spheres." In *The Making of a European Public Sphere: Media Discourse and Political Contention*, edited by Ruud Koopmans and Paul Statham, 195–222. Cambridge: Cambridge University Press. https://doi.org/10.1017/CBO9780511761010.012.

Meyer, Lukas, and Pranay Sanklecha, eds. 2017. *Climate Justice and Historical Emissions*. Cambridge: Cambridge University Press.

Neuhoff, Karsten. 2011. *Climate Policy after Copenhagen: The Role of Carbon Pricing*. Cambridge: Cambridge University Press.

Newell, Peter, Harriet Bulkeley, Karen Turner, Christopher Shaw, Simon Caney, Elizabeth Shove, and Nicholas Pidgeon. 2015. "Governance Traps in Climate Change Politics: Re-Framing the Debate in Terms of Responsibilities and Rights." *WIREs Climate Change* 6 (6): 535–40. https://doi.org/10.1002/wcc.356.

Newell, Peter John, and Matthew Paterson. 2010. *Climate Capitalism: Global Warming and the Transformation of the Global Economy*. Cambridge: Cambridge University Press.

Newell, Peter, Matthew Paterson, and Martin Craig. 2021. "The Politics of Green Transformations: An Introduction to the Special Section." *New Political Economy* 26 (6): 903–6. https://doi.org/10.1080/13563467.2020.1810215.

Niemi, Jari Ilmari. 2008. "The Foundations of Jürgen Habermas's Discourse Ethics." *The Journal of Value Inquiry* 42 (2): 255–68https://doi.org/10.1007/s10790-008-9119-7

O'Brien, Karen, Asunción Lera St Clair, and Berit Kristoffersen. 2010a. "The Framing of Climate Change: Why It Matters." In *Climate Change, Ethics and Human Security*, edited by Karen O'Brien, 3–22. Cambridge: Cambridge University Press.

O'Brien, Karen, Asuncion Lera St. Clair, and Berit Kristoffersen, eds. 2010. *Climate Change, Ethics and Human Security*. Cambridge: Cambridge University Press.

Oels, Angela. 2012. "From 'Securitization' of Climate Change to 'Climatization' of the Security Field: Comparing Three Theoretical Perspectives." In *Climate Change, Human Security and Violent Conflict. Challenges for Societal Stability*, edited by Jürgen Scheffran, Michael Brzoska, Hans Günter Brauch, Peter MIchael Link, and Janpeter Schilling, 185–205. Hexagon Series on Human and Environmental Security and Peace. Berlin: Springer.

Okereke, Chukwumerije. 2011. "Moral Foundations for Global Environmental and Climate Justice." *Royal Institute of Philosophy Supplements* 69: 117–35. https://doi.org/10.1017/S1358246111000245.

———. 2018. "Equity and Justice in Polycentric Climate Governance." In *Governing Climate Change: Polycentricity in Action?* edited by Andrew Jordan, Dave Huitema, Harro van Asselt, and Johanna Forster, 320–37. Cambridge: Cambridge University Press.

Okereke, Chukwumerije, and Philip Coventry. 2016. "Climate Justice and the International Regime: Before, during, and after Paris." *Wiley Interdisciplinary Reviews: Climate Change* 7 (6): 834–51. https://doi.org/10.1002/wcc.419.

Paterson, Matthew. 2021a. *In Search of Climate Politics*. Cambridge: Cambridge University Press.

———. 2021b. "'The End of the Fossil Fuel Age'? Discourse Politics and Climate Change Political Economy." *New Political Economy* 26 (6): 923–36. https://doi.org/10.1080/13563467.2020.1810218.

Pennings, Paul. 2002. "The Dimensionality of the EU Policy Space: The European Elections of 1999." *European Union Politics* 3 (1): 59–80. https://doi.org/10.1177/1465116502003001004.

Pickering, Jonathan, and John S. Dryzek. 2019. *The Politics of the Anthropocene.* Oxford Scholarship Online. New York, NY: Oxford University Press.

Rayner, Tim, and Andrew Jordan. 2013. "The European Union: The Polycentric Climate Policy Leader?" *Wiley Interdisciplinary Reviews: Climate Change* 4 (2): 75–90. https://doi.org/10.1002/wcc.205.

Rebich-Hespanha, Stacy, Ronald E. Rice, Daniel R. Montello, Sean Retzloff, Sandrine Tien, and João P. Hespanha. 2015. "Image Themes and Frames in US Print News Stories about Climate Change." *Environmental Communication* 9 (4): 491–519https://doi.org/10.1080/17524032.2014.983534

Rustin, Charles. 1999. "Habermas, Discourse Ethics, and International Justice." *Alternatives* 24 (2): 167–92. https://doi.org/10.1177/030437549902400202.

Schäfer, Mike, and Saffron O'Neill. 2017. "Frame Analysis in Climate Change Communication." In *Oxford Research Encyclopedia.* New York: Oxford University Press. https://doi.org/10.1093/acrefore/9780190228620.001.0001/acrefore-9780190228620-e-487.

Schlichting, Inga. 2013. "Strategic Framing of Climate Change by Industry Actors: A Meta-Analysis." *Environmental Communication* 7 (4): 493–511. https://doi.org/10.1080/17524032.2013.812974.

Schmidt, Vivien A. 2008. "Discursive Institutionalism: The Explanatory Power of Ideas and Discourse." *Annual Review of Political Science* 11 (1): 303–26. https://doi.org/10.1146/annurev.polisci.11.060606.135342.

———. 2010. "Taking Ideas and Discourse Seriously: Explaining Change through Discursive Institutionalism as the Fourth 'New Institutionalism.'" *European Political Science Review* 2 (1): 1–25. https://doi.org/10.1017/S175577390999021X.

Schön, Donald A., and Martin Rein. 1995. *Frame Reflection: Toward the Resolution of Intractable Policy Controversies.* New York: Basic Books.

Sjursen, Helene. 2006. "The EU as a 'Normative' Power: How Can This Be?" *Journal of European Public Policy* 13 (2): 235–51. https://doi.org/10.1080/13501760500451667.

Stern, Nicholas. 2007. *The Economics of Climate Change: The Stern Review.* Cambridge: Cambridge University Press.

Surel, Yves. 2000. "The Role of Cognitive and Normative Frames in Policy-Making." *Journal of European Public Policy* 7 (4): 495–512. https://doi.org/10.1080/13501760050165334.

Vliegenthart, Rens. 2012. "Framing in Mass Communication Research—An Overview and Assessment." *Sociology Compass* 6 (12): 937–48. https://doi.org/10.1111/soc4.12003.

Vreese, Claes H. de. 2012. "New Avenues for Framing Research." *American Behavioral Scientist* 56 (3): 365–75. https://doi.org/10.1177/0002764211426331

Weathers, Melinda R., and Brenden E. Kendall. 2016. "Developments in the Framing of Climate Change as a Public Health Issue in US Newspapers." *Environmental Communication* 10 (5): 593–611. https://doi.org/10.1080/17524032.2015.1050436.

Wehling, Elisabeth. 2016. *Politisches Framing: Wie Eine Nation Sich Ihr Denken Einredet - Und Daraus Politik Macht*. Edition Medienpraxis. Köln: Herbert von Halem Verlag.

Wendler, Frank. 2016. *Debating Europe in National Parliaments: Public Justification and Political Polarization*. Palgrave Studies in European Union Politics. London: Palgrave Macmillan.

———. 2022. "Contesting the European Union in a Changing Climate: Policy Narratives and the Justification of Supranational Governance." *Journal of Contemporary European Studies* 30 (1): 67–83. https://doi.org/10.1080/14782804.2021.1882107.

Wittmayer, J. M., J. Backhaus, F. Avelino, B. Pel, T. Strasser, I. Kunze, and L. Zuijderwijk. 2019. "Narratives of Change: How Social Innovation Initiatives Construct Societal Transformation." *Futures* 112: 102433. https://doi.org/10.1016/j.futures.2019.06.005.

Wurzel, Rüdiger, James Connelly, and Duncan Liefferink, eds. 2017. *The European Union in International Climate Change Politics: Still Taking a Lead?* Routledge Studies in European Foreign Policy. London: Routledge, Taylor & Francis Group, 2017–; ZDB-ID: 2885275-8 1. London: Routledge, Taylor & Francis group.

CHAPTER 3

Climate Change Policy in the EU: From the Paris Agreement to the European Green Deal

The proclamation of a European Green Deal (EGD) in a public address by EU Commission President Ursula von der Leyen to the European Parliament (EP) on 11 December 2019[1] was generally perceived as a breakthrough for more stringent action against climate change in the EU. How did this announcement come about, and how is it connected to previous stages of the EU policy-making process? And turning to the main question of this book, what is the discursive justification proposed by the Commission and other policy-makers in the EU for moving the goal of carbon neutrality until mid-century to the top of the EU agenda?

Addressing these questions, the main rationale of this chapter is to reconstruct how the European Green Deal and the subsequent debate on a European Climate Law (EPRS 2020a) fit into the policy-making discourse on climate change of the EU since the conclusion of the Paris Agreement. We aim to show that while the announcement of the EGD as a centerpiece of the Commission's agenda moves EU climate action to a new stage and brings into sharper focus the linkages between issues of

---

[1] The full text and video coverage of von der Leyen's full address to the European Parliament on 11 December 2019 can be retrieved from the European Commission's website at: https://ec.europa.eu/commission/presscorner/detail/en/speech_19_6751 (June 6, 2022).

© The Author(s), under exclusive license to Springer Nature Switzerland AG 2022
F. Wendler, *Framing Climate Change in the EU and US After the Paris Agreement*, Palgrave Studies in European Union Politics, https://doi.org/10.1007/978-3-031-04059-7_3

economic, energy, structural and environmental policy, its main rationale is closely linked to previous initiatives and policy-making procedures since the conclusion of the Paris Agreement. In this light, the EGD represents policy continuity rather than a disruptive breakthrough or innovation. We proceed in two steps: First, we reconstruct the evolution of EU climate action as a policy cycle reaching from the implementation of the Paris Agreement and feedback to a new phase of agenda-setting and policy formulation at the present stage. Applying this cycle as a heuristic framework allows us to bring into sharper focus the respective roles of the main EU institutions as agenda-setter, policy entrepreneur and legislative decision-maker during this period. Second, and turning to the analysis of policy discourse, we apply our approach of framing analysis as discussed in previous chapters to evaluate how the climate action agenda advocated by the EU institutions has been justified in their public political discourse. Going beyond, the present analysis will investigate more closely what linkages between different discursive frames of climate change and forms of contestation are discernible within this debate.

Overall, the present review demonstrates that the policy cycle from the Paris Agreement to the European Green Deal shows a progression not just towards an increased stringency of policy ambitions as expressed mainly by raising targets for the reduction of greenhouse gas (GHG) emissions. It also represents an expansion of the scope of discourse on climate change in which the overall ambition of achieving a net zero-carbon economy is no longer defined just as an environmental goal but one that is defined as a set of deeply transformative policies. In this sense, climate action is conceptualized as catalytic for a cross-cutting transformation of entire modes of production, investment and consumption, with implications for the entire internal agenda of the EU and its role as a global actor. This point underlines the critical importance of linkages between policy fields and their connection to an overarching framework of justificatory reasons, envisaged here through the approach of framing analysis.

In the subsequent sections, we reconstruct this policy development in two steps. First, the evolution of the EU policy cycle from the conclusion of the Paris Agreement to the current stage is reviewed through a systematic qualitative analysis of key documents and decisions by the main EU institutions. Here, we follow a sequential analysis based on the distinction between the EU's main executive, legislative and civil society agents and their respective role in the policy cycle (Sects. 3.1 through 3.4). This first part of the chapter aims to establish a detailed understanding of the various components of the climate policy framework proposed by the EU institutions since the Paris Agreement to the present stage. Second, we turn to the evaluation of discourse based on our conceptual approach of framing analysis. This part proceeds by presenting the results of a quantitative content analysis as discussed in the first part, based on our typology of six frames of climate change distinguished by their reference to economic, political, risk-based, ecological, justice and societal criteria (Sect. 3.5). The concluding section summarizes our main findings and prepares the ground for the subsequent comparative discussion (Sect. 3.6).

3.1 The EU Climate Policy Cycle Since the Paris Agreement

The year 2020 marks an important point in the evolution of the EU climate policy cycle, for two main reasons. First, the overall package of energy and climate legislation adopted by the EU to achieve a reduction of greenhouse gases (GHG) within its jurisdiction is set in decadal time frames in line with the overall proclamation of climate targets declared by the European Council; this package of policies comprises components such as emissions trading (ETS), the promotion of renewable energies and energy efficiency, and GHG reduction targets for Member States in non-ETS sectors (cp. DelbekeVis 2015: 29–108; 2019: 66–165; Wurzel et al. 2017a; Boasson and Wettestad 2013; Tröltzsch 2017). Therefore, the year 2020 marks the transition from the first period of major climate action goals, as defined through the easily memorable 20–20–20 targets,[2] to the so-called Phase IV of EU Climate Action, running from 2021 to the next target date of major pledges set for 2030. A major round of revisions of existing legislation were started around the year 2015 to adjust established regulatory instruments for the period reaching from

---

[2] This target, adopted by the EU in 2007, sets the threefold target of achieving a reduction of GHG emissions by 20% relative to 1990 levels, an increase of 20% in energy efficiency and an increase of renewable energies to 20% of the overall energy supply in EU Member States (cp. DelbekeVis 2015: 18–21; 2019: 12ff.), and overview of EU Climate Action on the website of the European Commission, https://ec.europa.eu/clima/policies/strategies/2020_en.

2021 to 2030 (cp. EPRS 2018a, b, 2019a, b). In this context, the European Green Deal did not emerge from a policy vacuum but was launched from the foundation of the EU's previous policy record and with a view to provide a specification of the longer-term goal of climate neutrality. In this sense, its main innovation consists of reaching beyond the intermediate time frame covered by current legislation reaching to 2030 and setting the agenda for longer-term targets set by the EU towards the year 2050.

Second, the year 2020 marks an important transition in the global climate policy regime, in several respects. Concerning the overall framework of international agreements on GHG emissions, the year marks the endpoint of the second commitment period of the previous Kyoto Protocol, as established by the (non-ratified) Doha Amendment in 2013 (Gupta 2014: 77–144). Set in this context, it therefore establishes the point in time marking the full transition of the global climate regime towards the more comprehensive, but also primarily voluntary and bottom-up framework of pledges by signatory states to enact reductions of GHG emissions as prescribed by the Paris Agreement (Popovski 2019; Oberthür 2016; Luterbacher and Sprinz 2018). Within this framework, the year 2020 is the target date for reaching the yearly volume of 100bn$ of contributions to climate finance, managed particularly through the Green Climate Fund (Delbeke and Vis 2019: 30ff.). In addition, the year 2020 marks a critical point for the scope of the agreement in terms of its membership, covering both the anticipated exit of United States and reversal of that decision after the presidential election in November. Finally, this year also marks the passage of the first five-year period since the adoption of the agreement, and hence the starting point for the review of the first five-year cycle of measures pledged by signatory states through their respective National Determined Contributions (NDCs). This review, as sanctioned through the cycle of pledge and review prescribed by the Paris Agreement (Popovski 2019: 23–31) was originally envisaged to start with the COP 26 conference in November 2020 but postponed by one year due to the pandemic situation. Due to its relevance for the ambition cycle of global climate governance envisaged by the Paris Agreement, this most recent global climate conference merits some closer attention.

Taking place in Glasgow between 13 October and 13 November 2021, the COP26 global climate summit was a highly publicized event. This was due both to the conjunction between responses to the climate crisis and economic recovery from the Covid pandemic, and the presence of a range of civil society organizations and activists accompanying negotiations with numerous public protests, events and statements, including Greta Thunberg's widely perceived commentary on COP negotiations as further worthless talk.[3] Concerning specific content of negotiations, initial summaries analyzing the proceedings and outcomes of the COP26 conference have focused on three major points: the inclusion of language requiring the phasing down of coal and reduction of fossil fuel subsidies, the requirement for countries to 'revisit and strengthen' their climate pledges by the end of 2022 as part of the so-called Glasgow Climate Pact, and intense controversy on several aspects of climate finance including the contentious issue of loss and damage (IISD 2021; Carbon Brief 2021; Aykut et al. 2022; Mechler et al. 2018). Concerning the empirical focus on the EU and US in this book, the most relevant aspect of the conference is probably the return of the United States to global climate negotiations, including appearances of both former President Obama[4] and an address by incumbent President Biden,[5] as well as a joint declaration of the US and China expressing their joint commitment to tackle the climate crisis.[6] By comparison, a brief spoken intervention by Commission Vice-President Timmermans[7] to the COP26 plenary received less attention, while the centrality of the UK presidency of the conference was perceived as standing apart from, or even in competition with the EU due to Brexit. At least in terms of media coverage and public commentary, the EU seemed to assume only a secondary role at the conference and was

---

[3] Extended coverage of the day-to-day events at COP26 and documentation of numerous events and speakers remain available through the New York Times climate hub at: https://climatehub.nytimes.com/.

[4] A video of former President Obama's address to COP26 in Glasgow is available at: https://www.youtube.com/watch?v=69EMd4csZRY.

[5] The text of the address by President Biden is published on the White House website at: https://www.whitehouse.gov/briefing-room/speeches-remarks/2021/11/01/remarks-by-president-biden-at-the-cop26-leaders-statement/; a video of the address is available at: https://www.youtube.com/watch?v=yExsEw6ZbGY.

[6] The text of the declaration in English can be found on the State Department website at the following https://www.state.gov/u-s-china-joint-glasgow-declaration-on-enhancing-climate-action-in-the-2020s/; further commentary on the declaration by the New York Times is available at: https://www.nytimes.com/2021/11/10/climate/china-us-climate-deal-kerry-xie.html?referringSource=articleShare.

[7] The full text of the speech by Timmermans can be found on the EU Commission's website at: https://ec.europa.eu/commission/presscorner/detail/en/SPEECH_21_6022; a video of this speech is available at: https://www.youtube.com/watch?v=I-ViCOPv4fU.

even accused of being the 'missing leader' at COP26,[8] in spite of its status as the region with the relatively most stringent climate targets to date.

Against the background of these global developments, the launch of the European Green Deal as the longer-term programmatic framework for EU Climate Action in the year 2019/2020 is set within a context of transitions to a new stage, both within the EU-internal climate policy cycle and the wider context of developments in the global climate policy regime. Accordingly, we conceptualize the development of EU climate policy from the Paris Agreement to the present stage as the progression through a policy cycle, using a heuristic systematization of decision-making stages familiar from the policy-making literature (Weible and Sabatier 2017). The period starting just before and following the adoption of the Paris Agreement establishes a process of policy re-formulation, aiming at the revision of key components of the EU climate and energy package; this process involves the revision of legislation on emissions trading in 2015 (Wettestad and Jevnaker 2016) and adjusting the EU framework for regulating renewable energy, effort sharing between Member States and rules to promote energy efficiency between 2016 and 2018. After the subsequent implementation of the respective directives and the overarching regulation on the governance of the energy union until the end of 2018, the EU policy process has entered into a new stage of evaluation and feedback from Member States and stakeholders. Following on this feedback, a new round of agenda-setting has started after the EP elections in 2019 and the nomination of a new Commission particularly through the announcement of the European Green Deal in December. Its proclamation has prompted the start of a next round of policy formulation, leading to the negotiation and subsequent adoption of the European climate law. Therefore, the empirical focus of this case study is focused on a sequence of steps in the policy cycle with a particular significance for the framing of policy discourse: namely, the transition from the stages of implementation and feedback to a new round of agenda-setting implying a potential modification of policy-making approaches, involved agents and institutional settings (cp. Daviter 2011). This review starts with the executive agenda-setting of the

---

[8] Cp.: EU accused of being the 'missing leader' at COP26 climate summit, Politico, November 11, 2021, https://www.politico.eu/article/eu-missing-leader-cop26-climate-talks-glasgow/.

European Council and Commission, before covering the European Parliament and its role as the EU's legislative institution in conjunction with the Council of the EU, and reviewing key inputs from civil society.

3.2 Problem Definition and Agenda-Setting: EU Council and Commission

This survey starts with the European Council (EC) as the main agenda-setter of the EU and its key agent to authorize the setting of mid- to longer-term political targets such as the reduction of GHG emissions (Oberthür and Dupont 2015). For climate policy, the EC is a key boundary institution to mediate between two interrelated levels of decision-making, taking into account the evolution of climate change policy as a key example of globalized multi-level governance (Zürn 2012, 2018: 53–61): namely, the internal dimension of EU policy-making, enacted mainly through regulatory legislation; and its global dimension, pursued mainly through climate diplomacy and the involvement of the EU and its Member States in the negotiation and adoption of international agreements on climate change (Dupont and Oberthür 2017; Oberthür et al. 2010). In this sense, conclusions adopted by the EC both authorize the setting of overall climate ambitions and targets for the EU and provide the foundation for the representation of EU positions at international negotiations, particularly in the framework of the annual Conference of the Parties (COPs). A survey of the most relevant Council conclusions therefore leads to a distinction between two main sets of documents: First, statements by the EC to address challenges of the global climate regime and to define the position taken by the EU within a forthcoming COP in the context of global climate policy, usually adopted each October; and second, formal declarations taken to endorse or authorize programmatic decisions concerning the contents of internal EU climate action, adopted particularly around the period of transition of the policy cycle from implementation to a new round of agenda-setting described here.

Based on this distinction between decisions concerning the global climate agreements and internal EU climate policy, decision-making of the European Council after the adoption of the Paris Agreement comprises two main phases and corresponding groups of conclusions (cp. EPRS 2020b). First, a series of Council conclusions between 2014 and 2019 deal with the adoption of the Paris Agreement, its implementation and conclusions proclaimed to define the position of the EU concerning annual negotiations about the practical application ('rulebook') of the Agreement (European Council 2016b, c, 2017b, 2018b). In addition, decisions by the EC during this time also cover the broader context of climate policy on a global level, particularly questions of climate diplomacy (European Council 2014, 2016a, 2017a, 2018a). In this context, issues of particular relevance are the 'mainstreaming' of climate in EU external action and responses to the decision by US President Trump to withdraw the United States from the Paris Agreement, announced in June 2017 and formally submitted to the UNFCCC two months later to take effect in November 2020 (an issue echoed although not directly discussed in conclusions of 23 June 2017, European Council 2017a). In summation, EC conclusions within this first phase are primarily outward-looking, by dealing with the global context of climate change policy.

Second, starting with the Spring Council of March 2019, the thematic focus of EC conclusions shifts back to priorities of climate action within the EU. After being addressed by several meetings of the Council through this and the following year, the Council proceeded to adopt conclusions endorsing the overall target of climate neutrality—i.e., a reduction of GHG emissions to net zero—in a time frame reaching to the year 2050, and debated the European Green Deal as a policy framework to achieve this goal. In this context, particularly the EC conclusions of 12 December 2019 deserve further scrutiny as the main decision taken paving the way for the formal endorsement of the approach outlined by the Commission (European Council 2019).

A striking feature of these conclusions is the brevity as well as the concise, factual, almost technical character of the conclusions, in spite of the far-reaching and potentially very contentious political content. Of the 11 recitals dedicated to the topic of climate change (comprising some 600 words), the first opens with the simple statement: 'In the light of the latest available science and of the need to step up global climate action, the European Council endorses the objective of achieving a climate-neutral EU by 2050, in line with the objectives of the Paris Agreement' (European Council 2019: 2). While the following sentence recognizes the factual opt-out of one Member State (i.e., Poland) from the joint commitment of Member States to the goal of climate neutrality, mainly three important policy advances are endorsed in the subsequent recitals: First, the Council takes note of the European Green Deal, endorsing its key argument that a transition to carbon neutrality can be realized that reconciles economic opportunity and growth with principles of social fairness and an adequate form of effort sharing and compensatory measures between Member States. In this vein, a subsequent recital recognizes the need for revisions of existing policy by pointing out that all relevant EU legislation needs to be consistent with the climate neutrality objective, inviting the Commission to scrutinize existing rules of the Single Market as well as state aid. While these conclusions indicate support for a mainstreaming of climate action and therefore endorse a considerable expansion of climate policy objectives to related policy areas, regulatory competence by the EU is limited by recognizing the right of Member States to decide on their own energy mix, including the use of nuclear energy (recital 6).

Following on this initial statement, the Council proceeds to authorize several initiatives for an expansion of EU climate finance. The most significant point beyond a renewed commitment to the build-up of international climate finance is that the conclusions authorize an expansion of EU-internal adjustment funds. In this context, both the engagement of the European Investment Bank (EIB) through investments in the amount of 1 trillion Euro, and initiatives by the EU Commission to facilitate 100 billion Euros through the Just Transition Fund are endorsed (recital 4). The politically most contentious pledge in this context is that the forthcoming multi-annual financial framework, the 7-year overall budget plan for the EU, will 'significantly contribute' to climate action. In this part of its conclusions, the Council addresses the perhaps most difficult set of EU-internal negotiations, with considerable potential for political conflict between Member States and virtually unavoidable linkages to other policy areas such as agriculture, research, cohesion funds and even policies on the rule of law.

In the concluding paragraphs, the Council addresses the international dimension of climate policy by emphasizing the relevance of a strong engagement by the EU for climate action on the international level, and calling on the High Representative of the EU to commit to a strong engagement in climate diplomacy. This point takes up a long-standing discussion of integrating climate policy into the priorities of the EU's External Action Service and the further development of its financial and human resources through focal points (BiedenkopfPetri 2019; Torney 2013). Concerning the external dimension of EU action, a point of major political relevance is that the Council proceeds to 'take note' of the Commission's proposal to introduce a carbon border adjustment mechanism for carbon-intensive sectors, based on the intention to limit the effect of 'carbon leakage' from the EU (i.e., the evasion of energy-intensive production from the EU to countries not covered by its legislation). Such a mechanism would introduce a price on imports whose production is cheaper outside the EU due to less stringent regulations or prices on carbon emissions. This is certainly the most politically contentious aspect of the European Green Deal in its international dimension, with considerable implications for trade relations and even wider political relations of the EU with third countries around the world (Kuik and Hofkes 2010).

In summation, during the period of analysis reviewed here, particularly the European Council conclusions of 12 December 2019 stand out as relevant as the decision at the highest political level to endorse key ideas and components of the Green Deal, marking the transition of EU climate policy into a new stage of agenda-setting and policy formulation at the current stage. As the previous discussion of these conclusions demonstrates, the Council endorses a broad programmatic framing of climate policy as a cross-cutting issue requiring substantial changes and revision of existing legislation and expenditure in a broad range of policy areas, including many aspects of EU external action. Furthermore, the conclusions adopt a relatively broad temporal and geographical perspective, envisaging the year 2050 as the reference point for climate action and setting EU climate action in a wider global context. As such, these landmark conclusions complete a sequence of decisions by the European Council since the Paris Agreement, summarized in Table 3.1.

Beyond the adoption of the relatively fundamental, longer-term policy goals and programmatic approaches covered here, the conclusions of the European Council address more specific policy details only in passing. More specific adjustments of regulatory policy, such as the revision of climate legislation undertaken between 2015 and 2018, were briefly authorized by the EU Council in conclusions adopted already before the Paris Agreement (particularly those of 26/27 June 2014). Even the intermediate targets for 2030 were mostly raised in the context of longer-term strategies envisaged by the Council: namely, those adopted to achieve climate neutrality within the longer-term perspective until 2050, resulting in the upward adjustment of intermediate goals following from the replacement of the previous 80% reduction goal until 2050 by the goal of climate neutrality.

Table 3.1 Overview of European Council conclusions on climate change; abbreviations in order of appearance: PL = Poland; COP = Conference of the Parties; NDC = Nationally Determined Contributions

Date	Key topic	Main conclusions
12 December 2019	EU Green Deal	Climate neutrality to 2050 endorsed (PL opt-out) Takes note of European Green Deal, including Carbon Border Adjustment Mechanism
9 October 2018	COP 24 (Katowice)	Calls for reinforcing NDCs to meet Paris goals Endorses Renewable Energy and Energy Efficiency targets (32/32.5%) to 2030
26 February 2018	Climate diplomacy	Commitment to multilateralism and COP process Calls for mainstreaming in external relations
13 October 2017	Climate diplomacy	Commits to climate finance and global stocktake Commits to Global Climate Action Agenda and Sustainable Development Goals
23 June 2017	Paris Agreement	Reaffirming commitment to Paris Agreement Stresses cooperation (international/non-state)
30 September 2016	COP 22 (Marrakesh)	Expresses concern that NDCs are insufficient Commits to climate finance goals and mechanisms
15 February 2016	Climate diplomacy	Welcomes Paris Agreement, commits to High Ambition Coalition Calls for stronger climate diplomacy by European External Action Service
23 October 2014	2030 targets	Endorses 40% GHG reduction to 2030 27% target for Renewable Energies and Energy Efficiency

In contrast to the European Council's role as agenda-setter and boundary agent between the global and EU domestic level, the Commission is focused predominantly on the internal dimension of climate action within the EU (Skjaerseth 2017). Limiting our focus on cross-cutting, programmatic policy documents, three main groups of documents are relevant for evaluating the Commission's climate policy discourse in this regard.

First, as a framework for the shorter-term, more immediate implementation of climate policies, particularly two documents are relevant: namely, the communication on the Energy Union Package, published on 4 March 2015 and hence prior to the conclusion of the Paris Agreement (COM 2015); and a relatively brief document entitled 'The Road from Paris' (COM 2016b), released on 2 March 2016 as an explanatory document for the proposal submitted to the Council for the adoption of the Paris Agreement. Here, the Commission outlines its approach for the 2030 Climate Action Plan and its contribution to the pledge and review process enacted by the Agreement, starting from the submission the EU's Intended Nationally Determined Contribution (INDC) in March 2015. Set in context of the policy cycle, these documents provide a framework for the ongoing policy formulation and implementation of the renewed climate policy pledges of the EU in the post-2020 stage following the expiry of the Kyoto Protocol, as envisaged through its 2030 Climate and Energy Package.

Second, building on this international commitment, several communications by the Commission outline the EU's intermediate strategy for a decarbonization of the economy until 2030, including broader programmatic approaches beyond specific legislative proposals. A centerpiece of this discourse is the communication 'Accelerating Europe's transition to a low-carbon economy', published in 20 July 2016 (COM 2016a). The document is drafted primarily to accompany several legislative proposals on effort sharing between Member States for a reduction of GHG emissions, on land use and the reduction of emissions from transport. Together with the individual legislative proposals and explanatory documents for the various components of EU Climate Action, this document explains and enacts the intermediate 2030 framework adopted by the European Council in October 2014. In terms of specific policy, it also complements an earlier document on the policy framework for climate and energy published by the Commission before that Council decision (COM 2014/2015). Taken together, these documents are the most comprehensive statements by the Commission on the process of policy formulation pursued to enact the EU's intermediate climate policy goals until 2030.

Finally, several documents published from 2018 onwards kick off the new cycle of agenda-setting concerning the longer-term climate goals of the EU. Particularly, two of these publications deserve further scrutiny. The first is the communication 'A Clean Planet for All' (COM 2018). Here, several pathways and scenarios are outlined for the climate strategy of the EU until the year 2050. This document establishes the main preparatory step before the proclamation of the European Green Deal in December 2019 towards the EP and its immediate follow-up, the publication of the Commission document on the Green Deal on 12 December (COM 2019). Both documents are relatively comprehensive in scope, comprising some 25 pages and therefore providing a much more detailed explanation of the strategy for dealing with climate change in the period between 2030 and 2050 and specific policy instruments. As the key documents establishing the Commission's policy discourse on the future strategy of climate action, these two documents therefore deserve closer review and scrutiny, as presented in the subsequent paragraphs.

The Commission publication 'A Clean Planet for All[9]' is the first detailed attempt to lay out policy options for following a trajectory towards the goal of achieving net-zero GHG emissions. It was published on 28 November 2018, together with a set of documents including an in-depth study of some 400 pages[10] on the impact of various approaches to reducing net carbon emissions.[11] What makes this document specific is the way it lays out a choice of political options for policy-makers: The document starts out with a relatively detailed introductory section making the case for immediate action, referring to the conclusions of the IPCC and presenting a survey of the expected impacts of climate change, specified through a distinction of seven climate regions of Europe. From this point of departure, a set of eight (potentially compatible) approaches are discussed that could be applied for reducing the net emission of

---

[9] The full title of the document is: 'A Clean Planet for all. A European strategic long-term vision for a prosperous, modern, competitive and climate neutral economy', Brussels, 28.11.2018, COM (2018) 773 final; https://eur-lex.europa.eu/legal-content/EN/TXT/PDF/?uri=CELEX:52018DC0773&from=EN (last accessed: 19 June 2020).

[10] The full title of the study is: 'In-depth analysis in support of the Commission Communication COM82018) 773. A Clean Planet for All. A European long-term strategic vision for a prosperous, modern, competitive and climate neutral economy', Brussels, 28 November 2018, https://ec.europa.eu/clima/sites/clima/files/docs/pages/com_2018_733_analysis_in_support_en_0.pdf (last accessed: 19 June 2020).

[11] The entire set of documents, including the study, several fact sheets and press releases can be retrieved at the https://ec.europa.eu/clima/policies/strategies/2050_en (last accessed: 19 June 2020).

GHGs until mid-century; these are labeled, somewhat confusingly, as both 'scenarios' and 'pathways' as potential policy options for decision-makers. These include (1) the electrification of economic processes and relevant sources of GHG emissions such as buildings and transport, (2) the comprehensive use of hydrogen to replace carbon-based fuels, (3) the application of power-to-X technologies where electricity is used to generate emission-free fuels such as methanol or hydrogen, (4) efforts to increase energy efficiency across all sectors of economic production and individual consumption, (5) introducing concepts of the circular economy particularly through reduction of waste and increased recycling, (6) an approach combining the technologies of the points 1 through 4 enumerated here, (7) the use of natural carbon sinks and biomass technology in addition to all measures envisaged in approach number 6, and (8) finally, the combination of all these approaches in addition to a widespread introduction of lifestyle changes in fields such as air travel and dietary choices (Commission 2018: 53ff., for a summary, see UBA 2018).

Taken together, the first five of these approaches represent technologies that can be applied across economic sectors and a wide range of forms of consumption (including mobility, services and residence). In comparison, approaches 6 through 8 represent different variants of political choices of combining these technologies, including more far-reaching social change in the scenario discussed as the eight and final option. The communication states that only this last, comprehensive approach is expected to deliver the goal of climate neutrality until the year 2050, whereas scenarios 5 and 6 are estimated to reach a reduction of 80 and 90% in GHG emissions, respectively. While the distinction of these eight scenarios is based on insights of the above-mentioned background study, the Commission document goes on in some depth to discuss seven fields of application (termed 'building blocks') for pursuing the scenarios outlined above. These include the expansion of renewable energy, changes in mobility, as well as changes in industry and infrastructure such as grids and networks, as well as carbon markets and technologies for CO_2 capture and storage (COM 2018: 8–15). While not every detail of the communication can be explained here, what this overview demonstrates is how the argument made here is framed in mainly technological, rather than political terms: In spite of the dramatic call for action at the outset of the document, the Commission mainly limits its case to presenting options and mapping their potential impacts rather than to prescribe one particular set of political choices. Particularly, the several sets of enumerations presented in the November 2018 package invite a pick-and-choose approach, while suggesting the feasibility of realizing the target of achieving a complete decarbonization. In this sense, the document presents a toolbox rather than a vision.

In comparison, the communication on the European Green Deal is much more unequivocal in its preference for a specific trajectory of climate policy in the longer term: From the outset, the document proclaims the goal of achieving climate neutrality—a net-zero balance between the emission and removal of GHG from the atmosphere—in the European Union until the year 2050. Presenting a much more detailed and comprehensive outline of a potential strategy against climate change than the Council conclusions, the approach outlined by the Commission consists mainly of the following five components.

First, and most importantly, the communication proposes a universal scope of the EU's future climate strategy. Acting against climate change, in this view, requires efforts that include all relevant sectors of the economy, as well as everyday forms of consumption, residential life and mobility, and is envisaged as a process affecting society and relations between its members as a whole, concerning questions of justice, inclusiveness and well-being. From this point of departure, the form through which the document defines the challenge posed by climate change is most adequately described as one of economic and social modernization: namely, to harness the potential of a transformation towards a decarbonized economy for increased competitiveness and growth on the one hand, and to manage changes effected by this transition in a way that increases social inclusion and justice, on the other (for related, very similar accounts of a Green Deal, cp. Rifkin 2020). Consequently, climate action is to be integrated into macro-economic governance mechanisms of the EU, particularly within the framework of the European Semester (Commission 2019: 3). Stating that 'the EU has the collective ability to transform its economy and society towards a more sustainable path', the communication affirms that necessary investments are an 'opportunity to put Europe firmly on a new path of sustainable and inclusive growth' (COM 2019: 2). Action against climate change, in other words, is to be presented not as an act of individual or collective self-restraint, but as an opportunity of positive change. In this sense, two main ideas—namely, opportunity and transformation—frame the Commission's approach to the issue of climate change policy. Indirectly, this approach confirms a major point of criticism highlighted particularly from civil society organizations: namely, that a fundamental adherence to the paradigm of economic growth is not questioned but confirmed (cp. also Ajl 2021: 42ff.).

Second, the communication spells out the various policy areas and streams of legislation requiring a revision if the European Green Deal is realized: In this sense, it is defined as a project of designing 'a set of deeply transformative policies' (COM 2019: 4). For reasons of space, the enumeration of policies included in the scope of the Green Deal can only be discussed in the briefest of terms here. However, a key to the understanding of these fields lies in the reflection of each individual step in the sequence of processes from the supply to the use and potential recycling of socially and economically important goods and services. In this sense, the production of energy is the first point addressed, taking up the agenda for a transition to renewable energies and related efforts to modernize infrastructure (particularly transmission networks) and energy markets. The second main area addressed concerns the entire field of industry production as a process involving both the use of energy and the production of waste and other externalities (e.g., pollution or degradation of ecological habitats). In this context, the concept of a circular economy is raised both as a sustainable and economically profitable vision, particularly in terms of efficiency, and as a source of job creation. The third field addressed in the document shifts the focus to energy demand, focusing on buildings (e.g., renovation and use of more efficient heating and cooling technologies) and transport, particularly emission-friendly fuels and vehicles. This discussion of economic cycles from supply to demand is also envisaged for land use and agriculture, promoting the concept of 'farm to fork' to express the idea of a sustainable link between sustainable food production (covering issues such as pesticides, antibiotics and land use) and consumption, including strategies to influence consumer behavior and the production of waste. The fifth and final policy area addressed in this context is to integrate climate policy goals with established policies of environmental protection, particularly the preservation of biodiversity, habitats and ecosystems more generally. Both a potential strength and obvious point of criticism are laid open in this discussion of the broad range of policies requiring further adjustment: Virtually of the fields mentioned are covered by various forms of EU regulation, hence providing the regulatory tools needed to enact change but also clarifying the magnitude of the challenge arising from the need for their revision aimed at an increased stringency of GHG emission reductions.

While these two first points are key to define the Green Deal's overall approach and ambition, three additional points are discussed in the document to describe some of its governance mechanisms and to give credence to its potential for realization. The first of these issues is the strengthening of two instruments—namely, the promotion of climate-related science and increased funding for climate finance—as supporting instruments of general relevance across individual policy areas. The communication identifies a volume of 260 billion Euros annually as the volume required even for the pursuit of the current 2030 climate goals and recommends a 25% target of expenditure across all spending programs of the EU for climate mainstreaming (COM 2019: 15). Also mentioned are the InvestEU Fund, a new investment plan entitled Sustainable Europe and the initiative to raise the climate target of the European Investment Bank (EIB) to 50% of its lending. A second issue are proposals to increase the EU's visibility as a global leader of climate action, particularly through bilateral agreements with other key actors on the global stage (particularly, China), the inclusion of climate goals in multilateral strategies (such as the EU-Africa strategy) and green conditionality in trade agreements. A particularly important point in this context is the announcement that the Commission will propose a carbon border adjustment mechanism if 'differences in levels of ambition worldwide persist' (COM 2019: 5). As mentioned above, the possible introduction of this mechanism is a point of considerable relevance and wide resonance in the climate policy community and beyond, including from representatives of major international institutions including the World Bank. Finally, in terms of a political signal, the document proposes the establishment of a European Climate Pact to support the initiatives outlined here by outreach to the public, including the creation of online forms of involvement and support for grassroots activities (COM 2019: 22f.). Summing up, and without prejudging the future course of decisions taken to enact the Green Deal, it seems justified to appraise it as a politically ambitious, longer-term act of agenda-setting with considerable potential implications for a wide range of EU policies, including its expenditure, mechanisms of macro-economic governance ('European Semester'), market regulation, cohesion policy, and not least, external relations and trade policy.

To conclude, this section demonstrates how the EU's executive institutions—the European Council and Commission—have addressed climate change proceeding from a stage of policy formulation and implementation following the Paris Agreement to a phase of agenda-setting with an ambitious long-term perspective: namely, to realize the objective of climate neutrality (i.e., net-zero GHG emissions) until the year 2050 as envisaged by the European Green Deal and specified through the European climate law. Both of these stages, but particularly the political entrepreneurship of the Commission expressed through its advocacy of the Green Deal agenda prompt political responses and controversy at the level of the EU legislative, discussed in the following section.

3.3 Parliamentary Discourse on Climate Change: Resolutions by the European Parliament

The European Parliament (EP) is typically characterized as a pioneer and early advocate of climate policy in Europe (Burns and Carter 2010; Burns et al. 2013). In fact, the EP can be considered a first mover during the first stages of EU climate policy, having adopted its first resolutions on the subject even before the conclusion of the Kyoto Protocol. From this point of departure, the subsequent review confirms that the EP usually supports more stringent targets for the reduction of GHG emissions than the Council, and also frequently goes beyond proposals by the Commission, even though a more 'pragmatic' stance concerning specific questions of policy has been identified in more recent accounts (cp. Burns 2017, 2019; Wendler 2019, 2020).

Beyond the relatively simple characterization as a leader or pioneer, the EP is a versatile institution, engaged in more phases of the policy cycle and levels of climate policy than the other EU institutions. The rationale of this section is to evaluate these various functions of the EP to prepare the ground for our subsequent analysis of parliamentary discourse and its framing of climate change. In this sense, the EP is involved in decision-making about climate governance in three respects: first, in its role as legislative decision-maker; second, as a diplomatic agent addressing issues of forthcoming global climate negotiations; and finally, as a discursive agent aiming to communicate its stance concerning the strategic and longer-term targets of EU climate action, however without legally binding effect on legislation (Kreppel and Webb 2019). In addition to providing a survey of these functions, the subsequent review also seeks to explain why the present study concentrates its empirical focus only on the two latter of these functions.

First, and most importantly in terms of concrete policy-making influence, the EP acts as a co-legislator with the Council on climate and energy legislation, governed through the Ordinary Legislative Procedure since the adoption of the Lisbon Treaty. The most important recent development in this regard, and one signaling the transition of the Green Deal from agenda-setting to the next stage of policy formulation, is the adoption of a European Climate Law, proposed by the Commission to the EU's legislative institutions on 4 March 2020 (COM 2020/80). Within the EP, legislative negotiations were led by the environmental committee ENVI and its main rapporteur Jytte Guteland (S&D), with additional input through the provision of opinions by six other committees including those on industry (ITRE), economic and monetary affairs (ECON), regional development (REGI) and agriculture[12] (AGRI). Following an agreement in trilogue negotiations on 21 April 2021 and approval by the EP plenary on 24 June 2021, the European climate law has been adopted as EU regulation 2021/1119 and entered into force on 29 July 2021 (EPRS 2021). Its centerpiece is the climate-neutrality objective (Article 2), creating a legally binding mandate for the EU and its Member States to achieve net-zero greenhouse gas emissions by 2050, and to take necessary measures at the EU and national level to enable the collective achievement of this objective. From this point of departure, particularly three aspects of the European climate law created controversy during legislative negotiations, both between competing EP party groups and EU Member States represented in the Council.

First, a major point in negotiations was how to define the intermediate GHG reduction targets of the EU to be achieved by 2030, which were previously set at 40%; legislative negotiations included calls for raising this target to 60% by the EP (and its environmental committee ENVI even calling for 65%). Following political resistance especially from some of the Member States in the Council, the intermediate targets was ultimately set at a value of at least 55% (Article 4), thereby prompting an initiative by the Commission to revise and update existing EU legislation for the reduction of GHG emissions to meet this benchmark (the so-called "Fit for 55"

---

[12] Full details about the legislative procedure of the European Climate Law covering documentation and involved agents and institutions can be accessed at the EP's legislative observatory at the https://oeil.secure.europarl.europa.eu/oeil/popups/fichep rocedure.do?reference=2020/0036(COD)&l=en.

package[13]). Concerning intermediate targets, moreover, the regulation also requires the Commission to make a legislative proposal for defining a climate target for 2040 within six months after the first global stocktake required under the Paris Agreement (Article 4,3).

Second, controversy emerged over how to empower EU institutions to manage the transition to carbon neutrality and potentially impose legally binding rules of action on Member States. While the legislative proposal initially envisaged a mandate for the Commission to act through delegated acts requiring necessary adjustments of ongoing policies on a path towards carbon neutrality, the relevant provisions of the regulation were changed to require such corrective action to proceed through the ordinary legislative route requiring consent from the EP and Council. According to these provisions, the Commission is mandated to assess both individual and collective progress made by Member States as well as the consistency of EU measures with the climate-neutrality objective by 30 September 2023 and every five years thereafter. Where inconsistency between the goal of carbon neutrality and existing measures is identified, the Commission is empowered to 'take measures in accordance with the Treaties' concerning relevant EU measures such as proposing revisions of existing legislation, and to issue recommendations to Member States where national measures have been evaluated as insufficient (Article 6 and 7).

Finally, a major innovation introduced by the climate law is the establishment of the European Scientific Advisory Board on Climate Change, tasked with providing scientific advice and reports on relevant Union measures and their coherence with envisaged targets of the European climate law and the EU's international commitments (Article. 3). This provision seems relevant particularly because it creates a link between the calculation of carbon budgets on the trajectory towards climate neutrality (referred to in the regulation as 'indicative greenhouse gas budgets' in Article 3,2) and the evaluation of existing Union policies. Concerning Member States, the climate law only contains a provision formally 'inviting' them to establish a national climate advisory body responsible for providing expert advice on policies of relevant national authorities (Article 3,4).

---

[13] The measures relevant in this regard are summarized on the Commission website at: https://ec.europa.eu/clima/eu-action/european-green-deal/delivering-european-green-deal_en.

Relating to the European climate law as an overarching framework for EU climate action, the EP has also been involved in the establishment and revision of specific legislation covering the various regulatory tools employed by the EU for a reduction of carbon emissions. Within the context of these legislative negotiations, informal negotiation with the Council and Commission through trilogue (cp. Brandsma et al. 2021) have become standard practice and are commonly led on behalf of the EP by its two committees on the environment (ENVI) and industry (ITRE), with varying forms of involvement and varying assignments of lead roles depending on the dossier in question. Broad support for compromise agreements by 'mainstream' EP party groups and a pragmatic stance in inter-institutional negotiations are typical for decision-making on legislation on key pieces of the EU Climate and Energy package for Phase IV[14] of its climate action (2021–2030).

This negotiation of EU climate change regulation establishes an important field of research for studies interested in policy influence of the EP, party-political contestation of climate policy and advocacy coalitions within the EP and their interaction through negotiation and decision-making (cp. Wendler 2019, 2020). While a full account of these legislative processes cannot be provided here for reasons of space, two observations are relevant for the purposes of the present study.

The first is that within the legislative processes surveyed here, those parliamentary functions of the EP aiming at a broader public and citizens—namely, the representation of competing, or even polarized party-political stances within the EP and their communication towards a wider political public through plenary debate—are less developed than the role of the EP as negotiator and policy-shaper (for this typology of parliamentary functions, cp. Hefftler et al. 2015). Legislative procedures within the EP are largely conducted through non-public forms of negotiation and decision-making, particularly through bargaining on policy positions at committee level within the EP and through so-called trilogues at the inter-institutional level (for broader accounts of these

---

[14] As mentioned above, this package covers EU legislation on emissions trading, agreement between Member States on the reduction of GHG emissions in non-ETS sectors such as agriculture, buildings and transport ('effort sharing'), legislation covering the reduction of carbon emissions through energy, both with regard to its supply (renewable energies) and demand (energy efficiency), and finally, legislation prescribing targets for the reduction of CO_2 by vehicles and the increase of zero- and low-emission vehicles.

processes, cp. Ringe 2010; Ripoll Servent 2015). Trilogue as a form negotiation between Council, Commission and the EP was applied to reach preliminary inter-institutional agreement in all five of the legislative acts summarized above (EPRS 2018a, b, 2019a, b). While plenary debate in the EP on climate legislation is held regularly, mostly before the vote on proposed inter-institutional agreements, and documented on the EP website with speeches by MEPs (and frequently, members of the Commission) in their original language (without English translation), these debates fail to reach larger publics and tend to stay within the 'Brussels bubble' (Nitoiu 2015). Another is the absence of clear partisan polarization on climate change issues between the EP party groups. Votes in the plenary, particularly on pieces of specific legislation such as emissions trading, are not clearly split between party lines but mostly carried by oversized majorities of the 'mainstream' groups (EPP, S&D, ALDE/Renew and Greens), opposed only the more climate- and Eurosceptic groups ID and END but suggesting no evident pattern of party polarization (Wendler 2019, 2020).

The second is that the involvement of the EP within these legislative procedures is only roughly appraised by assuming a stable, unidimensional political space and locations positions of the EP or individual party groups and MEPs somewhere in the spectrum between 'less' and 'more' stringent climate policy. While some key political targets of climate policy—particularly the definition of overall reduction targets for GHG emissions—can be used to distinguish between more and less ambitious approaches to climate change mitigation, legislative bargaining involves more than a single dimension between the principles of environmental protection and economic freedom (for a classical account of party politics and issue dimensions in the EP; cp. Hix et al. 2007). Mainly two additional issue dimensions emerge within the legislative procedures surveyed here which the EP uses to negotiate compromise with its interlocutors from the Council: First, controversy emerged between demands for an increased authority of supranational institutions and mechanisms as opposed to more flexible mechanisms providing leeway for Member States or economic sectors. An example of this is the prescription of legally binding reduction targets instead of indicative national contributions, or intervals in which progress has to be reported and is potentially sanctioned by the Commission. Second, a distributive dimension emerges between different Member States and their respective stakes in particular industries, as most directly negotiated in legislation on effort sharing and climate finance but also present in issues such as carbon leakage and indirectly, the inclusion of economic sectors in emissions trading (Wendler 2019).

The dimensions of political conflict addressed here arguably vary with the specific legislative issue negotiated. One of the potential merits of framing analysis is to explore the emergence of these various issue dimensions in a closer investigation and comparison of different legislative procedures, beyond the scope of this current chapter. The point made here, however, is that legislative decision-making by the EP on specific aspects of legislation needs to be distinguished carefully in terms of its scope, institutional procedures and issue dimensions from another area: namely, acts adopted primarily aiming at discursive agency as realized by the EP through resolutions adopted to communicate general programmatic positions to other EU institutions, stakeholders and political publics (cp. Kreppel and Webb 2019).

The first of these discursive functions of the EP relate to the external dimension of EU climate diplomacy (Biedenkopf 2015). At this level, communication by the EP comprises parliamentary statements addressing the role of the EU as an actor of global climate governance, and the involvement of its representatives and Member States in negotiations at the international level, primarily in the framework of the Conferences of the Parties (COPs). In terms of legally binding decision-making, the role of the EP in this field is very limited: Neither the EP as a whole nor its members are formally involved within negotiations of global climate agreements; furthermore, positions adopted by the Member States or the EU Council concerning these negotiations cannot be influenced or sanctioned by the EP. In this sense, the only legal authority the EP has in the field of external climate diplomacy is the endorsement or authorization of agreements entered by the EU on the global level. This may include statements of intent and legally formalized and binding documents such as the Paris Agreement. Relating to this point, the EP decision formally endorsing the Paris Agreement on behalf of the EU, adopted on 4 October by the EP plenary (2016/0184), is only a very brief document formally declaring that the EP gives its consent to the Agreement. More relevant as documents communicating the stance of the EP towards global climate negotiations, however, are the non-legislative resolutions adopted just prior to the annual gathering of the COPs as the main forum of negotiation about the key contents, mechanisms and implementation of the global climate regime. Within the period of our analysis, these resolutions include those on the COP 21 in Paris (adopted 14 October 2015,

EP 2015b), the COP 22 in Marrakesh (adopted 6 October 2016, EP 2016), the COP 23 in Bonn (4 October 2017, EP 2017), the COP 24 in Katowice (adopted 25 October 2018, EP 2018c) and the COP 25 in Madrid (adopted 28 November 2019, EP 2019c). While these resolutions address key elements of the evolving regime of agreements at the global level as well as evaluations of commitments by signatories around the world, their main target are primarily policies adopted by the EU and its Member States. Here, EP resolutions cover the ambition of the respective national action plans of Member States, the stringency and credibility of EU climate targets and its commitments to climate finance. In addition, the EP has also adopted a general resolution on climate diplomacy (adopted 3 July 2018). The document calls for strengthening the financial and personal resources for the external representation of climate targets within the EU External Action Service; furthermore, a key point of the resolution is to call for a mainstreaming of climate targets across all areas of external action such as trade, development and political partnerships with third countries and regions (EP 2018a).

Taken together, these resolutions on the role of the EU in global climate governance appear more suitable for the purposes of the present analysis than specific acts of legislation, considering its main rationale: namely, to evaluate the discursive framing of broader, programmatic approaches towards the mitigation of climate change rather than very specific aspects of regulatory policy-making inviting a broad range of more technical, sector-specific issues. All resolutions listed above cover relatively general visions of climate action and relate to the same overall framework of agreements and commitments. Another distinctive aspect recommending these resolutions for our present analysis is their primarily discursive purpose and institutional origin as documents representing only the views of the EP: Adopted through the own-initiative procedure of the EP and hence not following on a proposal by the Commission or negotiations with the Council, the resolutions discussed here have no legally binding effect but are primarily addressed at the other EU institutions, civil society organizations and the wider political public.

Third, and in addition to its resolutions on global climate negotiations, the EP also acts as a discursive agent communicating its programmatic positions on EU domestic policy on climate change. As in the previous example, these resolutions are adopted through the own-initiative procedure, representing the views of the EP without additional direct input from the other EU institutions. Within the period of analysis chosen here, especially the resolution adopted by the EP as a response to the announcement of the European Green Deal by the Commission stands out as the most prominent example. Following on the publication of written positions by each of its parliamentary party groups, the EP adopted a plenary resolution on 15 January 2020, endorsing the overall concept of a European Green Deal as proposed by the Commission but asking for stringent follow-up and adding more stringent targets (EP 2020i). Most importantly, these include the call to aim for a GHG reduction of 55% until the year 2030 and legally binding commitment to the goal of climate neutrality until 2050, a clearer commitment to reaching the limit of 1.5° warming enshrined in the Paris Agreement, and the adoption of a legally binding climate law. As a comprehensive statement covering the entire range of policies involved in the realization of the Green Deal, the resolution is a good representative example of how the EP frames its broader vision of climate action in a longer-term perspective.

Another EP resolution aimed at the communication of general positions towards the issue of climate change, rather than a policy-specific problem, is the declaration of a climate emergency, adopted by the EP plenary on 28 November 2019, just prior to the (delayed) arrival into office of the new Commission (EP 2019a). Within this resolution, supported by about two thirds of MEPs (429–225), the EP stresses the need for immediate stringent action to limit global warming to 1.5 °C relative to the pre-industrial age and calls on the other EU institutions to engage in action to achieve this target. The main ambition of the resolution is to mainstream climate change into all relevant policy fields of the EU: In this sense, the Commission is requested to consider the climate impacts of all legislative and budgetary proposals and to consider inconsistencies between related fields of policy-making, such as agriculture, trade, transport, between each other and the overall aim of climate action. Finally, other EP resolutions covering EU climate action as a whole are the resolutions on the EU Energy Union adopted on 15 December 2015 (EP 2015a), on the role of the regions concerning climate change adopted on 13 March 2018 (EP 2018b), and finally, a resolution simply dealing with the challenge of climate change adopted on 14 March 2019 (EP 2019b). Within this latter resolution, the EP mainly responds to the Commission document 'A Clean Planet for All' and its distinction of eight pathways into the future. In the document, the EP endorses the most stringent of the strategies proposed and calls for action to realize the target of climate neutrality in the EU by 2050 and to support efforts to achieve his goal at a global level by 2067. As this brief survey should make clear, the EP resolutions reviewed here are primarily programmatic and discursive—in the sense of addressing relatively general visions and challenges of climate change towards a broader political public and the other EU institutions, but without having any immediate effect on more specific acts of legislative decision-making. As stated above, and considering the three forms of EP involvement in EU climate policy discussed here, the subsequent analysis will focus on these EP resolutions, hence excluding controversies on specific pieces of legislation mainly for theoretical and methodical considerations.

3.4 Civil Society: Stakeholders, Advocacy Groups and Activists

Climate change governance attracts an increasing range of highly visible responses from a wide spectrum of civil society agents and organizations, prompting an academic debate about their potential for a democratization of global climate governance (Stevenson and Dryzek 2014). In fact, the sheer diversity of mobilization and involvement of civil society organizations require the analysis of their public communication and framing strategies to be delegated to a separate study. For the purpose of reconstructing the policy discourse of EU institutions on climate change, we therefore limit our observations to giving a survey of the various forms of involvement of civil society agents in the development of the EU strategy on climate change. Mainly, three layers of involvement need to be distinguished in this respect.

First, a relatively formalized structure of consultations has been established to allow the input of affected stakeholders, defined as a collective term for groups representing the broad range of economic and societal areas involved in the transition to a zero-carbon economy. As in several other fields of EU policy-making, the Commission regularly holds public consultation processes, opening an online forum for interested stakeholder organizations and individuals to send comments about selected topics related to the EU's climate agenda. Recent consultations include topics such as the 2030 Climate Target Plan, the European Climate Pact as part of the Green Deal, the longer-term strategy to reduce GHG emissions or on climate adaptation. On its website, the Commission offers full access to contributions made to the consultation and a report of the results.[15]

Second, a broader representation of environmental interests is created by the group of well-established ecological NGOs with broad public visibility and membership, and a more general mandate to communicate ecological concerns than the more issue-specific stakeholder groups. These cross-cutting groups are loosely organized in the so-called group of 10 and include well-known organizations such as Friends of the Earth, Greenpeace, the World Wildlife Foundation (WWF), Climate Action Network (CAN) Europe and the European Environmental Bureau (EEB). Comments and positions about EU climate policy are communicated through a wide variety of channels and formats, including public events and campaigns, briefing papers, press releases and online communication (cp. Bennett et al. 2014). Capturing particularly these latter forms of communication would require a separate study, tailored more specifically to the formats and expressions of advocacy used by NGOs both on- and offline.

Finally, a much more decentralized but nevertheless highly visible network of activists with a broad resonance within civil society has obviously emerged through the public protests and statements of Fridays for Future and related groups such as Scientists for Future, as well as more activist forms of protest through Extinction Rebellion and related groups. Concerning Fridays for Future as the most prominent group, the EU is not necessarily the main target of public protests, particularly in comparison to national governments. Nevertheless, several public appearances at the EU institutions by the movement's most prominent member, Great Thunberg, suggest efforts by policy-makers within the Commission and EP to signal an attitude of openness or even cooperation with the movement. These occasions include a public address by Greta Thunberg to the European Parliament on 21 April 2019, which the activist started with the much-cited words: 'My name is Great Thunberg, I am 16 years old, I come from Sweden, and I want you to panic.[16]' She was again invited

---

[15] A list of recent consultation procedures in the field of climate action is available online: https://ec.europa.eu/clima/consultations_en (last accessed: 29 September 2020).

[16] Video of Thunberg's full speech is available at: https://www.youtube.com/watch?v=cJAcuQEVxTY.

to speak to the European Parliament about the European Green Deal on 4 March 2020.[17]

The various types of civil society group arguably establish a broad range of settings and agents articulating strongly variegated, and at least partly also highly visible claims about the urgency to act against climate change towards a wider general public. Mainly two arguments, however, matter as points for consideration to exclude them from the subsequent analysis of framing. The first is the highly dispersed and multi-level form of organization and communication about climate change by civil society groups, including within online communities and fora. Doing justice to the complexity of the various formats and channels of communication within these various levels requires a separate approach and study, both in conceptual and methodical terms. Second, while the present study focuses on public communication about climate change, it also concentrates on elements of discourse directly involved in the policy-making process. Exploring the wider context of inputs into this process from a range of agents at the level of civil society would require also considering inputs from political parties, expert communities as well as from debates in institutional agents such as national parliaments and executives.

3.5 Framing Climate Change in EU policy Discourse: Structure, Linkages and Contestation

Having set out the overall trajectory of climate policy since the Paris Agreement, this section focuses on the evaluation of the main question addressed at the outset: How is climate change framed in policy discourse of EU institutions, and what linkages and patterns of contestation emerge within controversies on policy between political agents? In the following paragraphs, we present the main findings from a survey of policy documents covered in the previous discussion: namely, particularly the conclusions of the European Council, communications by the Commission and resolutions of the European Parliament from the Paris Agreement in 2015 to the current debate on the European Green Deal. In this context, the subsequent discussion establishes a first survey of data for this case study, to be presented in the same form for the subsequent

---

[17] Video of Thunberg's speech is available at: https://www.youtube.com/watch?v=ayqYBVJfp_I.

US case study and then scrutinized in more detail in the comparative chapter.

Concerning the selection of empirical material, the survey covers four types of document. First, the analysis includes eight thematically relevant conclusions of the European Council since 2015, covering all of the annual global climate negotiations within the Conferences of the Parties (COPs), as well as general statements on the mid-term 2030 climate targets, on climate diplomacy, and on the issue of climate change in general (cp. Council 2014–2019, overview in EPRS 2020b). Second, we present a survey of the five most relevant policy documents from the European Commission since the Paris Agreement, including those covered in detail above: namely, the communications on 'A Clean Planet for All' and on the European Green Deal, in addition to three more documents discussing the implementation of the Paris Agreement ('Road from Paris' and 'Transition to a Low Carbon Economy') and the Energy Union (COM 2015–2019). Third, we cover a set of eleven resolutions adopted by the EP plenary, covering each of the annual COPs since the adoption of the Paris Agreement, and several thematically broader resolutions on climate change. Finally, in order to tap more directly into party-political controversy, the subsequent discussion covers the motions for a resolution on the European Green Deal[18] tabled by each of the seven major EP party groups (in alphabetical order, by the EPP, ECR, ID, Greens, NGL, Renew and S&D group, EP 2020b, c, d, e, f, g, h); and furthermore, a joint resolution supported by four of these groups (namely, jointly by the EPP, Greens, Renew, and S&D, EP 2020a). Taken together, the documents chosen for the empirical analysis comprise some 132,000 words. Within this selection, the EU Council conclusions are more concise (with a length of about 9,600 words) than the policy documents of the European Commission (23,900 words) and particularly the

---

[18] As discussed above, these motions were tabled just prior to the adoption of the plenary resolution on 15 January 2020 and each present a full communication on the Green Deal following a roughly similar structure of thematic points. In this sense, the motions cover the EU's overall approach and ambition in the field of climate action as well as the following more specific policy challenges: the transition to clean energy and more efficient energy use, to a circular economy and 'smart' mobility, the realization of a carbon-neutral approach to production chains 'from farm to fork', the preservation of biodiversity, questions of climate finance and a socially fair transition, technological innovation and the role of the EU as a global leader in climate action.

much more comprehensive resolutions and motions by the European Parliament (98,700 words).

The dictionary used for automated coding contains 130 keywords assigned to a particular frame and to one of the three levels of justificatory concepts and ideas distinguished in the theoretical discussion (cp. this chapter): namely, paradigmatic terms establishing highly generalized, fundamental rationalizing concepts and principles; programmatic terms and ideas used for identifying general political strategies applied to tackle climate change; and finally, policy-specific instruments and approaches proposed to realize proposed political targets. Based on this approach, the six discursive frames distinguished at the outset—namely, the rationalization of climate change based on economic, political, risk- and justice-based, ecological and societal concepts and criteria—are each covered with a roughly equal number of 21–23 terms used for automated coding.[19] The coding procedure returned an overall result of 7,920 coded text segments covering the policy documents from all three major EU institutions, with the greatest number coded for the EP, then the Commission, and a smaller number for the European Council due to the concise form of its conclusions.[20] Our review of empirical results proceeds through a three-step approach discussed in the theoretical part:

---

[19] These terms often consist of a single keyword (such as 'investment' or 'solidarity'), but also frequently consist of compounds of two or more words (such as 'carbon price' or 'effects of climate') in order to target specific meanings and contexts of the discussion on climate change. A particularly relevant example for using compound terms (consisting of more than one single word) to target the specific context of a term is the word 'climate'. Unsurprisingly, this term is the most frequently used word within the policy documents (excluding words such as pronouns, articles and propositions blocked by the stop list). Applied on its own, the word 'climate' is used far too often and in too many contexts to evoke a particular framing of the issue of climate change, and therefore unsuited to indicate the use of a particular frame. A solution to this problem is to search for combinations of this word with other terms to uncover more specific uses of the term, such as 'climate justice', 'Climate diplomacy' or 'climate emergency'. As the overview of keywords shows, corresponding word combinations including the term 'climate' were identified through word frequency screens and included in the dictionary. Other terms too unspecifically used to evoke a particular frame on their own, but useful for analysis when screened as part of a word combination include 'efficiency', 'sustainable', 'adaptation', 'green' or 'growth'.

[20] The data gained from the coding of documents comprises 609 coded text segments for the EU Council, 1,406 for the European Commission, and 5,905 for the European Parliament; for the latter, this figure includes 3,362 segments for resolutions adopted by the plenary and 2,543 for the party group motions on the European Green Deal.

namely, the *structure* of EU climate policy discourse, as measured by the relative salience of the six different climate frames; the *linkages* between frames in a comparison of various institutional settings; and finally, the *contestation* of climate policy, considering different resolutions of EP party groups on the European Green Deal within the European Parliament.

3.5.1 Structure of Discourse: Framing Climate Change in EU Policy Documents

The first global survey of our empirical results leads to two main insights: First, a clearer distinction between discursive frames used as primary, supplementary, and more marginal justification of climate policy in the EU; and second, more distinct profiles of the various EU institutions and the way their policy documents engage with the different aspects and layers of discourse about climate change. A survey of results covering the relative strength of each of the six different climate frames, both at the aggregate level and for each of the EU institutions is shown in Graph 3.1.

Based on these results, two discursive frames emerge as the main foundation for justifying climate action in the EU: In addition to the promotion of ecological frames, particularly economic concepts and ideas are advanced in EU policy documents to make the case for action against climate change. Taken together, both frames establish a perception of climate change as an ecological reality and economic opportunity as the dominant framing in the policy discourse of EU institutions. Closer insight about the use of these two master frames is gained from the rank order of most frequently coded keywords. This ranking identifies the term 'investment' as the most frequent keyword from the dictionary, followed by the keywords 'environment', 'market' and 'biodiversity' within the first five ranks. An additional insight in this context is that both the ecological and economic aspect of climate change are addressed primarily by reference to highly generalized, paradigmatic terms and concepts (such as industry, market or ecosystem) rather than more specific programmatic or even policy-specific terms. This observation confirms the role of the two frames as foundational frames used to establish a broad, generalized case for acting against climate change; taken together, arguments framed in economic or ecological terms comprise almost half (namely, 47%) of the statements coded in the policy documents, with almost exact equal weight given to both types of frame.

STRUCTURE OF FRAMES IN EU CLIMATE POLICY DISCOURSE

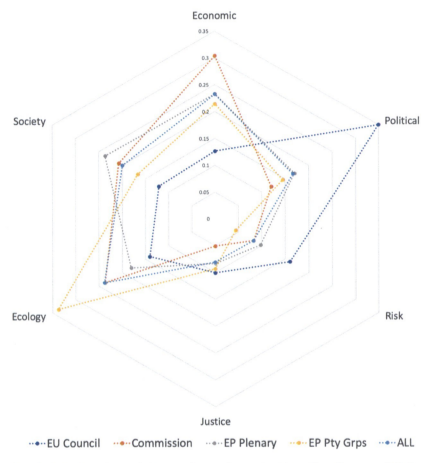

Graph 3.1 Structure of climate change frames in EU policy discourse (EP Pty Grps = European Parliament Party Groups)

In addition to these two master frames, particularly arguments framed in political and societal terms establish the second most important form of justification, comprising just over a third of all arguments coded. This dimension of policy discourse mainly addresses questions about how policies against climate change will be put into practice—emphasizing keywords such as 'implementation' and 'climate action'; they also address the various levels and context of political action such as 'region', 'city', and 'local' or 'urban' agents, as well as agents and participants of the policy process, such as 'citizens' or 'people', 'legislative' actors, 'communities' as a well as actors within 'civil society'. These claims made about the political and societal framing of climate action are proposed mainly in programmatic terms, involving relatively specific references to climate objectives, targets, diplomacy or agenda items rather than more paradigmatic references to the global framework of cooperation in the framework of UN institutions.

Finally, the least weight in quantitative terms is given to two frames closely associated with some of the potentially most contentious, ethical aspects of action against climate change: namely, its implications for questions of justice and the provision of security in relation to a broad range of individual and societal forms of risk. Both frames occur in roughly the same frequency and together comprise about 16% of all arguments coded in the empirical material. In this sense, it is evident that many terms coded within the justice frame—particularly keywords such as 'poverty', 'gender' and 'women' or references to 'least developed' or 'most vulnerable' regions and societies address highly relevant and politically sensitive questions of climate action; this aspect will be taken up again when we turn to the contestation and party-political aspect of framing climate change. It is, however, perhaps a surprise that references to the numerous threats established by climate change to individuals and society are relatively rare in policy documents of the EU, with relatively general mentions of 'risk' and 'security' still the most frequent mentions of this thematic dimension. This point probably reflects the fact that most EU documents are not primarily engaged in arguing the case that climate change establishes a threat to society, but rather moving on to more specific questions of policy.

Summing up this first set of findings leads to the conclusion that EU policy discourse on climate change is primarily framed in economic terms of growth, opportunity and investment—and secondarily in political and societal criteria of targets, decision-making implementation and reference to specific contexts of action such as regions and cities. Beyond this global survey, more specific insights into the structure of EU policy discourse are gained by distinguishing between the EU institutions and their respective framing of climate change. Here, we can draw insights from presenting a

Table 3.2 Rank order of frames in policy documents of the three main EU institutions

	EU Council	COM	EP plenary	EP party groups
Economic	(4)	(1)	(2)	(2)
Political	(1)	(4)	(4)	(4)
Risk	(2)	(5)	(5)	(6)
Justice	(6)	(6)	(6)	(5)
Ecology	(3)	(2)	(3)	(1)
Society	(5)	(3)	(1)	(3)
Dominant frames (>50%)	Political and risk	Economic and ecology	Society, economic and ecology	Ecology and economic

rank order of the frames used by the EU Council, Commission and Parliament, and identifying their respective dominant form of framing: namely, the combination of discursive frames that together comprises more than half of their coded statements. Table 3.2 summarizes the findings.

This comparative survey provides some differentiation but also fits to the established roles of each of the three main institutions within the EU policy-making process. In this sense, the EU Council assumes its role as a programmatic leader for the mid- to longer-term political strategy of the EU. It does so by adopting language that frames climate action primarily in terms of political targets and agendas, combined with additional references to general sources of risk posed by climate change. Against this background, the Commission spells out the more specific approaches to climate policy by framing climate policy as an opportunity for economic growth and modernization strategy, as reflected in its predominant use of these two frames. While this framing approach is reflected in EP party group motions on the European Green Deal, it is noteworthy that the primary frames used in resolutions adopted by the EP plenary is societal—namely, referring to the involvement of regions, citizens, and various levels of political decision-making including cities and private entities into the realization of climate change policy. This latter finding can be taken as an indication that the institutional role of the EP as the primary forum of democratic representation in the EU is strongly reflected in its language about the future course of climate action.

Overall, this first cut through the data is proof that the issue of climate change reaches beyond the environmental in EU policy discourse but is addressed as a much broader political, economic and societal challenge by the various EU institutions according to their respective role in the policy-making process. To conclude, this survey demonstrates the differentiation of tasks between the EU institutions within the policy-making process rather than different, or even competing views on climate change as an issue: With regard to this latter question, our insights confirm that the mitigation of climate change is defined primarily as an opportunity for economic investment and growth, resonating with an approach described as eco-modernization (cp. Rifkin 2020).

3.5.2 Linkages: Proximity and Interconnections Between Frames

The second part of our analysis turns to the linkages between frames: The question which sets of concepts and ideas about climate change are more frequently used in combination or connection with each other, and which are more distant and therefore more likely to present opposing interpretations. In this sense, we can expect closely interconnected clusters of concepts associated with various frames to be more relevant for establishing dominant framings of climate change than single but isolated data points indicating frequent use of a particular component.

Concerning the choice of methods, the relative proximity of frames and their interconnections are evaluated here using quantitative distance measures; for better accessibility, these are visualized for the subsequent discussion through code maps produced through an output function of the text analysis software. These code maps can be read to understand both the relative importance and mutual interconnections between frames: In addition to indicating the relative frequency of codes assigned to text segments (indicated by the size of plot markers), the maps also demonstrate the relationship of codes to each other. The more frequently two or more codes have been assigned to the same text segment— and each coded segment comprises the sentence in which a keyword occurs and the following sentence—the closer they are represented in the diagram. In addition, coincidences of frames exceeding a certain number are shown through linkages in the form of lines within the diagram. Taken together, these aspects are combined to identify clusters of interconnected frames within the data. These surveys include three aspects: first, the proximity of frames in the public discourse of each of the three main EU institutions; second, the overall scope of discourse and number of clusters identifiable within the code maps; and finally, the density of linkages between various clusters.

The first code map demonstrates the relatively narrow, focused, and tightly integrated policy discourse of the European Council (Graph 3.2). Within its center, the two frames identified as dominant for its discourse—namely, the setting of political targets addressing the risk and security dimension of climate change—are closely interlinked with each other, establishing a central core of the conclusions adopted both at the highest level of Heads of State and Government and the Foreign Affairs Council. This core covers only a relatively small scope within the code map, connecting the three components of the dominant, political frame with several other frames, but particularly the risk-based justification of climate action. In addition to this core of the Council's discourse, only one additional cluster of economic arguments can be identified as a second main point of reference within the Council conclusions, albeit applied with less emphasis. A final observation about the data points plotted here is

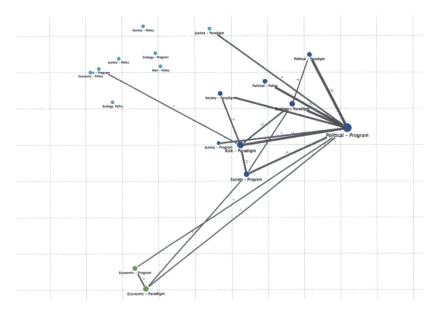

Graph 3.2 Code map of frames in EU Council conclusions on climate change

the strong emphasis on claims at the paradigmatic and program level, resulting in a clear separation between this sort of highly general claims and more policy-specific arguments. References to policy, by contrast, are framed neither have considerable weight nor strong linkages to the main, primarily political-programmatic arguments of the Council.

Moving on from general agenda-setting to more specific policy formulation, both an expansion and re-framing of climate discourse is observable with regard to the European Commission (Graph 3.3). The two dominant frames used here—namely, the framing of climate as both an economic opportunity and ecological challenge—emerge as more distinct clusters that are further apart from each other and less directly interlinked. Both clusters are also connected with other types of justification, particularly with terms associated with the societal frame. In comparison of both clusters, the economic framing of climate action has stronger emphasis and more interlinkages with additional frames,

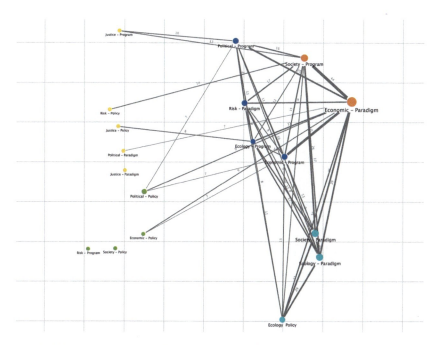

Graph 3.3 Code map for EU Commission policy documents on climate change

confirming this approach as the dominant perspective in Commission documents on the issue. Finally, it is striking how one of the most sensitive and contentious aspects of climate change—namely, its justice dimension involving questions of finance, development, gender and social protection of vulnerable groups—is de-emphasized and detached from the core of the Commission's framing.

Finally, and covering resolutions adopted by the EP plenary, the third code map demonstrates the degree to which parliamentary statements broaden and diversify discourse about climate change in the EU (Graph 3.4). Overall four main clusters of arguments are mapped in the visual presentation, with different weight and degrees of interconnection between various frames not all of them are identifiable as clusters of more tightly interlinked forms of references to climate change: First, the strongest cluster depicted on the right side of the map combines the generally predominant, economic framing with a discursive approach

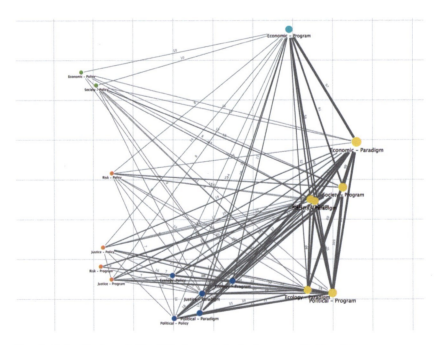

Graph 3.4 Code map for EP plenary resolutions on climate change

more typical for the EP, namely, references to specific contexts of action, stakeholders and citizens comprised in the societal frame. In addition, economic arguments also establish a second, more detached cluster of arguments in the EP's resolutions. References to an ecological frame combined with political terms—expressed mainly through a call for action, based on a sense of urgency to act against the climate crisis— establishes a third cluster of arguments in declarations of the EP. Finally, an intriguing aspect is the emergence of references to justice as part of an additional cluster, pictured at the bottom left of the code map: Here, references to justice gain in salience, emerging both at a more paradigmatic but also policy-specific level of discourse; these references are integrated relatively closely with claims that are framed in political and ecological terms. This suggests that the EP emerges as a primary discursive agent concerning more normative and politically contentious aspects of climate action.

This finding is further corroborated in the code map covering the motions for resolution on the European Green Deal (Graph 3.5). Here, the close interlinkages between the dominant framing of climate action through economic, ecological and societal criteria reflect discourse by the Commission on the EGD as previously discussed. In addition, however, references to both justice and risk emerge as more distinct clusters that are also relatively coherent in terms of references to the various levels of discourse at the paradigm, program and policy level. Put more simply, it is almost exclusively in EP party group motions that we find more condensed and visible discussions of aspects of climate justice and about questions of risk, while the predominant framing of climate action in economic terms is still upheld and closely interlinked with the discussion of ecological concerns.

In comparison, this survey of the EU institutions demonstrates a gradual broadening and diversification of climate discourse through the different stages of the policy-making process: Starting with the very narrow, focused declaration of targets through the EU Council, both the use of frames and their relative density gradually expand in policy discourse by the Commission as the main policy entrepreneur of the European Green Deal but particularly in resolutions of the European Parliament. Here, particularly frames covering aspects of risk, society and justice are added to broaden the dominant framing of climate change discourse in economic terms. Especially this latter point brings up the question to what degree and how the use of climate frames is linked

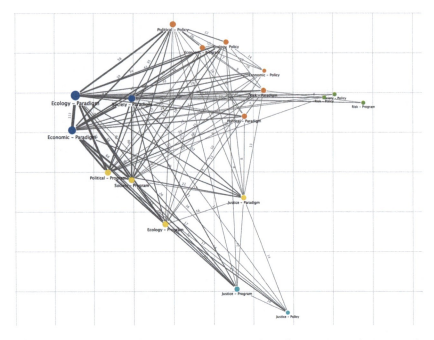

Graph 3.5 Code map for EP party group motions for an EP resolution on the European Green Deal

to political contestation, considering ideological stances of party groups within the EP.

3.5.3 Contestation: How Political Party Groups Frame Climate Change

An important question for the present analysis is how different forms of framing open insights into the contestation of climate policy, and particularly its party-political dimension (cp. Carter et al. 2018). In this regard, we concentrate our analysis on the motions for resolution on the European Green Deal tabled by each of the EP's seven main party groups in January 2020. These motions have advantages in terms of comparability, by presenting a full and relatively comprehensive (about 6,000 words each) appraisal and following an overall similar sequence of topics and

Table 3.3 Framing of motions for the EP resolution on the European Green Deal by EP party groups; NGL = Nordic Green Left, S&D = Socialists and Democrats, EPP = European People's Party, ECR = European Conservatives and Reformists, ID = Identity and Democracy Group

	NGL	Greens	S&D	Renew	EPP	ECR	ID	ALL
Economic	13.9	20.2	22.0	24.9	30.4	20.8	22.0	21.4
Political	8.8	13.1	13.9	18.0	18.1	18.7	6.4	14.5
Risk	6.6	4.5	3.2	3.9	1.5	7.5	5.6	4.4
Justice	15.4	12.3	9.8	5.1	6.5	8.0	2.1	9.3
Ecology	38.4	35.9	34.3	33.9	23.5	26.2	32.0	33.7
Society	17.1	13.9	16.7	14.4	20.1	18.7	32.0	16.6
N	410	449	304	334	204	187	141	2543

headings. Based on this empirical material, it is therefore possible to establish a direct comparison about how political party groups represented in the EP frame their position towards the overall programmatic direction of climate policy as embodied in the European Green Deal. Table 3.3 shows an overview of the results.

This survey provides several insights about how the framing of climate change corresponds with party-political positions towards the issue. Mainly three observations stand out: First, several of the climate frames discussed here are associated with particular party groups or components of the spectrum of political positions represented within the EP. An economic framing of climate issues is emphasized particularly by the EPP and Renew groups and hence, parties on the center-right usually associated with a position leaning towards free market competition (Hix et al. 2007). A similar observation is made within the political frame, where particularly parties of the center-right (EPP, Renew and ECR) use stronger emphasis than those on the left. A combined economic and political framing of climate issues is identified as a typical frame associated with centrist positions leaning to the center-right and relatively market liberal positions. By contrast, the climate frame most clearly associated with parties on the left side of the political spectrum is the one based on ideas of justice: Particularly the left party group NGL, Greens and the center-left S&D are identified as groups emphasizing this frame associated with questions of gender, climate finance and various aspects of energy poverty to a stronger degree than parties on the right. However, this insight gains in significance when compared to variation of the ecological frame, which equally receives more support from parties on the left but does not show the drastic degree of variation between both sides of the spectrum if compared in relative terms. The justice frame is emphasized by the three left-of-center parties to considerably higher degrees than by the four parties right-of-center. In comparison, the same degree of variation is not reached within the ecological framing of climate policy, where only the EPP and ECR are shown to use significantly less emphasis, and all other parties show values within a relatively narrow corridor.

Second, and building on the previous insights, an ecological framing of climate change is shared across the political spectrum and is even identified as the relatively strongest form of justification across all parties compared (with the single exception of the EPP, where an economic framing is stronger). Arguably the use of an ecological frame does not necessarily suggest that a progressive position towards a reduction of GHG emissions is taken—references to sustainability, global temperature, ecosystems and biodiversity can be made by debating or even disputing the impact climate change. Nevertheless, it is remarkable how much a common language consisting of numerous key terms of an ecological framing are shared across party groups. In fact, the use of this frame by the Green party group is not significantly higher than by the far-right ID group (35.9 and 32.0%, respectively). Obviously, it is a highly important question for the comparative aspect of our study whether this commonality of ecological terms and concepts in the political discourse across party groups is also observable in the US case (cp. Hayes and Knox-Hayes 2014).

Finally, the data shows some loose ends that deserve further scrutiny in future research into the party politics of climate change policy. The most important question in this context is how framing is linked to positions expressing skepticism about climate change, particularly more fundamental forms of rejecting concepts to reduce GHG emissions. This question deserves careful scrutiny as 'climate skepticism' and denial is hardly reducible to a single, ideologically coherent position but comprises a variety of critical stances towards the scope, consequences, severity and possible remedies of climate change. Turning to the empirical data presented here, it is a surprising finding that the framing of climate change in terms of risk—established by referring to the effects and impacts of climate change, threats such as extreme weather and floods, and issues of public health, food security and migration—has no visible association with party-political orientations; on the contrary, the use of this frame shows both relatively little salience and highly mixed variation across the political spectrum. Against this background, however, an intriguing observation is the heavy emphasis laid on a societal framing by Identity & Democracy (ID), the arguably most climate skeptical group in the EP, and equally elevated values of this frame by parties on the right. This observation suggests that objections to climate action in the EU are framed primarily through concepts of political autonomy and identity: namely, by referring to ordinary citizens, their culture, identity and tradition, and the adverse impacts that initiatives towards a decarbonisation have on their daily lives, particularly if these measures are not imposed in voluntary or flexible form. This being said, it is also noteworthy that typical keywords of positions expressing a hard version of climate denial—such as hoax, hysteria, exploitation, deception or tyranny—were not detected in the screening of keywords, and therefore appear largely absent from political discourse by and between EU institutions.

3.6 Conclusions: Framing Climate Change in EU Policy Discourse

Summing up, this chapter has reconstructed policy developments and discourse communicated by the main EU institutions leading from the Paris Agreement to the European Green Deal and its legislative operationalization through the European climate law. Asking how the EU institutions frame the issue of climate change, and how perspectives established by various frames are both interlinked and contested in the policy debate, our analysis has revealed the following three insights.

First, this review of the structure of EU policy discourse identifies a dominant framing of policies to mitigate climate change: namely, a project of eco-modernization defined as a vision to combine the idea of ecological sustainability with economic opportunity and growth. In this sense, particularly ecological and economic terms were identified as the most frequently coded references of political discourse, with a secondary role assigned to political terms related to climate targets and implementation, and references to a variety of societal groups and contexts of action mainly to address issues of implementation and evaluation. Beyond this general survey, a further distinction between the main EU institutions reveals their more distinct, and complementary forms of framing public communication on climate change: namely, through a focus on political target-setting by the EU Council, a more detailed policy discourse spelling out the mutual integration of ecological and economic principles by the Commission, and a more variegated form of framing that engages with aspects of risk, society and concerns of justice by the European Parliament. Ecological concerns are addressed throughout the policy documents but are emphasized especially strongly in the EP party group motions on the European Green Deal. Overall, it fits to these observations that the most frequently coded keywords in the entire empirical material were 'investment', 'environmental', 'market' and 'region', while the respective main keyword for the EU institutions were 'implementation' (EU Council), 'investment' (Commission), 'region' (EP plenary resolutions) and 'environmental' (EP party group motions).

Second, analyzing the linkages between frames suggests that EU discourse on climate change is highly integrated through relatively close linkages between a limited set of clusters, even though gradual expansion and diversification are observable following the policy process and related EU institutions. Here, our review has demonstrated the gradual expansion of discourse from the very narrow framing in conclusions of the EU Council to the specification of climate policy initiatives by the Commission and the broader framing in political debate in the European Parliament. While the respective choice of frames by each EU institution can be seen to correspond with their roles in the policy-making process as agenda-setter, policy entrepreneur and arena of democratic representation, the survey also suggests a tight integration of different frames in EU policy discourse. In this respect, identifiable clusters of frames are connected with sufficient overlaps and linkages as to establish connected, mutually compatible perspectives on climate change.

Finally, our review of motions for resolution on the European Green Deal provides insights about how framing is linked to the party-political contestation of climate change policy. In this context, a relevant finding is that two frames arguably central for the appraisal of climate change as a political problem—namely, its evaluation according to criteria of ecological sustainability as well as individual and societal risk—are used relatively indistinctly across the spectrum of political parties. In this sense, they do not appear as reliable indicators of ideological position within the left/right spectrum, or even of skepticism towards the issue of climate change. One implication of this finding is that parties represented in the EP share a common language—by using ecological terms, concepts and ideas to address some of the most fundamental aspects of global warming and how it creates a threat to both the environment and human society.

In comparison, other frames included in this analysis appear as more closely associated with the position of political parties within the political spectrum. In this sense, an economic framing based on a concept of climate change as an emerging opportunity structure for investment, technological competitiveness and growth is associated with parties on the center-right, whereas particularly the framing of climate change in terms of justice—addressing the gender, development and poverty dimension of its implications—is used by parties of the left. As discussed above, more climate critical parties seem to adopt a societal framing of climate change, referring to issues of culture, identity, sovereignty and tradition.

Taken together, these findings provide a substantial foundation for the comparative evaluation of the political space of climate policy in comparison to other political entities such as the US. Taken for themselves, however, they also contribute to a critical assessment of the claim that the EU has emerged as a leader of global climate policy particularly within a discursive and cognitive definition of the term (Wurzel et al. 2017b; Rayner and Jordan 2013; Bretherton and Vogler 2010). Some of the key criteria to assess leadership by an institution or agent in discursive terms—particularly the coherence, consistency and inclusiveness of arguments proposed to combat climate change—substantiate the positive appraisal of political leadership in this regard, both by the EU as a whole and its different institutions. At the same time, a critical addition is that a discourse of economic modernization typical for EU governance has largely been expanded to the realm of climate policy, however marginalizing to a relatively strong degree the aspect of climate justice particularly in a global perspective. Leaving this point for consideration in future research debates, the following chapter proceeds to the second of our two case studies, presenting a reconstruction of climate change politics in the United States.

References

Ajl, Max. 2021. *A People's Green New Deal*. London: Pluto Press.
Aykut, Stefan C., Christopher Pavenstädt, Alvine Datchoua-Tirvaudey, Emilie d'Amico, Max Braun, Ella Hinks, Felix Schenuit, Jan Wilkens, and Simone Rödder. 2022. "Circles of Global Climate Governance. Power, Performance and Contestation at the UN Climate Conference COP26 in Glasgow." CSS Working Paper Series No 4, Hamburg. https://doi.org/10.25592/css-wp-004.

Bennett, W. Lance, Sabine Lang, and Alexandra Segerberg. 2014. "European Issue Public Online: The Cases of Climate Change and Fair Trade." In *European Public Spheres. Politics Is Back*, edited by Thomas Risse, 108–38. Cambridge: Cambridge University Press.

Biedenkopf, Katja. 2015. "The European Parliament in EU External Climate Governance." In *The European Parliament and Its International Relations*, edited by Stelios Stavridis and Daniela Irrera, 92–108. https://doi.org/10.4324/9781315713984-6.

Biedenkopf, Katja, and Franziska Petri. 2019. "EU Delegations in European Union Climate Diplomacy: The Role of Links to Brussels, Individuals and Country Contexts." *Journal of European Integration* 41 (1): 47–63. https://doi.org/10.1080/07036337.2018.1551389.

Boasson, Elin Lerum, and Jørgen Wettestad. 2013. *EU Climate Policy: Industry, Policy Interaction and External Environment*. Farnham [u.a.]: Ashgate.

Brandsma, Gijs Jan, Justin Greenwood, Ariadna Ripoll Servent, and Christilla Roederer-Rynning. 2021. "Inside the Black Box of Trilogues: Introduction to the Special Issue." *Journal of European Public Policy* 28 (1): 1–9.

Bretherton, Charlotte, and John Vogler. 2010. *The European Union as a Global Actor*. 2nd ed. London [u.a.]: Routledge.

Burns, Charlotte. 2017. "The European Parliament and Climate Change: A Constrained Leader?" In *The European Union in International Climate Change Politics*, edited by Rüdiger Wurzel and James Connelly, 2nd ed., 52–65. https://doi.org/10.4324/9781315627199-16.

———. 2019. "In the Eye of the Storm? The European Parliament, the Environment and the EU's Crises." *Journal of European Integration* 41 (3): 311–27. https://doi.org/10.1080/07036337.2019.1599375.

Burns, Charlotte, and Neil Carter. 2010. "The European Parliament and Climate Change: From Symbolism to Heroism and Back Again." In *The European Union as a Leader in International Climate Change Politics*, edited by Rüdiger Wurzel and James Connelly, 1st ed., 58–73. https://doi.org/10.4324/9780203839959-13.

Burns, Charlotte, Neil Carter, Graeme A. M. Davies, and Nicholas Worsfold. 2013. "Still Saving the Earth? The European Parliament's Environmental Record." *Environmental Politics* 22 (6): 935–54. https://doi.org/10.1080/09644016.2012.698880.

Carbon Brief. 2021. "COP26: Key Outcomes Agreed at the UN Climate Talks in Glasgow." https://www.carbonbrief.org/cop26-key-outcomes-agreed-at-the-un-climate-talks-in-glasgow.

Carter, Neil, Robert Ladrech, Conor Little, and Vasiliki Tsagkroni. 2018. "Political Parties and Climate Policy: A New Approach to Measuring Parties' Climate Policy Preferences." *Party Politics* 24 (6): 731–42.

COM (EU Commission). 2015. "Energy Union Package. The Paris Protocol—A Blueprint for Tackling Global Climate Change beyond 2020." Brussels, COM(2015) 81 final. https://eur-lex.europa.eu/resource.html?uri=cellar:e27fdb4d-bdce-11e4-bbe1-01aa75ed71a1.0003.03/DOC_1&format=PDF.

———. 2016a. "The Road from Paris: Assessing the Implications of the Paris Agreement and Accompanying the Proposal for a Council Decision on the Signing, on Behalf of the European Union, of the Paris Agreement Adopted under the United Nations Framework Convention on Climate Change." Brussels, COM(2016a) 110 final. https://eur-lex.europa.eu/legal-content/EN/TXT/PDF/?uri=CELEX:52016aDC0110&from=EN.

———. 2016b. "Accelerating Europe's Transition to a Low-Carbon Economy." Brussels, COM(2016b) 500 final. https://eur-lex.europa.eu/legal-content/EN/TXT/PDF/?uri=CELEX:52016bDC0500&from=EN.

———. 2018. "A Clean Planet for All. A European Strategic Long-Term Vision for a Prosperous, Modern, Competitive and Climate Neutral Economy." Brussels, COM(2018) 773 final. https://eur-lex.europa.eu/legal-content/EN/TXT/PDF/?uri=CELEX:52018DC0773&from=EN.

———. 2019. "The European Green Deal." Brussels, COM(2019) 640 final. https://eur-lex.europa.eu/resource.html?uri=cellar:b828d165-1c22-11ea-8c1f-01aa75ed71a1.0002.02/DOC_1&format=PDF.

Daviter, Falk. 2011. *Policy Framing in the European Union*. Palgrave Studies in European Union Politics. Basingstoke [u.a.]: Palgrave Macmillan.

Delbeke, Jos, and Peter Vis. 2015. *EU Climate Policy Explained*. Abingdon, OX [u.a.]: Routledge.

———. 2019. *Towards a Climate-Neutral Europe: Curbing the Trend*. London: Routledge.

Dupont, Claire, and Sebastian Oberthür. 2017. "The Council and the European Council: Stuck on the Road to Transformational Leadership?" In *The European Union in International Climate Change Politics. Still Taking a Lead?* edited by Rüdiger Wurzel, James Connelly, and Duncan Liefferink, 66–80. Abingdon: Routledge.

EP (European Parliament). 2015a. "Towards a New International Climate Agreement in Paris (2015a/2112(INI))." Brussels, P8_TA(2015a)0359. http://www.europarl.europa.eu/sides/getDoc.do?pubRef=-//EP//TEXT+TA+P8-TA-2015a-0359+0+DOC+XML+V0//EN.

———. 2015b. "Towards a European Energy Union (2015b/2113(INI))." Brussels P8_TA(2015b)0444. https://www.europarl.europa.eu/doceo/document/TA-8-2015b-0444_EN.pdf.

———. 2016. "UN Climate Change Conference in Marrakesh, Morocco (COP22) (2016/2814(RSP))." Brussels, P8_TA(2016)0383. http://www.europarl.europa.eu/sides/getDoc.do?pubRef=-//EP//TEXT+TA+P8-TA-2016-0383+0+DOC+XML+V0//EN.

———. 2017. "UN Climate Change Conference in Bonn, Germany (COP23) (2017/2620(RSP))." Brussels, P8_TA(2017)0380. http://www.europarl.europa.eu/sides/getDoc.do?pubRef=-//EP//TEXT+TA+P8-TA-2017-0380+0+DOC+XML+V0//EN.

———. 2018a. "The Role of EU Regions and Cities in Implementing the COP 21 Paris Agreement on Climate Change (2017/2006(INI))." Brussels P8_TA(2018)0068. https://www.europarl.europa.eu/doceo/document/TA-8-2018-0068_EN.pdf.

———. 2018b. "Climate Diplomacy (2017/2272(INI))." Brussels, P8_TA(2018b)0280. https://www.europarl.europa.eu/doceo/document/TA-8-2018b-0280_EN.pdf.

———. 2018c. "UN Climate Change Conference in Katowice, Poland (COP24) (2018c/2598(RSP))." Brussels, P8_TA-PROV(2018c)0430. http://www.europarl.europa.eu/sides/getDoc.do?pubRef=-//EP//TEXT+TA+P8-TA-2018c-0430+0+DOC+XML+V0//EN.

———. 2019a. "Climate Change—A European Strategic Long-Term Vision for a Prosperous, Modern, Competitive and Climate Neutral Economy in Accordance with the Paris Agreement (2019a/2582(RSP))." Brussels, P8_TA(2019a)0217. https://www.europarl.europa.eu/doceo/document/TA-8-2019a-0217_EN.html.

———. 2019b. "Climate and Environmental Emergency (2019b/2930(RSP))." Brussels P9_TA(2019)0078. https://www.europarl.europa.eu/doceo/document/TA-9-2019-0078_EN.pdf.

———. 2019c. "UN Climate Change Conference (COP25)—Thursday, 28 November 2019c (2019c/2712(RSP))." Brussels, P9_TA(2019c)0079. https://www.europarl.europa.eu/doceo/document/TA-9-2019c-0079_EN.html.

———. 2020a. "Motion for a Resolution on the European Green Deal on Behalf of the ID Group, 10 January 2020." https://www.europarl.europa.eu/doceo/document/B-9-2020-0046_EN.html.

———. 2020b. "Motion for a Resolution on the European Green Deal on Behalf of the PPE Group, 10 January 2020." https://www.europarl.europa.eu/doceo/document/B-9-2020-0042_EN.html.

———. 2020c. "Motion for a Resolution on the European Green Deal on Behalf of the Renew Group, 10 January 2020c." https://www.europarl.europa.eu/doceo/document/B-9-2020c-0043_EN.html.

———. 2020d. "Motion for a Resolution on the European Green Deal on Behalf of the S&D Group, 10 January 2020d." https://www.europarl.europa.eu/doceo/document/B-9-2020d-0045_EN.html.

———. 2020e. "Motion for a Resolution on the European Green Deal on Behalf of the Verts/ALE Group, 10 January 2020." https://www.europarl.europa.eu/doceo/document/B-9-2020-0040_EN.html.

———. 2020f. "Motion for a Resolution on the European Green Deal on Behalf of the GUE/NGL Group, 10 January 2020 (2019/2956(RSP))." Brussels B9-0044/2020/REV. https://www.europarl.europa.eu/doceo/document/B-9-2020-0044_EN.html.

———. 2020g. "Joint Motion for a Resolution on the European Green Deal on Behalf of the PPE, S&D, Renew and the Verts/ALE Group." https://www.europarl.europa.eu/doceo/document/RC-9-2020a-0040_EN.html.

———. 2020h. "The European Green Deal—European Parliament Resolution (2019/2956(RSP))." Brussels, P9_TA(2020b)0005. https://www.europarl.europa.eu/doceo/document/TA-9-2020b-0005_EN.html.

———. 2020i. "Motion for a Resolution on the European Green Deal on Behalf of the ECR Group, 10 January 2020 (2019/2956(RSP))." Brussels, B9-0041/2020. https://www.europarl.europa.eu/doceo/document/B-9-2020-0041_EN.html.

EPRS. 2018a. "Post-2020 Reform of the EU Emissions Trading System; Limiting Member States' Carbon Emissions, Briefing: EU Legislation in Progress." European Parliament Research Service, Briefing, Brussels. http://www.europarl.europa.eu/RegData/etudes/BRIE/2018b/621902/EPRS_BRI(2018b)621902_EN.pdf.

———. 2018b. "Effort Sharing Regulation, 2021–2030: Limiting Member States' Carbon Emissions, Briefing: EU Legislation in Progress." European Parliament Research Service, Briefing, Brussels. http://www.europarl.europa.eu/RegData/etudes/BRIE/2016/589799/EPRS_BRI(2016)589799_EN.pdf.

———. 2019a. "Promoting Renewable Energy Sources in the EU After 2020 Briefing: EU Legislation in Progress." European Parliament Research Service, Briefing, Brussels. http://www.europarl.europa.eu/RegData/etudes/BRIE/2017/599278/EPRS_BRI(2017)599278_EN.pdf.

———. 2019b. "Revised Energy Efficiency Directive; Briefing: EU Legislation in Progress." European Parliament Research Service, Briefing, Brussels. http://www.europarl.europa.eu/RegData/etudes/BRIE/2017/595923/EPRS_BRI(2017)595923_EN.pdf.

———. 2020a. "European Climate Law." European Parliament Research Service, Briefing: Legislation in Progress, Brussels. https://www.europarl.europa.eu/RegData/etudes/BRIE/2020a/649385/EPRS_BRI(2020a)649385_EN.pdf.

———. 2020b. "European Council Conclusions. A Rolling Check-List of Commitments to Date." European Parliament Research Service, Brussels. https://www.europarl.europa.eu/RegData/etudes/STUD/2020/642816/EPRS_STU(2020)642816_EN.pdf.

———. 2021. "European Climate Law." Briefing: EU Legislation in Progress, Brussels. https://www.europarl.europa.eu/RegData/etudes/BRIE/2020/649385/EPRS_BRI(2020)649385_EN.pdf.

European Council. 2014. "Conclusions European Council 23/24 October 2014." General Secretariat of the Council EUCO 169/14. https://www.consilium.europa.eu/media/24561/145397.pdf.

———. 2016a. "Conclusions on European Climate Diplomacy After COP 21, 15 February 2016." General Secretariat of the Council 6061/16. https://data.consilium.europa.eu/doc/document/ST-6061-2016-INIT/en/pdf.

———. 2016b. "Council Decision on the Conclusion, on Behalf of the European Union, of the Paris Agreement Adopted under the United Nations Framework Convention on Climate Change." Official Journal of the European Union L 282/1. https://eur-lex.europa.eu/legal-content/EN/TXT/PDF/?uri=CELEX:32016D1841&from=ES.

———. 2016c. "Preparations for the United Nations Framework Convention on Climate Change Meetings in Marrakech (7–18 November 2016c)." General Secretariat of the Council 12807/16. https://data.consilium.europa.eu/doc/document/ST-12807-2016c-INIT/en/pdf.

———. 2017a. "Conclusions European Council 22/23 June 2017." General Secretariat of the Council EUCO 8/17. https://www.consilium.europa.eu/media/23985/22-23-euco-final-conclusions.pdf.

———. 2017b. "Council Conclusions on Paris Agreement and Preparations for the UNFCCC Meetings (Bonn, 6–17 November 2017)." General Secretariat of the Council, Press Office. https://www.consilium.europa.eu/en/press/press-releases/2017/10/13/conclusions-paris-agreement-and-unfccc-meetings/pdf.

———. 2018a. "Conclusions on Climate Diplomacy 26 February 2018a." General Secretariat of the Council 6125/18. https://data.consilium.europa.eu/doc/document/ST-6125-2018a-INIT/en/pdf.

———. 2018b. "Preparations for the UNFCCC Meetings in Katowice (2–14 December 2018a)." General Secretariat of the Council 12901/18. https://www.consilium.europa.eu/media/36619/st12901-en18.pdf.

———. 2019. "Conclusions European Council 12 December 2019." General Secretariat of the Council, EUCO 29/19. https://www.consilium.europa.eu/media/41768/12-euco-final-conclusions-en.pdf.

Gupta, Joyeeta. 2014. *The History of Global Climate Governance*. Cambridge: Cambridge University Press.

Hayes, Jarrod, and Janelle Knox-Hayes. 2014. "Security in Climate Change Discourse: Analyzing the Divergence Between US and EU Approaches to Policy." *Global Environmental Politics* 14 (2): 82–101. https://doi.org/10.1162/GLEP_a_00230.

Hefftler, Claudia, Christine Neuhold, Olivier Rozenberg, and Julie Smith, eds. 2015. *The Palgrave Handbook of National Parliaments and the European Union*. Palgrave Handbooks. Basingstoke [u.a.]: Palgrave Macmillan.

Hix, Simon, Abdul Noury, and Gérard Roland. 2007. *Democratic Politics in the European Parliament*. 1. publ. Themes in European Governance. Cambridge [u.a.]: Cambridge Univ. Press.

IISD—International Institute for Sustainable Development. 2021. "Earth Negotiations Bulletin—COP26 Final." https://enb.iisd.org/sites/default/files/2021-11/enb12793e_1.pdf.

Kreppel, Amie, and Michael Webb. 2019. "European Parliament Resolutions—Effective Agenda Setting or Whistling into the Wind?" *Journal of European Integration* 41 (3): 383–404. https://doi.org/10.1080/07036337.2019.1599880.

Kuik, Onno, and Marjan Hofkes. 2010. "Border Adjustment for European Emissions Trading: Competitiveness and Carbon Leakage." *Energy Policy, Energy Security* 38 (4): 1741–48. https://doi.org/10.1016/j.enpol.2009.11.048.

Luterbacher, Urs, and Detlef F. Sprinz, eds. 2018. *Global Climate Policy: Actors, Concepts, and Enduring Challenges*. Cambridge, MA: The MIT Press.

Mechler, Jonas, Laurens Bouwer, Thomas Schinko, Sonja Surminski, and JoAnne Linnerooth-Bayer. 2018. *Loss and Damage from Climate Change*. New York, NY: Springer Berlin Heidelberg.

Nitoiu, Cristian. 2015. "Supporting the EU's Approach to Climate Change: The Discourse of the Transnational Media Within the 'Brussels Bubble.'" *Journal of European Integration* 37 (5): 535–52. https://doi.org/10.1080/07036337.2015.1019879.

Oberthür, Sebastian. 2016. "Reflections on Global Climate Politics Post Paris: Power, Interests and Polycentricity." *The International Spectator* 51:4: 80–94.

Oberthür, Sebastian, and Claire Dupont. 2015. *Decarbonization in the European Union: Internal Policies and External Strategies*. Basingstoke: Palgrave Macmillan.

Oberthür, Sebastian, Marc Pallemaerts, and Claire Roche Kelly. 2010. *The New Climate Policies of the European Union: International Legislation and Climate Diplomacy*. Brussels: VUB Press Brussels University Press.

Popovski, Vesselin. 2019. *The Implementation of the Paris Agreement on Climate Change*. Law, Ethics and Governance Series. London: Routledge.

Rayner, Tim, and Andrew Jordan. 2013. "The European Union: The Polycentric Climate Policy Leader?" *Wiley Interdisciplinary Reviews: Climate Change* 4 (2): 75–90. https://doi.org/10.1002/wcc.205.

Rifkin, Jeremy. 2020. *The Green New Deal. Why the Fossil Fuel Civilization Will Collapse by 2028, and the Bold Economic Plan to Save Life on Earth*. New York: St Martin's.

Ringe, Nils. 2010. *Who Decides, and How?: Preferences, Uncertainty, and Policy Choice in the European Parliament*. Oxford [u.a.]: Oxford University Press.

Ripoll Servent, Ariadna. 2015. *Institutional and Policy Change in the European Parliament: Deciding on Freedom, Security and Justice*. Palgrave Studies in European Union Politics. Basingstoke: Palgrave Macmillan.

Skjaerseth, Jon Birger. 2017. "The Commission's Shifting Climate Leadership: From Emissions Trading to Energy Union." In *The European Union in International Climate Change Politics: Still Taking a Lead?* edited by Rüdiger Wurzel, James Connelly, and Duncan Liefferink, 37–51. Abingdon: Routledge.

Stevenson, Hayley, and John S. Dryzek. 2014. *Democratizing Global Climate Governance*. Cambridge: Cambridge University Press.

Torney, Diarmuid. 2013. "European Climate Diplomacy: Building Capacity for External Action." *FIIA Briefing Paper 141*, October, 8.

Tröltzsch, Jenny. 2017. "Die Europäische Union." In *Handbuch Globale Klimapolitik*, edited by Georg Simonis, 302–33. Paderborn et al.: UTB.

UBA (German Environment Agency). n.d. "Fact Sheet: EU 2050 Strategic Vision 'A Clean Planet for All.'" Umweltbundesamt, Dessau. https://www.umweltbundesamt.de/sites/default/files/medien/376/publikationen/eu_2050_strategic_vision_a_clean_planet_for_all.pdf.

Weible, Christopher M., and Paul A. Sabatier, eds. 2017. *Theories of the Policy Process*, 4th ed. New York, NY: Westview Press.

Wendler, Frank. 2019. "The European Parliament as an Arena and Agent in the Politics of Climate Change: Comparing the External and Internal Dimension." *Politics and Governance* 7 (3): 327–38. https://doi.org/10.17645/pag.v7i3.2156.

———. 2020. "Framing Climate Change in the European Parliament: Political Contestation, Issue Dimensions, and Coalition-Building." Paper for ECPR General Conference, Panel P 395. https://ecpr.eu/Events/Event/PaperDetails/54829.

Wettestad, Jørgen., and Torbjorg Jevnaker. 2016. *Rescuing EU Emissions Trading: The Climate Policy Flagship*. London: Palgrave Macmillan.

Wurzel, Rüdiger, James Connelly, and Duncan Liefferink, eds. 2017a. *The European Union in International Climate Change Politics: Still Taking a Lead?* Routledge Studies in European Foreign Policy. London: Routledge, Taylor & Francis Group, 2017a; ZDB-ID: 2885275-8 1. London: Routledge, Taylor & Francis group.

Wurzel, Rüdiger, Duncan Liefferink, and James Connelly. 2017b. "Introduction: European Union Climate Leadership." In *The European Union in International Climate Change Politics: Still Taking a Lead?*, edited by Rüdiger Wurzel, James Connelly, and Duncan Liefferink, 3–19. Abingdon: Routledge.

Zürn, Michael. 2012. "Global Governance as Multi-Level Governance." In *The Oxford Handbook of Governance*, edited by David Levi-Faur, 731–45. Oxford University Press.

———. 2018. *A Theory of Global Governance: Authority, Legitimacy, and Contestation*. First edition. Oxford: Oxford University Press.

CHAPTER 4

US Climate Politics Since the Paris Agreement

Approaching US climate change policy with a focus on its discursive framing engages particularly with two aspects of its development since the adoption of the Paris Agreement. First, a central feature is that measures to curb GHG emissions in the United States remain fragmentary: No comprehensive policy package has so far been enacted at the federal level with the scope and stringency sufficient to achieve decarbonization even in the most relevant domains such as industry emissions, vehicle standards and energy production. Instead, policy initiatives in this regard have remained incomplete, often pending in their implementation and resulted in a patchwork of rules and standards particularly in a comparison across different state jurisdictions within the US (Selin and VanDeveer 2021; Karapin 2016; Houle et al. 2015; Brewer 2015; Andrews 2020; Bailey 2015; Rabe 2018; Weibust and Meadowcroft 2014; Mormann 2017; Carlarne 2010). Moreover, and contrary to common perception (cp. Kramer 2020), policy developments from the second term of the Obama through the Trump presidency have not been characterized by sharp policy reversals or resulted in a full replacement or dismissal of the entire set of regulatory standards enacted to address climate change. Instead, efforts to reduce carbon emissions have evolved through gradual modifications of a loose policy core centered on provisions particularly of the Clean Power Plan and successor framework, the Affordable Clean

© The Author(s), under exclusive license to Springer Nature Switzerland AG 2022
F. Wendler, *Framing Climate Change in the EU and US After the Paris Agreement*, Palgrave Studies in European Union Politics, https://doi.org/10.1007/978-3-031-04059-7_4

Energy Act, both launched through executive action and moved towards mostly unsuccessful implementation through the Environmental Protection Agency (EPA). In this sense, the discussion of policy developments in this chapter identifies greater degrees of continuity at the level of specific policies, particularly as resulting from incremental and incomplete decision-making than could be expected given the stark ideological differences in the perception of climate change by both administrations (cp. Carlson and Burtraw 2019; Mehling and Vihma 2017; Danish 2018; Freeman 2013). As the strongly contrasting ideological views and agendas of both administrations and political parties have to deal with a policy development that is frequently stalled and fragmented, however, the linkage between political discourse and policy is looser than in the EU case. It is therefore aimed more frequently at the advocacy of envisaged agendas whose realization remains speculative than at the justification of actual decision-making.

Second, it is evident that discourse on climate change and policies envisaged to reduce carbon emissions is more variegated in terms of the approach, scope and ambition of proposals and substantially more polarized than in the European case (Zhou 2016; Vezirgiannidou 2013; Sussman and Daynes 2013; Mann 2021: 22ff.; Fisher et al. 2013; Klein 2020). In this context, a relevant point is that in spite of its ineffectual role as a policy-maker, US Congress emerges as a central setting for the advocacy of a wide range of competing proposals for action against climate change. This role is expressed through a range of resolutions and bills reaching from specific proposals for carbon pricing to much broader programmatic proposals. While controversies within Congress often respond to actions taken and public communication promoted by the respective US President, particularly the House of Representatives is an important setting for advocacy and coalition-building on competing approaches towards the establishment of a federal climate policy (Vandeweerdt et al. 2016). Proposals in this regard range from resolutions raising objections against the Paris Agreement on the grounds of sovereignty to the promotion of the Green New Deal as a departure towards a broad agenda of transformative social and political change. Controversy on climate change in the US therefore reaches beyond a simple dichotomy between proponents and adversaries of climate action or between the denial of climate change as a hoax versus its framing as an issue of sustainability and progressive change. In fact, the subsequent discussion shows that the crude rejection of global warming as a hoax, prominent as it may be in public perceptions of the Trump administration, is mostly irrelevant in competing legislative proposals, and also at the level of presidential announcements and speeches.

The key observation for the present case study—namely, the contrast between relative continuity of policies caused by stalled decision-making on one hand, and much greater volatility and sharp contrasts between competing forms of discourse on climate change, on the other—are also reflected in the membership of the United States in the Paris Agreement since its adoption in December 2015. Evidently, a clear contrast is created between the advocacy in favor of the agreement by President Obama, and the highly publicized announcement by his successor to withdraw based on claims about the allegedly unfair, unnecessary and ineffective nature of the agreement. However, at the level of specific policy provisions, the impact of the temporary exit of the US has remained limited, for two reasons. First, the Paris Agreement did not impose legally binding requirements on the United States to implement a particular policy aiming at emission reductions, leaving the impact of the withdrawal announcement mainly at the discursive and programmatic level rather than specific policies (Jotzo et al. 2018; Zhang et al. 2017). Second, the actual period of withdrawal remained limited to just over three months, with US withdrawal taking effect on 4 November 2020, the day after the Presidential Election, until 19 February 2021, when the proclamation by newly inaugurated President Biden to rejoin the agreement took effect. Having rejoined the terms of the agreement, the US returned to take part in the global climate governance negotiations in the framework of the COP 26 at Glasgow in November 2021, as briefly covered in the previous chapter.

In order to evaluate political discourse on climate change in its relation to policy-making since the Paris Agreement, this chapter proceeds through the same set of steps as the previous case study. The following section presents a survey of major policy developments to establish the framework for investigating the politics of climate change in the US since the Paris Agreement (Sect. 4.1). The following two sections then review the discursive framing of climate policy by policy-making actors; this review starts with programmatic announcements and policy documents by the federal executive (Sect. 4.2) and moves on to both chambers of Congress, covering relevant bills and resolutions and their respective sponsors (Sect. 4.3) and backing by civil society groups and think tanks (Sect. 4.4). The chapter then proceeds to the analysis of the frames promoted in political discourse and their structure, linkages and contestation (Sect. 4.5), before our main findings are summarized in the conclusion (Sect. 4.6).

4.1 Stages of US Climate Policy-Making Since the Paris Agreement

In the introductory chapters of this book, several broad institutional similarities were identified between the political systems of the US and EU. These relate particularly to their structure as multi-level systems and a bicameral legislature working independently from majority control by the executive. For the reconstruction of more specific developments of policies aiming at the reduction of GHG emissions, however, two features of the US political system shaping the trajectory of major policies in this field deserve attention that set it apart from the EU case study: namely, the emergence of the administrative presidency as a term used for the shift of policy-making from legislative rule-setting to the enactment of executive mandates through delegated acts and independent agencies on the one hand (Thompson et al. 2020; Resh 2015; Hollibaugh 2016); and a shift towards more contested federalism and corresponding processes of litigation between federal and state-level agents and related partisan polarization, on the other (Rabe 2011; Conlan 2017; Konisky and Woods 2018, for comparative perspectives on this aspect between the EU and US, cp. also Fabbrini 2005; Menon and Schain 2006; Sbragia 2008; Gehler 2005). The relevance of both concepts is demonstrated in a review of key decisions and policies against climate change enacted in the second term of the Obama presidency.

The operating principles of the administrative presidency are reflected in the involvement of the US in climate agreements at the international level. In this context, the general approach and content of the Paris Agreement seem modeled to demands by the US, and more specifically to constraints of action encountered by its presidential executive. In this context, a defining feature of the Paris Agreement is its inherent switch of global climate policy from a system of legally binding, specified obligations addressed to specific countries to meet reduction targets as enshrined in the previous Kyoto agreement, and towards a voluntary commitment towards GHG reductions to contribute to a global effort of limiting global warming to below two degrees Celsius (Milkoreit 2019; Ahmad et al. 2017). From a US perspective, the negotiation of the Paris

Agreement seems to draw on lessons from the previous Kyoto Protocol, which was signed by President Clinton in 1997 but subsequently not submitted to the US Senate for consent due to common expectation that ratification there would fail (cp. Brewer 2015: 228f.). From this point of departure, the governance framework established by the Paris Agreement seems designed to accommodate particularly three requirements of US climate policy as resulting from its institutional and political foundation in the administrative presidency and contested federalism (Rabe 2011).

First, a key rationale for the Obama administration's involvement in the Paris Agreement framework was to design its legal status in a form that would avoid a ratification procedure in the US Senate and the evident risk of a veto raised by its Republican members. Therefore, the Obama administration was compelled to negotiate an agreement based on a voluntary pledge and review system; hence, it would be one that did not formally establish new legal obligations for the US, particularly by not prescribing a specific target or instrument of emission reductions and not making pledges in NDCs legally binding or enforceable. In the same vein, contributions to the Green Climate Fund are targeted to reach an annual volume of 100bn $ by 2020 but remain formally voluntary, in spite of rhetoric by Republican policy-makers against the allegedly exploitative financial contributions required from the United States (Ahmad et al. 2017: 284; Bodansky and O'Connor 2015). Adopting this argumentation, US President Obama signed the Paris Agreement as an executive agreement on 29 August 2016 without ratification by US Congress (Durney 2017: 234). This approach created a departure from previous ratification procedures and the adoption of the 1997 Byrd-Hagel resolution, a measure establishing criteria for the adoption of international agreements on climate change and seen as a major reason for why the US never ratified the Kyoto Protocol[1] (cp. Milkoreit 2019: 1024f.).

---

[1] This resolution (S.Res. 98 of the 105th Congress), named after its two sponsors Chuck Hagel (R-NE) and Robert Byrd (D-WV), was adopted unanimously in the US Senate on 25 July 1997 (97-0) and requires that the US should not ratify international agreements on climate change requiring a reduction of GHG emissions from Annex I countries (ie., advanced industrialized countries such as US) without the inclusion of new commitments for developing countries, or one that can be seen to result in serious harm to the economy of the United States. Furthermore, the resolution also requires the US government to accompany any agreement on climate change submitted to the Senate for ratification by a detailed explanation of 'any legislation or regulatory actions that may be required (...) and should also be accompanied by an analysis of the detailed financial

The political contentiousness of the decision by the Obama administration to negotiate and adopt the Paris Agreement as an executive act is reflected in several motions launched by Republican members of the Senate requesting a formal consent procedure, to be discussed in more detail in a later section of this chapter (cp. Leggett 2019; Leggett and Lattanzio 2016; Durney 2017).

Second, through its quasi-universal scope in terms of signatory states and ambition of keeping global atmospheric warming to as close to 1.5 degrees Celsius as possible, the agreement creates political momentum for launching a renewed political agenda to work towards the reduction of carbon emissions at the US federal level. The central point of departure for this re-launch of US climate policy is its commitment to specify a broader framework of action towards climate change mitigation through the Nationally Determined Contribution (NDC) as required by the Paris Agreement. In this sense, the first NDC submitted to the UNFCCC in September 2016[2] established the pledge of achieving an economy-wide reduction of GHG emissions by 26–28% below 2005 levels by 2025. These targets are stated in a brief document of five pages that lists previous initiatives by the US to cut carbon emissions and refers to (then) ongoing programs launched under the auspices of the Clean Air Act. These include particularly EPA-led initiatives to reduce emissions from power plants, to be discussed in more detail as the Clean Power Plan (UNFCCC 2016). While clearly affecting the perception of the US as an agent of global climate policy, the hiatus of US involvement caused by the Trump administration has effectively not led to the removal but a reinforcement of pledges submitted under the framework of the Paris Agreement. Having rejoined the Paris Agreement after the end of the Trump presidency, the US has submitted a second NDC in April 2021, renewing the intermediate pledge to 2025 but adding a secondary mid-term target of achieving a reduction of 50–52% below 2005 levels by 2030 (UNFCCC 2021). While the second, updated NDC of 2021 does

---

costs and other impacts on the economy of the United States which would be incurred by the implementation of the protocol or other agreement'. The resolution is commonly seen as a major reason for why the US did not proceed to ratify the Kyoto Protocol through consent of the US Senate, even if it had no legally binding effect as a resolution expressing the 'sense of the Senate' (cp. Brewer 2015: 228f.).

[2] A country page for the United States containing both the 2016 and 2021 NDC can be found on the website of the NDC Registry of the UNFCCC at: https://www4.unfccc.int/sites/NDCStaging/pages/Party.aspx?party=USA (last accessed: 18 August 2021).

not spell out the details of any specific policy or regulatory approach to be entered into the legislative process or adopted as executive act, it enumerates several key fields of action. These include a move to carbon-free electricity by 2035, emission reductions for vehicles and buildings, and progress towards decarbonization of industry through increased research and technological innovation.

Finally, the Paris Agreement speaks to the fragmented character of climate policies in the US by complementing a framework of UN-based governance mechanisms that actively encourage a range of initiatives at the regional and local level, as well as pledges by business and other private actors (Ahmad et al. 2017: 289ff.). Supported by governance frameworks such as the Marrakesh Partnership for Global Climate Action and the Non-State Actor Zone (NAZCA), these aspects of the global climate regime as framed by the Paris Agreement can be seen to endorse multiple initiatives in the US at the state and business level. These include the setting of vehicle standards or emission trading approaches at state or regional level such as in California or through the Regional Greenhouse Gas Initiative (RGGI[3]), but also cover industry pledges and initiatives by private agents such as the Energy Breakthrough Initiative or networks of local entities such as the C40 city network[4] involving major US cities and mayors (cp. Bulkeley 2014; Arroyo 2017). In summation, the Paris Agreement creates a governance framework that accommodates significant concerns and positions held by the US towards the architecture of global climate governance and reflects the involvement of the Obama administration in its negotiation (Milkoreit 2019: 1020ff.; Parker and Karlsson 2018). Against this background, the agreement was also likely to reinforce aspects of fragmentation and contestation inherent in the specific institutional and political environment of US climate change

---

[3] The Regional Greenhouse Gas Initiative (RGGI) was established in 2009 and currently includes eleven states in the North-East of the US (Connecticut, Delaware, Maine, Maryland, Massachusetts, New Hampshire, New Jersey, New York, Rhode Island, Vermont and Virginia). The initiative establishes a cap on emissions by power plants and includes a system of auctions through which allowances are issued to producers and programs for the promotion of energy efficiency and clean energy programs funded through its revenues. More information is available at the RGGI website at http://www.rggi.org.

[4] A survey of initiatives launched by C40 can be found in its 2020 Annual report, available online at: https://c40-production-images.s3.amazonaws.com/other_uploads/images/2827_C40_Annual_Report_2020_vMay2021_lightfile.original.pdf?1622806882 (last accessed: 19 August 2021).

policy, precisely because of its passage as an element of executive action without full approval of the legislature.

The administrative presidency and adversarial relations between (groups of) states and the federal level as epitomized by the concept of contested federalism are also reflected in policies enacted against climate change at the domestic level. The centerpiece of these policies is the Clean Power Plan (CPP), a set of provisions requiring states to limit GHG emissions from power plants and oversee a transition to renewable energies within a framework of reduction targets set at the federal level (Glicksman 2017; Carlson and Burtraw 2019; Tomain 2017; Durney 2017; Holthaus 2015). While recognized as the most relevant effort of the Obama administration to work towards an energy transition, the CPP establishes what could be called a loose core of climate policy, as it never went into effect through a legal stay imposed by the Supreme Court and its subsequent repeal by the Affordable Clean Energy (ACE) act by the Trump administration. Ironically, the latter policy initiative was also successfully challenged in court before going into effect and is currently likely to be replaced again by a countervailing policy proposal by the Biden administration.

The evolution of policies associated with the Clean Power Plan can be reconstructed in three stages: These reach from the program's launch and steps towards enactment to a second step of disintegration effected through litigation and subsequent diversification of approaches taken by US states to respond to the policy package proposed by the federal administration; a third stage is marked by the attempts of the Trump administration to dismantle and replace the provisions of the plan by a more permissive, but nevertheless similarly modeled approach to controlling carbon emissions.

The first of these stages was launched through the President Obama's proclamation of the Clean Power Plan (CPP) on 3 August 2015, just prior to the conclusion of the Paris Agreement. Considered a signature policy of his administration for a reduction of carbon emissions (Atkinson 2018), the plan links the ambition for a new global agreement with a re-launch of domestic policy, as reflected in the President's statement to the American public on this day: 'Climate change is (…) about the reality that we're living with every day, right now. (…) And that's why I committed the United States to leading the world on this challenge.… (T)oday, we're here to announce America's Clean Power Plan—a plan two years in the making, and the single most important step America has ever taken in the fight against global climate change' (White House 2015b).In terms of policy provisions, the plan harnesses a provision of the Clean Air Act (section 111d) to require states to reduce GHG emissions of power plants, covering fossil-fuel powered energy generating units (using coal, oil or natural gas) and aiming at a reduction of carbon pollution by the energy sector of 32% relative to 2005 levels by the year 2030. Applying various criteria relating to both the rate of carbon emissions as measured by pounds of CO_2 relative to energy produced and overall mass of emissions, the CPP sets individual emission goals for US states. These are subsequently required to develop and implement plans ensuring that power-generating units meet intermediate and final emission reduction rates for the period between 2022 and 2029 to be applicable either to individual power plants, state-wide energy production or regional and multistate cooperation frameworks between various states. Using a flexible approach, the CPP thereby establishes a concept of 'best system of emission reductions' (BSER), allowing different energy mixes by states but applying criteria of carbon intensity of energy production and the cost of substituting fossil-fuel energy with either lower-emitting natural gas or renewable sources. Further flexibility is given to states by allowing the selection of measures and pathways towards the reduction of carbon emissions. However, failure of states to adopt plans for a reduction of carbon emissions in compliance with the CPP is sanctioned with the threat of direct intervention by the EPA regulating the power generation of that particular state (EPA 2016; Tomain 2017: 11ff.; Glicksman 2017: 239f.).

Concerning the second stage of implementation, three aspects link the CPP to the two concepts of the administrative presidency and contested federalism. First, the CPP is a key example of a policy initiative launched through executive action without legislative involvement of Congress. Based on the Clean Air Act of 1970, it uses an existing legal frameworks to delegate action to the EPA as a specialized agency to act at arm's length from the presidential administration. Second, perhaps the most curious aspect of the CPP is that in spite of its status as a signature policy, it never achieved full legal effect, as the US Supreme Court ordered a stay on the plan's further implementation on 9 February 2016. In this sense, it could be argued that the main impact of the CPP is not primarily rooted in its legal authority or the political clout represented by the federal executive. Rather, its main impact can be seen to lie in its political and ideational quality of re-launching efforts to achieve decarbonization and identifying ways for doing so in a contested political environment. Finally, this latter aspect is corroborated further by the fact that during the legal stay imposed by the Supreme Court, the CPP prompted a variety of responses from states reaching from initiatives to go forward with its provisions regardless to passivity and statements of active resistance. The CPP, therefore, is considered one of the primary examples of contested federalism in a setting of multi-level environmental governance, prompting highly varied responses from states to the regulatory initiative of the federal level depending mostly on party-political affiliation of governorships in the respective states.

Finally, a third stage of efforts aiming at the repeal and replacement of the CPP's ambitions was created during the Trump presidency. Here, extended scrutiny of the possible scope of action that would withstand litigation by defenders of the CPP lasted through the time in office of first EPA administrator during the Trump presidency Scott Pruitt to his successor Andrew Wheeler[5]; the latter finally proposed an alternative set of regulations through the launch of the Affordable Clean Energy Plan (ACE) in August 2018. Reducing ambitions to cut carbon emissions by a far smaller degree (namely, 11 million tons of CO_2 or just between 0.7 and 1.5% by 2030), the plan was perceived to open the door for an

---

[5] In this context, only passing mention can be made of the fact that Scott Pruitt was a controversial figure as Administrator of the EPA from 17 February 2017 to 9 July 2018, primarily because of his well-known and critical stance towards the scientific consensus on climate change and its effects, but also his previous role as Attorney General of Oklahoma, during which he led numerous legal challenges against federal environmental legislation and the EPA itself. The departure of Pruitt was the EPA was accompanied by numerous accusations of fraud and legal investigations concerning his conduct in office, conflicts of interests, and use of personal privileges in office. His successor Andrew Wheeler served as his successor until the end of the Trump administration and was confirmed for the position of EPA Administrator in the US Senate on 28 February 2019. Having served as deputy administrator of the EPA since April 2018, Wheeler also has ties to political networks critical of climate science and climate policy, having worked for a law firm representing interests of the coal industry and as an aide for US Senator James Inhofe, one of the foremost critics of action against climate change and previous chairman of the Senate Committee on Environment and Public Works (cp. *New York Times*: "Trump Nominates a Coal Lobbyist to Be No. 2 at E.P.A.", 5 October 2017, URL: https://www.nytimes.com/2017/10/05/climate/trump-epa-andrew-wheeler.html, and *New York Times*: "Trump Says He'll Nominate Andrew Wheeler to Head the E.P.A.", 16 November 2018, URL: https://www.nytimes.com/2018/11/16/climate/trump-andrew-wheeler-epa.html).

increase in the burning of fossil fuels by focusing on the rate or relative efficiency of energy production in terms of carbon emissions, thereby setting an incentive to investment in coal plants at a larger scale. This plan was, however, also challenged in court and eventually ruled out by the US Court of Appeals for the District of Columbia on 19 January 2021, the last day in office of President Trump.

Therefore, both variants of emission regulation for the energy sector have influenced the pursuit of efforts towards an energy transition more in their function as a political and normative benchmark than as a legally binding regulatory framework. This guidance function of both the CPP and ACE becomes particularly clear in the specific context of multi-level governance established by US federalism: Here, individual states pursued different strategies on GHG emission reduction from power plants depending mostly on their respective party-political majorities at the level of governors and legislatures. In this sense, states differed in their approaches whether to fully abandon the renewable energy provisions of the CPP, to continue preparations in the anticipation of its re-enactment or to follow through with initiatives corresponding to the CPP's provisions regardless.

A second major field of controversy about the reduction of GHG emissions, and one that pulls together aspects of the administrative presidency and contested federalism, is the setting of emission standards for vehicles (Thompson et al. 2020: 24ff.; Freeman 2011; Richards 2016; Sneed 2016; Vogel and Swinnen 2011; Vogel 1995). While covering some 30% of carbon emissions in the US and therefore a greater share than both industry or power generation by current EPA figures,[6] the reduction of emissions from vehicles is considered politically sensitive by directly touching on individual forms of mobility as well as requiring major changes in infrastructure, particularly through loading stations for electric vehicles. As a point of reference for assessing the fuel economy of cars and related emission levels, the standard most commonly mentioned in public debate is the mileage reached by cars and trucks per gallon of combusted fossil fuel (MPG[7]), in addition to benchmarks quantifying the

---

[6] https://www.epa.gov/ghgemissions/sources-greenhouse-gas-emissions.

[7] For easier comparison of the miles per gallon (MPG) standard with those measured in liters consumed per 100 km as commonly used in a European setting, consider that 1 US gallon is 4.54609 L and 100 km corresponds to a distance of 62.1371 US miles (1 US mile is 1.60934 km). Obviously, this implies that higher figures relating to the miles per

percentage of low- and zero-emission vehicles (ZEVs) sold to consumers and used by public authorities.

At the level of policy, the setting of tailpipe standards is intriguing by involving three interrelated dynamics of decision-making, namely: first, the setting of emission standards and procurement provisions through executive rules and decrees at the federal level, based on provisions of the Clean Air Act of 1970 and enacted primarily through EPA standards; second, the provision of waivers for individual states (particularly, California) to deviate from these standards and establish their own, more stringent rules; and finally, the establishment of voluntary pledges by automakers to promote low- or zero-carbon emission technologies and achieve emission reductions within announced time frames, with effects on car sales markets across the US and partially resulting in legally binding agreements with individual states. Particularly this latter aspect results from the fact that as in the case of emission standards for energy production, this field also involves an important component of litigation especially between the federal government and individual states; the resulting situation of uncertainty over the mid- and longer-term development of emission limits clearly sets an incentive for automakers to adopt their own pledges in compliance with more stringent rules to avoid competitive disadvantages in car markets at the national level and beyond. Furthermore, the lowering of emissions due to ecological concerns can be perceived as being aligned with economic incentives both at the individual level due to the reliance of most commuters on cars and the high visibility of price signals for fuels, and at the corporate level considering longer-term profit margins resulting a comprehensive renewal of vehicle fleets. Considering these aspects, it is therefore evident both why the setting of tailpipe emission standards is politically charged and shows signs of a highly dynamic, but also volatile and ambivalent development. From this point of departure, the most relevant developments within the three levels identified above can be summarized in a concise form as follows.

First, a framework for the regulation of tailpipe emissions was set during the Obama presidency on 29 July 2011, when the administration

---

gallon (MPG) standard mean stricter fuel efficiency standards. More specifically, a reach of 20 miles per gallon as typical for bigger pick-up trucks and SUVs corresponds to a consumption of about 14.1 L per 100 km; other corresponding values of both standards are: 30 MPG = 9.4 L/100 km, 40 MPG = 7.1 L/100 km, 50 MPG = 5.7 L/100 km, and 60 miles per gallon = 4.7 L/100 km.

announced an agreement with thirteen automakers to increase the average fuel economy of annually sold passenger car fleets to a value of 54.5 mpg (or 163 grams CO_2 per mile) by the year 2025.[8] As in the energy sector, these standards were established through executive action based on a rulework known as the Corporate Average Fuel Economy (CAFE) standards and administered through the National Highway Traffic Safety Administration (NHTSA). This framework included annual target values for different types of car to be reached by producers and became subject to a mid-term review by the EPA, the NHTSA and California Air Resources Board (CARB), resulting in a mixed assessment that shed some doubt about the feasibility of the 2025 targets considering market developments and consumer behavior. A rollback of federal rules was then introduced by the EPA and Department of Transportation during the Trump presidency, resulting in a freeze of fuel economy goals to the 2021 target of 37 mpg and lower the longer-term targets to a more permissive standard of 40.4 mpg by model year 2026. As in the previous period, this revision of standards was launched through executive action by the EPA and NHTSA, and specified in the Safer Affordable Fuel-Efficient (SAFE) Vehicle Rules, specifying emission targets for the period 2022–2026 and spelling out the reasons for this decision based on impacts of rules for consumer costs, safety of vehicles and environmental standards as described in the Clean Air Act.[9] A second reversal of this framework of rules has come about with the Biden presidency, particularly through its announcement to switch the procurement of vehicles for federal government agencies fully to electric vehicles by 2035, and through the announcement of plans by the EPA and the Department of Transportation in December 2021 to raise the fuel efficiency of passenger cars to 55 mpg by 2026. This target requires considerable modification to the currently applicable standard of 38 mpg and aims at a slightly stricter standard than the one

---

[8] Cp. the announcement on the website of the National Highway Traffic Safety Administration (NHTSA): https://web.archive.org/web/20130305181919/http://www.nhtsa.gov/About+NHTSA/Press+Releases/2011/President+Obama+Announces+Historic+54.5+mpg+Fuel+Efficiency+Standard.

[9] See the SAFE regulations factsheet on the NHTSA website at: https://www.nhtsa.gov/corporate-average-fuel-economy/fact-sheet-safe-vehicles-rule.

set by the previous Obama administration.[10] In this most recent stage, the debate on tailpipe emission reductions also stands in close relation with announced investments into the buildup of infrastructure for electric car charging stations, as envisaged through the infrastructure bill passed by Congress in November 2021 and potentially to be extended through additional spending in the framework of legislative initiatives for social and infrastructure spending ('Build Back Better'). As this very brief overview demonstrates, the framework for the setting of emission standards at the federal level has been unstable and subject to reversals due to changing political majorities both in the presidency and within Congress. At the same time, policy reversals are neither sudden nor radical but are announced in gradual steps, as the setting of rules is based on executive action that in the case of revisions is continuously subject to legal challenges in the courts.

Second, the setting of vehicle emissions standards is further complicated by the fact that since their introduction at the state level in 1968, the state of California has reserved the right to adopt more stringent rules and has been granted a corresponding waiver to deviate from federal legislation. Given the size of the car sales market in California as the most populous state in the US, and considering that many other states have often tied their own standards to those set by California, the creation of stricter standards in this state has effects reaching beyond its borders, particularly as automakers try to avoid additional planning and production costs by having to adapt to different levels of emission standards. As a consequence, the right of California to deviate from federal rules is equally contested as part of the overall framework of emissions regulation governed by the federal level. The same reversals caused by swings in the presidency as discussed above therefore apply: The 'waiver' provision for California described above was accepted during the Obama presidency and an extension was granted through the year 2025 in January 2017 just before the transition to the successor administration. During this time, a set of almost two dozen US states tied their vehicle emission standards to those set in California. After the changeover to the Trump administration, the EPA introduced new regulations prohibiting California to establish its own emission levels in September 2019 by revoking

---

[10] Cp. coverage in the *New York Times* article: "E.P.A. Announces Tightest-Ever Auto Pollution Rules", 20 December 2021, URL: https://www.nytimes.com/2021/12/20/climate/tailpipe-rules-climate-biden.html.

the waiver provision[11]; as a consequence, California lead a legal suit against the federal government's decision joined by many other US states, including some Republican-leaning ones such as Nevada, New Mexico, Wisconsin, Pennsylvania and Michigan.[12] At this time, California rules required automakers to reduce the fuel efficiency of vehicles to an average range of 54.5 miles per gallon by 2025, the value adopted as benchmark by the Obama administration from California to launch its 2011 agreement with automakers; by contrast, the Trump administration insisted on lowering this value to only 37 miles per gallon.[13] Observers of this legal challenge at the time noted that while the EPA has sometimes successfully refused the introduction of new, more stringent standards by states in the past, no previous case had existed of the EPA actively revoking existing regulation at the state level based on a waiver. The attempted rollback of emission standards during this time demonstrates the close link between the loosening of regulations at the federal level and the removal of rights for states to set their own rules, as both were included in the same package of EPA measures. The subsequent legal challenges raised by the state of California against the rules introduced by the Trump administration subsequently became moot with the election of President Biden and the reversal to more stringent fuel standards.

Finally, a third component of developments in this field is the announcement of fuel efficiency standards by automakers, responding to apparent shifts in consumer orientation and partly in response to the uncertain regulatory environment arising from reversals and contestation described in the previous two points. As with regulatory action by the state, the adoption of these voluntary standards relates to different aspects of emissions regulation, namely both the right of states to deviate from federal rules and the definition of fuel standards themselves. As stated above, the 2011 initiative by the Obama administration to set

---

[11] Cp. coverage in the *New York Times*: "Trump to Revoke California's Authority to Seet Stricter Auto Emissions Rules", 17 September 2019, URL: https://www.nytimes.com/2019/09/17/climate/trump-california-emissions-waiver.html.

[12] Cp. coverage in the *New York Times*: "California Sues the Trump Administration in Its Escalating War Over Auto Emissions", 20 September 2019, URL: https://www.nytimes.com/2019/09/20/climate/california-auto-emissions-lawsuit.html?action=click&module=RelatedLinks&pgtype=Article.

[13] For easier comparability with European measurements, these standards correspond to a consumption of about 7.6 L per 100 km (37mpg) and 5.2 L per 100 km (54.5 mpg).

stricter emission standards through 2025 was based on an agreement with thirteen automakers covering a major share of the US market.[14] More recently, the two most publicized initiatives include the conclusion of a legally binding agreement between a group of five automakers (namely, BMW, Ford, Honda, Volkswagen and Volvo) and the state of California, in which these carmakers agreed to comply with the state's strict tailpipe standards.[15] This settlement followed a previous, informal agreement with four of those car manufacturers with the state and went directly against the loosening of emission rules issued by the Trump administration on the national level. The scope of this agreement concluded during the Trump presidency is demonstrated by the fact that the automakers involved cover some 30% of the market in car sales in the US, and thereby strengthen the standing of vehicle emission rules applied at that time by 13 other US states. In addition, a group of major automakers including Toyota and Fiat Chrysler as well as General Motors announced in early 2021 that they would drop legal efforts to stop California from imposing its own vehicle emission standards, removing its last obstacle after the election victory of President Biden in November 2020.[16] A development related to the discussion of fuel efficiency standards is the announcement by an increasing number of car producers to switch their passenger car fleets to fully electric zero-emission vehicles in the intermediate future. These initiatives have picked up speed around the year 2020 and are often brought in relation with the growing market share of Tesla sales in the US auto market. Most prominently, this includes a pledge by the automaker General Motors to sell only zero-emission vehicles by the year 2035.[17] Another recent, highly publicized event in this regard is the introduction in early 2021 of an electric version of the Ford F-150 pickup, the

---

[14] According to the NHTSA declaration of 29 July 2011, an agreement on 2025 targets was made with Ford, GM, Chrysler, BMW, Honda, Hyundai, Jaguar/Land Rover, Kia, Mazda, Mitsubishi, Nissan, Toyota and Volvo (URL: https://web.archive.org/web/20130305181919/http://www.nhtsa.gov/About+NHTSA/Press+Releases/2011/President+Obama+Announces+Historic+54.5+mpg+Fuel+Efficiency+Standard).

[15] Cp. *New York Times* article: "Defying Trump, 5 Automakers Lock in a Deal on Greenhouse Gas Pollution", 17 August 2020, URL: https://www.nytimes.com/2020/08/17/climate/california-automakers-pollution.html.

[16] Cp. *New York Times* article: "Automakers Drop Efforts to Derail California Climate Rules", 2 February 2021, URL: https://www.nytimes.com/2021/02/02/climate/automakers-climate-change.html.

[17] See footnote 11.

most frequently sold vehicle in the US market, and the announcement by the carmaker to invest in production facilities to push sales of electric vehicles to about 40–50% of all global sales by 2030 according to public statements by the company.[18]

This brief survey demonstrates the dynamics of change towards a reduction of emissions, but also the great degree of contentiousness, complexity and volatility of this field of regulation. While a distinction between the three dynamics discussed—namely, developments through rule-setting at the federal and state level, as well as through voluntary pledges made by automakers—has been made above for analytical purposes, these are closely intertwined and interdependent in political reality. Through its combination of executive action at the federal level, and deviations from it both through state and business initiatives, the regulation of emissions from cars and trucks represents some of the main features of the highly fragmented forms of action towards a green energy transition in the United States.

In summation, the contestation of standards between the US federal government and states is a feature that connects the regulation of GHG emissions from power plants and vehicles, as both case studies involve controversy and litigation concerning the authority of federal agencies to hold states to binding standards. In this context, agents opposed to more stringent regulation have taken sides to both defend and oppose the regulatory authority of the federal level. An example is stances taken by EPA director Scott Pruitt claiming that individual states should not be exempted from federal rules governing vehicle emissions; in contrast to this stance, he was known for previously arguing that states should have discretion concerning the regulation of power plants in relation to rules imposed at the US federal level (Thompson et al. 2020: 82ff.). This point underlines that federal relations in the US have become a subject of intense party-political contestation. To summarize, the two policy packages introduced here, aiming to govern the reduction of carbon emissions from power plants and vehicles, establish the two main pillars of energy and climate policy at the US federal level. In addition, elements of carbon pricing exist particularly through extraction taxes, and forms

---

[18] Cp. the company's public statement 'Ford to Lead America's Shift to Electric Vehicles' covering the creation of a new 'Mega Campus' in Tennessee and twin battery plans in Kentucky, 27 September 2021, URL: https://media.ford.com/content/fordmedia/fna/us/en/news/2021/09/27/ford-to-lead-americas-shift-to-electric-vehicles.html.

of emissions trading have been realized on a smaller scale at the state level, where additional regulation on energy production and usage as well as energy efficiency standards for buildings have also been developed (Karapin 2016; Rabe 2018).

Beyond the realm of policies explicitly framed as part of action against climate change, a field of major importance for the development of carbon emissions is the regulation of the extraction, transport and sale of fossil fuels (Guliyev 2020; Mehling 2017; Selby 2019; Thompson et al. 2020; Zevin 2018, 2019). This field covers three main areas of regulation: first, decision-making on permits for extraction of fuels from natural habitats and offshore sites, as sanctioned by federal regulation; second, the deregulation of extraction methods and resources to include a broader range of fossil fuels produced within the US, particularly through the extended use of fracking; and finally, the controversy surrounding the granting of permits for the construction of pipelines for the transport of oil and natural gas, specifically concerning Keystone XL and the Dakota pipeline project. At the level of political discourse, addressing these efforts to expand the use of fossil fuels is mostly the flip side of arguments raised in favor of introducing more stringent rules for climate action: While mostly excluding the issue of climate and GHG emissions in terms of explicit references, advocacy in favor of lifting restrictions against coal and gas extraction adds to political discourse opposing climate action. For this reason, references to this aspect of energy policy are considered as the third main component of controversy surrounding climate change in the US case, in addition to international agreements and the regulation of carbon emissions through power plants and vehicles.

To summarize this very brief review of US climate policy since the adoption of the Paris Agreement, its most defining feature appears to be its fragmentation, in a dual sense: first, in terms of the relatively weak and contested basis of policy action at the federal level, prompting a wider range of responses at the state level reaching from support and partial adoption to open resistance and legal challenges; and second, in terms of the lack of a broader policy framework to integrate and synergize the various aspects of climate and energy governance, covering carbon emissions by industry, agriculture, buildings and individual consumption. The highly incomplete set of policy approaches stands in notable contrast with the pledge of the Paris Agreement to contribute to a limitation of global warming below two degrees, requiring stringent and timely action by the US as the entity with the highest per capita-emissions of

GHG in the world. This incongruence puts an onus on the presidential executive to explain how this misfit between global commitments and domestic action could be resolved, facing the American public as an audience in which substantial majorities do support the perception of global warming as a serious threat (Saad 2017, 2019). Two strongly contrasting approaches for resolving this incongruence have been communicated through policy documents and public speeches by the Obama and Trump administrations, as discussed in the subsequent section.

4.2 Presidential Discourse: The Contested Nexus of Climate, Energy and Industry

Presidential discourse about energy and climate policy is reviewed in this study by covering programmatic documents issued by the White House, as well as major public addresses about decisions concerning the Paris Agreement and domestic policies covering the three main aspects of energy and climate policies as described above (cp. Kincaid and Roberts 2013). Two features are typical for this sort of programmatic discourse. First, considering the inevitable mismatch between the scope of climate change and the limited reach of policies established or proposed to cut carbon emissions, discourse in favor of more stringent climate action has to refer to existing programs as a first step, to be complemented later by more far-reaching action. In a reverse perspective, an effect is created where claims raised against existing measures adopted in the US as a consequence of the Paris Agreement exaggerate their adverse impacts and political consequence, such as foreign domination, economic decline or economic injustice. A discursive effect of 'angel' or 'devil shifts' is therefore a common feature of presidential discourse about climate policy; this term is used for the effect of agents exaggerating both the benevolence and positive effect of their own actions and the harm, malicious intent and political clout of adversaries within the theoretical model of the Advocacy Coalition Framework (ACF) and Narrative Policy Framework (NPF, cp. Shanahan et al. 2011; Jenkins-Smith et al. 2017; Jones and McBeth 2010; Sabatier and Weible 2007). Second, the subsequent review demonstrates that executive discourse on climate policy is almost necessarily framed in terms of the administrative presidency—namely, in terms of steps taken by the presidential executive as an act taken on behalf of the American people and without further outreach or negotiation with other branches of government. An adversarial element is therefore inevitable as announcements of policy-making even if explicit references to political adversaries are not made.

Comparing President Obama and his successor Trump, clear differences emerge with regard to the arenas, audiences and discursive framing chosen for their respective speeches and announcements (cp. Brown and Sovacool 2017). The subsequent section provides a structured overview of the major public addresses by both presidents related to the Paris Agreement and climate policy, as transcripts of these speeches are included in the framing analysis presented later in this and in the subsequent comparative chapter.

A distinctive feature of President Obama's public communication about climate change is that it includes speeches within the framework of global negotiations on a climate agreement and addressed at an international audience of policy-makers. Focusing on those announcements most directly associated with the run-up and conclusion of the Paris Agreement, the selection of speeches covered here include remarks at the UN climate summit on 23 September 2014 and, of course, the statement made towards the participants of the COP 21 in Paris on 30 November 2015 (White House 2015a). In a brief characterization of these speeches, two things stand out. The first is that both adopt various of the climate frames distinguished in our analysis to make a very comprehensive, broad-based case for action against climate change. This framing includes references to justice in terms of responsibility towards future generations, a political framing stressing the support for climate action and support for a multilateral framework to act, and economic arguments about investments in infrastructure, jobs and returns from greater energy efficiency. Both speeches also include references to Martin Luther King and his saying about action never being too late to stress a sense of urgency to act against global warming. Second, however, both speeches open with a framing of the present situation that addresses climate change as a risk and material threat, referring to the 'urgent and growing threat of a changing climate' in the 2014 speech and drastic effects of global warming including sea level rise, submerged countries, and 'political disruptions that trigger new conflict' (White House 2014b). While suggesting urgency, this framing is focused more on material aspects of climate change and policy to human society—emerging threats from global warming, economic and security effects of climate action, and political momentum created for subsequent action—than ecological concerns or arguments of climate justice. This suggests the use of a discursive strategy by Obama to argue on a foundation of concerns that are more bipartisan by referring to issues of security and less prone to ideological positions and criticism as more typical leftist environmental or justice arguments.

In addition to these spoken addresses, a written joint presidential statement by the US and China issued on 11 November 2014 and declaring their shared commitment to an ambitious agreement during the Paris conference is included as a major statement of the Obama administration to both an international and domestic audience (White House 2014a). Finally, a link between the conclusion of negotiations at the global level by the US government and its communication towards a domestic audience is created by Obama's statement on the Paris Agreement, delivered from the White House just after the conclusion of the accord on 12 December 2015. Praising the adoption of the Paris Agreement as a 'tribute to American leadership' of which the American people can be proud (White House 2015c), the framing adopted in this address is mainly political and economic, emphasizing the ambition of global cooperation based on the agreement and the beneficial economic effects of climate action in terms of jobs, technological advances and economic growth. As above, climate change is referred to as 'carbon pollution that threatens our planet', adopting a risk-based approach to framing climate change (cp. Weathers and Kendall 2016).

A second major component of the Obama administration's public communication about climate change is a string of public speeches and publication of policy documents to announce and explain a re-launch of initiatives to cut carbon emissions during the President's second term. Among these appearances, particularly the address to faculty and students at Georgetown University on 25 June 2013 stands out as one of the most elaborate attempts by the 44th President to outline his agenda for action against climate change. About 45 minutes in length, the Georgetown speech is directly linked to the launch of the 2013 National Climate Action Plan. As in the previous examples, this address is framed in a way that addresses climate change primarily as a threat to the material well-being of society and further seeks to find claims and arguments that establish a bipartisan case for action rather than promoting arguments that may be prone to ideological polarization. Starting with a memorable reference to the first photo of Earth shot from space in 1968 ('Blue Marble'), the speech proceeds to identify the impacts of climate change in terms of draughts, sea level rise and other events causing costs 'as measured in lost lives and lost livelihoods' (White House 2013). The President then goes on to discard arguments about the economically damaging effects of environmental policies by referencing a Climate Declaration issued by 500 major US companies and stressing that a 'low-carbon, clean energy economy can be an engine of growth for decades to come' (White House 2013: 10). In political terms, Obama frames his initiative as bipartisan by pointing out that the Clean Air Act—the legal basis for the launch of his Clean Power Plan—was promoted by a Republican President and adopted by unanimity in the Senate and a near-unanimous vote in the House, subsequently receiving legal approval by the Supreme Court. The adoption of the deliberately non-ideological, pragmatic framing by Obama is epitomized in his statement about the possibility of tackling climate change: 'So, obviously, we can figure this out. It's not an either/or, it's a both/and' (White House 2013).

Several subsequent announcements to the general public complement the Georgetown speech. One relevant appearance in this context is remarks to proclaim the launch of the Clean Power Plan delivered at the White House on 3 August 2015 covered in some detail already in the previous section. In addition, a public statement on energy and climate change delivered at the Department of Energy on 19 March 2015 is also included in our empirical analysis. Finally, two of the weekly addresses by the President dedicated to the issue of climate change—namely, those delivered on 29 June 2013 accompanying the launch of the National Action Plan against climate change and on 29 August 2015 just prior to a highly publicized trip to Alaska to explore the impacts of climate change—are included as two major examples of Obama's communication about climate change to the American public.

A considerable change in presidential discourse about climate change has evidently come about with the transition from the Obama to the Trump presidency, particularly through a shift of focus from the issue of climate change to an agenda defined by the priorities of American energy independence, deregulation and economic growth. As a consequence, relatively few public speeches by President Trump and members of his administration directly deal with the issue of climate change. More frequently, their policy discourse addresses how carbon-reduction policies touch on the issue of energy policy, shifting from an international to a primarily domestic focus. Within the small subset of more extensive speeches explicitly dealing with the issue of climate, particularly the announcement of the intention to withdraw from the Paris Agreement, delivered by President Trump in the Rose Garden of the White House on 1 June 2017 stands out as a programmatic statement. Considering its prominence in this regard, it seems adequate to review the argumentative structure of this address in some more detail, particularly with regard to how the issue of climate change is addressed and on what grounds the framework of international cooperation established by the Paris Agreement is rejected.

A main observation in this regard is that the problem of climate change itself—its existence, causes, severity or consequences—is not discussed at any length during the President's remarks. This includes the absence of any attempt to dispute or doubt the existence of anthropogenic climate change. Instead, the main objections raised by Trump against the Paris Agreement are framed in terms of political autonomy and in fact, based on arguments of justice. The key statement in this regard is the claim that the US is forced by the provisions of the Agreement to contribute to global climate finance and suffer economic costs through the closure of carbon energy plants, creating an unfair treatment in relation to emerging economies and particularly China. Concerning ecological considerations, the Paris Agreement is criticized not for advocating but failing to live up to 'environmental ideals', and subsequently for punishing the United States as the 'world's leader in environmental protection' (White House 2017). In this vein, the assumption that carbon emissions are indeed harmful in ecological terms is indirectly recognized by Trump's claim that the Paris Agreement allows China and other polluters to continue their use of coal. This is further confirmed by Trump's statement that even if 'implemented in full, (…) it is estimated that (the agreement) would only produce a two-tenths of one degree (…) Celsius reduction in global warming by 2100': a claim minimizing the effectiveness of existing carbon reductions but actually recognizing the causality linking carbon emissions and global warming. Trump's concluding statement that under his administration, the country will have 'the cleanest and most environmentally friendly country on Earth' (ibid.) further demonstrates a technique of cooptation of ecological arguments to question and reject the Paris Agreement. This point is not to deny that Trump's argument ignores, distorts and misrepresents accepted scientific claims about climate change and the provisions included in the Paris Agreement; it does so especially by conflating a reduction of carbon emissions with 'clean air', refusing to accept the need for reducing carbon emissions in the US and overstating the obligations imposed by the Paris accord. The point to be made here, however, is that Trump's approach to counter the case for a global climate policy framework is framed in terms of sovereignty, justice, and an appropriation of ecological arguments, but not by explicitly endorsing claims of climate change denial. In addition to this widely recognized appearance, few other public speeches were made by Trump to appraise climate change as a challenge, or to discuss policy approaches to deal with it. This implies, however, that no major public speech by President Trump goes into detail to challenge the existence of climate change, its anthropogenic causes, the severity of its consequences or the futility of existing policies to address its causes—the main elements of climate skepticism and denial (cp. Dunlap and McCright 2011; Collomb 2014).

In order to capture the Trump administration's discourse about the nexus between climate and energy policy, it is therefore not enough to simply review the few public statements explicitly dealing with climate or emission reductions. Politically at least as important are the more numerous public appearances and speeches by the 45th President discussing the future development of energy policy, particularly with regard to the extraction of fossil fuels and removal of regulatory restrictions. Public speeches of this kind typically combine three characteristic elements: First, lengthy and celebratory appraisals of the economic benefits and job creation garnered by the expansion of extraction sites and technologies, often combined with appearances of workers or local residents praising the President's efforts; second, a heavy emphasis on energy independence gained through increased exploitation of domestic energy sources and leading to reduced dependence on foreign supply and creating economic returns through the export of fossil fuels; and finally, the confident claim of the Trump administration's promotion of green values through the creation of clean air, water and the conservation of natural habitats. Once again, this aspect shows an appropriation rather than outright rejection of ecological arguments, however sidelining systemic changes of climate mechanisms and turning the focus to more tangible and local environmental problems and issues. This sort of environmental discourse is essentially based on a crude simplification: namely, one reducing the complex and systemic problem of climate change to a linear and local one by re-focusing environmental problems to pollution, especially of local water sources and habitats. The rationale of Trump's discourse about environmental issue is then to depict them as compatible with an aggressive agenda of deregulation aiming at the expansion of fossil fuel use and economic growth. To conclude this review, two specific features can be identified as typical for public discourse by President Trump about climate change. The first is a cooptation of ecological issues and arguments, achieved through a technique of simplifying and objectifying. A second is the aggressive adoption of a version of climate justice that combines an emphasis on economic freedom with a call for strengthening for national sovereignty, fitting to Trump's general aversion against multilateralism as epitomized through the slogan of 'Making America Great Again', and in this specific case, exaggerated to a point where claims to global leadership are combined with a sense of self-victimization.

So far, this review has practically equated executive discourse on climate change with statements by the US President, as seems justified given his public visibility and status as the leader of the federal executive with substantial powers over appointments and setting the direction of policy. However, it should not be left unmentioned that due to its size and functional differentiation, the US federal government includes Departments and agencies substantially contributing to climate-related public communication through reports based on their respective mandates. These reports are often seen as perspectives on climate change that are framed through the specific institutional mandate of agencies and therefore independent to some degree from political intervention by the President. Examples include studies about security implications of climate change both at the domestic level and in an international context, including potential consequences for military operations and deployment, published by the Departments of Defense, National Security Council and Homeland Security; such reports were issued particularly during the Obama presidency and are subsequently included in the empirical analysis as part of the administration's policy discourse due to their focus on the political implications of climate change. The most comprehensive account of the scope and impact of climate change from a scientific perspective, however, is published through a sequence of National Climate Assessment Reports, the fourth and most recent of which was published in 2018 during the Trump administration. While this report left no uncertainty about the severity of climate change and need for stringent political action, the publication of this report is also an indicator of the degree of independence of federal government agencies towards the central executive. Being a very extensive and mostly natural scientific report, the Fourth Climate Assessment was nevertheless excluded from the subsequent analysis of executive discourse about climate policy, also as it would be difficult to subsume it as part of the political discourse of the Trump administration on climate change.

4.3 Legislative Discourse: Framing Climate Policy in Motions of US Congress

The involvement of both chambers of US Congress in climate policy-making creates a contrast to its EU counterpart in one major aspect: namely, the fact that no major piece of legislation on the reduction of GHG emission could be passed into law with majorities of both the House of Representatives and the Senate. In terms of policy-making, this renders the function of Congress virtually irrelevant for establishing regulation on the reduction of carbon emissions. In fact, only a handful of legislative proposals covering action against climate change passed the House of Representatives in the last decade, however, to be stopped by the Senate. The most prominent example in this regard is the Markey/Waxman bill, a legislative proposal for the introduction of a cap-and-trade system for CO_2 at the federal level, which passed by the House in 2009 but was rejected by the Senate (Rabe 2018; Sussman and Daynes 2013; Holt and Robins 2009).

As a more recent example, especially the proposal for a Green New Deal comes to mind, as a vote on the bill was expected in the House; however, Republicans moved to reject it in the Senate with a majority of 57 votes, with all Democratic Senators withholding explicit consent by voting 'present'. Against this background, it is obvious that skepticism has been expressed about the ability of the incoming Biden administration to pass climate change legislation through both chambers of Congress given the extremely thin majority Democrats hold on the legislature. Most recent developments concerning the difficulties for the proposed social spending bill to pass the House given the announcement by Representatives Kyrsten Sinema and Joe Manchin corroborate this point, even if a first infrastructure bill involving measures to promote investment in green technologies passed Congress and was signed into law by President Biden in November 2021 (White House 2021).

Against this background, it is noteworthy how active members of both Congress have been in their efforts to propose bills and resolutions on climate change in the period of analysis covered here. Rather than considering its function as a legislator, therefore, the focus here shifts to the discursive and representative function of Congress: rather than acting as a legislator in cooperation with the executive branch, the main significance of Congress for the political debate about climate change in the US has emerged in its role as an arena for proposing and representing various competing concepts for action against climate change. These reach from very specific proposals for carbon pricing and energy policy to the proposal of broader political agendas covering the cooperation of the US in the global climate policy regime, but also how to relate the issue of climate change to questions of economic governance, public investment, and social justice and equality. Precisely because Congress does not succeed in passing legislation and an established, comprehensive policy-making framework for acting against climate change is missing, its role as a forum for the politics of climate change gains higher prominence than in the European case. As the subsequent review of legislative proposals will show, the resulting fault lines of controversy on climate change run along more than a single political dimension and are also not fully reducible to partisan distinctions between Democrats and Republicans. The resulting splits give rise to a debate between a more diverse set of groups and coalitions advocating for a broad diversity of proposals for policy-making against climate change.

As discussed at the outset of this book, several political and institutional factors promote the volatile and mostly discursive involvement of Congress in climate policy-making in comparison to the European Parliament. First, the US legislature establishes a weaker and more volatile institutional framework for the negotiation of legislative proposals on energy and climate policy. Both chambers of Congress have a diverse, more malleable and less thematically specialized structure of committees for legislation in the field of energy and climate policy. These include the Senate Committee for Energy and Natural Resources and the House Committees for Science, Space and Technology as well as the Committee for Energy and Commerce, none of which have a clear profile for environmental or climate legislation. Second, the fact that legislative proposals are not introduced by an external executive institution as in the EU but by members of Congress links their negotiation both to the political advocacy of individual or groups of legislators and aspects of partisan affiliation, including to currents and subgroups within one of the two major political parties. To better understand the political environment of climate policy debate within the US Congress, it therefore seems important to give a survey of at least the most relevant agents and caucuses responsible for legislative proposals in the field of climate and energy policy.

First, a group of legislators with a distinctive profile for its bipartisan composition is the Climate Solutions Caucus, for which a group has been created both in the House of Representatives and the Senate.[19] Founded and led by two Representatives of both parties—Democratic member Ted Deutch and Republican member Francis Rooney—and supported by the Citizens' Climate Lobby, a grassroot organization with the declared goal of building relationships with legislators and creating support for climate legislation, the caucus is among the biggest groups working on environmental legislation in the House. Comprising some 65 members with equal representation from both parties, the group's stated goal is to 'educate members on economically viable options to reduce climate risk and to explore bipartisan policy options[20]' concerning climate change. In a similar vein, the Climate Solutions Caucus in the Senate comprises some 14 members of both major parties and is led by both a Democratic (Chris Coons) and Republican senator (Mike Braun). While the Senate caucus does not involve some of the more high-profiled Senators recognized for important initiatives in climate legislation, some more influential Senators especially from the Republican side are members (including Marco Rubio, Mitt Romney, Lindsey Graham or Lisa Murkowski). In fact, the subsequent discussion of specific legislative proposals particularly in the realm of carbon pricing will show that some of the leading members of the group feature as proponents of legislation. The reputation of the group as an actual promoter of climate legislation in both chambers of Congress, however, is mixed, suggesting that many observers see the group primarily as a platform especially for Republican members to boost their environmental credentials without committing them to substantial contributions to policy initiatives. In this vein, criticisms of the Climate Solutions Caucus are mostly that it serves as a fig leaf for Republican members

---

[19] A website of the Climate Solutions Caucus in the US Senate hosted by Senator Chris Coons can be found at the following URL: https://www.coons.senate.gov/climate-solutions-caucus/; a website of the Climate Solutions Caucus in the House of Representatives hosted by House Member Ted Deutch can be found at the URL: https://teddeutch.house.gov/climate/; additional information is also provided on a website hosted by the Citizens' Climate Lobby at the URL: https://citizensclimatelobby.org/climate-solutions-caucus/ (all last accessed: 20 August 2021).

[20] Statement quoted from the Climate Solution Caucus website, URL: https://teddeutch.house.gov/climate/ (last accessed: 21 August 2021).

of the House on environmental issues (ClimateWire 2017, 2018, 2019a, 2019b). Critical views were boosted particularly by the accession of Matt Gaetz, a House member previously known for pushing for the abolishment of the Environmental Protection Agency (EPA). Prompted by these criticisms, the caucus debated adopting the requirement for its members to have endorsed at least one piece of environmental legislation in the House—a criterion evidently established in a way that does not impose very stringent conditions, or a strong track record of environmentalism for membership.

Second, a relevant platform for coordinating Democratic members of the House of Representatives is the Sustainable Energy & Environment Coalition,[21] created in 2009 with the re-launch of climate policy after the election of Obama and led by Democrat House Members Gerald Connolly, Doris Matsui and Paul Tonko. Overall, the group has some 70 members and sets out to promote 'policies that support clean energy innovation, address climate change, protect our natural environment and promote environmental justice', according to the mission statement. Interestingly, joint membership of the SEEC and the Climate Solutions caucus applies to several but overall only a minority of members about a just under quarter of members of this group.[22] Politically, the main relevance of this caucus can be seen in the connection it creates between a significant number of Democratic House Members and the Subcommittee on Environment and Climate Change, both of which are chaired by Rep. Paul Tonko (D-NY).[23] While not counting among the co-sponsors of the Green New Deal agenda, Tonko has gained prominence in policy debates about climate change by launching a 'framework for

---

[21] A website of the SEEC hosted by House Member Paul Tonko can be found at the following URL: https://seec-tonko.house.gov (last accessed: 20 August 2021).

[22] Based on membership lists of both the SEEC and the Climate Solutions Caucus on their respective websites, overall 16 of the 71 members of the SEEC can be identified as belonging also the Climate Solutions Caucus. These are, in alphabetical order of their last names: Don Beyer, Earl Blumenauer, Susanne Bonamici, Salud Carbajal, Matt Cartwright, Judy Chu, Jim Himes, Derek Kilmer, Ann Kuster, Alan Lowenthal, Jerry McNerney, Jimmy Panetta, Ed Perlmutter, Scott Peters, Robert Scott, and Peter Welch (for URLs of websites, see footnotes 4 and 6, last accessed and membership lists scrutinized on 21 August 2021).

[23] The composition and activities of the Subcommittee on Environment and Climate Change can be reviewed at: https://energycommerce.house.gov/subcommittees/environment-and-climate-change-117th-congress.

climate action' in March 2019 to guide action by Democratic lawmakers launching proposals for carbon pricing and other aspects of climate action. The framework includes a set of nine principles established as benchmarks for national climate legislation, announced as the result of an outreach to stakeholders, experts, businesses and labor organizations; among them is the requirement that targets should be set to achieve greenhouse gas neutrality by mid-century, but also that climate action should contribute to a strong and competitive economy, invest in America's future, deliver a just and equitable transition, protect low-income households, and create stable and predictable policies.[24] Within the political environment of intense debate about a re-launch of climate action after the Democratic mid-term election victory of 2018, the function of this policy framework and coordinating function is to create a pragmatist, moderate platform and counterweight to the more progressive agenda of initiatives around the Green New Deal (ClimateWire 2019a). In more specific terms of policy, carbon pricing and more recently, the agenda arising from the infrastructure bill form thematic emphases of the group.

Third, beyond these more formally organized groups and platforms, a significant role for the advancement of broadly recognized initiatives for climate legislation is often played by senior members of Congress with a strong profile in environmental issues. While no full overview in this sense can be given here, particularly the following legislators stand out: For the Senate, probably the most noteworthy member is Ed Markey (D-MS), who was involved in major initiatives to establish a more stringent climate policy at the federal level from both the House and Senate. His involvement includes advocacy for the failed cap-and-trade-bill in 2009, but also his leading role for plans to launch the Green New Deal in the Senate. Another Senator with a strong profile in environmental policy is Sheldon Whitehouse (D-RI), who assumed prominence for the advocacy of climate issues both as a book author and promoter of several bills promoting a carbon price. Covering both the House and Senate, one of the politically most prominent groups advocating for more stringent climate action during the 115th Congress is the network of Democratic

---

[24] A summary of the framework including a list of the nine key principles can be reviewed on Paul Tonko's House of Representatives website at: https://tonko.house.gov/news/documentsingle.aspx?DocumentID=829; the full document of the climate action framework is accessible at: https://tonko.house.gov/uploadedfiles/tonko_-_climate_principles_116th.pdf.

members pushing for the adoption of a Green New Deal. A central role for launching this agenda in the form of a legislative proposal in the House is played, of course, by Democratic House Member Alexandra Ocasio-Cortez,[25] who entered the House as its youngest member after the mid-term elections of 2018. Further discussion is included in a later section when this survey turns to the Green New Deal. Furthermore, members with a more active role in proposing climate-relevant legislation include John Larson (D-Conn.), Dan Lipinski (D-Ill.) or Jerry McNerney (D-Cal.). On the Republican side, several senators have gained a profile by strongly opposing any initiatives for more stringent climate legislation. These include, most prominently, Oklahoma Senator James Inhofe, previous chair of the Senate Environment Committee and author of a book rejecting climate change as a hoax (Inhofe 2012). Another prominent member of the Senate with skeptical views of climate policy is John Barrasso of Wyoming, who served as ranking member and chair of the Senate Environment Committee.

As this brief overview shows, legislative proposals to address climate change are launched from a range of different agents and platforms—including bi- and single-partisan groups, sets of individual Members of Congress with a strong backing of civil society groups and networks, and veteran policy-makers with an established track record of legislative proposals in environmental policy. It is, therefore, no surprise to find a very broad range of different proposals that differ particularly in two respects: namely, the balance struck between action to curb carbon emissions and economic principles of competition, growth and efficiency gains achieved through technological innovation, on the one hand; and the scope of proposals concerning the degree to which proposals for reducing carbon emissions are linked to agendas of action in fields beyond immediate relevance for climate change, particularly concerning social justice and international cooperation. A review of legislative bills and resolutions proposed in the 114th to 116th US Congress, covering the elective periods from early 2015 to 2021, reveals a considerable degree of activity, in spite of the almost complete lack of acts successfully passed into law during this period.

---

[25] A section of Ocasio-Cortez's website dedicated to the Green New Deal agenda can be found at the following URL: https://ocasio-cortez.house.gov/gnd (last accessed: 20 August 2021).

Four broad thematic areas can be identified in relation to the issue of climate change that were addressed by proposed legislative acts during this time, reaching from relatively specific to very broad approaches to framing the issue and involving both advocacies in favor of climate action and its rejection.

First, a topic prompting numerous initiatives from members of Congress is the participation of the United States in the Paris Agreement, and more specifically the terms and ambitions of its adherence to the agreement. A recurring theme of proposed resolutions is to express political opposition to the stance taken by the presidential administrations since the conclusion of the agreement, and the executive discretion assumed by both Presidents in this context. Particularly the decision by President Obama to adopt the Paris Accord as a legally non-binding instrument not requiring ratification in the Senate (Durney 2017) prompted a backlash of resolutions demanding its involvement and consent. This includes, among others, two resolutions expressing the sense that the President should submit the Paris agreement to the Senate for review and consideration (S. Res. 68); or a resolution expressing a sense of the Senate concerning the agreement (S. Res. 329), stating that any agreement under the UN framework convention shall have no effect and payments to the Green Climate Fund withheld. After the transition to the Trump presidency, the center of gravity for resolutions rejecting presidential actions on international climate agreements has shifted to the House and resolutions critical of the announcement of US withdrawal from the Paris Agreement. These include a resolution expressing strong disapproval of the President's notification to withdraw from the Paris Agreement (H.Res. 743), a resolution expressing the commitment of both chambers of Congress to the Paris Agreement (H.Con. Res. 15) and several resolutions recognizing anniversaries of it (such as H.Res. 660 for the second, H. Res. 762 for the fourth, and H.Res. 1260 for the fifth anniversary).

Within the range of resolutions expressing dissent from this exit decision, particularly a bill entitled Climate Action Now Act (H.R. 9) and passed in the House by the Democratic majority in May 2019 stands out. If enacted, the bill would have effectively forced the President to uphold obligations arising from the Paris Agreement and even pursue them in a more stringent than formally required manner. More specifically, this would have involved the requirement to draw up an annual plan on how the United States seeks to comply with its targets pledged under the agreement through the Nationally Determined Contribution, and prohibiting the use of federal funds for the use of withdrawal from the agreement. The main site for launching the initiative was the House Select Committee on the Climate Crisis, chaired by Rep. Kathy Castor (D-Fl.) and established after the Democratic victory in the 2018 mid-term elections.

Turning to the domestic dimension of US climate policy, carbon pricing is debated as a central element of any progress towards a mitigation of GHG emissions. Here, the most striking aspect of politics within the US Congress is the contrast between the virtually complete absence of any breakthroughs in terms of substantive legislation, and the numerous legislative proposals proposed during the last years of the Obama and throughout the Trump presidency. Surveys of relevant legislation published by the climate think tank C2ES cover nine proposals for carbon pricing during the 115th Congress (2017–2018) and eleven for the 116th Congress (2019–2020) alone (Ye 2014, 2018, 2020, cp. also Ramseur 2019), even if this count includes the re-introduction of previous failed bills. These proposals include initiatives launched by House members involved in the leadership of the Climate Solutions Caucus (the Energy Innovation and Carbon Dividend Acts of 2018, H.R. 7173, and of 2019, H.R. 763, introduced by T. Deutch and F. Rooney), but also bills introduced by joint initiative of members of the House and Senate (such as the Climate Action Rebate Act of 2019, S. 2284 and H.R. 405, sponsored by Senators Chris Coons and Dianne Feinstein, and House member Jimmy Panetta). Others were proposed by groups of Senators (such as the American Opportunity Carbon Fee Act of 2019, sponsored by Senators S. Whitehouse, B. Schatz, M. Heinrich and K. Gillibrand) or by individual members of the House (such as the America Wins Act of 2019 H.R. 4142). In terms of content, only one of these proposals is based on an approach of emissions trading (or 'cap and trade'), namely the Healthy Climate and Family Security Act (sponsored by Senator C. van Hollen and House member D. Beyer and introduced twice in 2018 (S.2352 & H.R. 4889) and again 2019 (S. 940 & H.R. 1960), while all others envisage the introduction of a carbon tax.

Two related criteria can be applied to systematize these proposals. First, on the revenue side of carbon pricing, the various initiatives differ with regard to the range of emissions covered and the relative stringency of carbon taxing, concerning both the entry price and subsequent trajectory of increases in carbon pricing (or 'escalation rate', cp. Ye 2020). In this regard, a range opens up between the (relatively moderate) Deutch-Rooney proposal with an entry price of 15$ per metric ton and potential annual increases of 10$, and more ambitious proposals such as the Larson proposal ('America Wins Act') with a starting price of 52$ per ton, or the Coons/Feinstein proposal ('Climate Action Rebate Act') that envisages steeper escalation rates of between 15 and 30$ of annual increases in the carbon tax (Ye 2020: 12ff.). Second, and more importantly concerning the political framing of the various carbon pricing proposals, the bills envisage different rationales and mechanisms for using the revenue raised from the introduction of a carbon price. Here, proposals present different visions concerning to what degree revenues from carbon taxing should be used to fund infrastructure and climate-friendly technologies, or whether they should be made available as a direct subsidy to individuals. Several of the proposals surveyed here contain a more distinct climate justice aspect in this context. The proposal tabled by House members Deutch and Rooney follows this logic by envisaging the use of revenues for a monthly dividend to individuals with a valid Social Security number, assigned as a pro-rata share for household members; similar approaches are taken up in the van Hollen/Beyer proposal (Healthy Climate and Family Security Act). By contrast, the proposal tabled by Senators Feinstein and Coons contains a clause to funnel revenues into a Climate Action Rebate Fund, 20% of which are intended to be used for infrastructure and additional funds to be available for research and carbon sequestration projects. Even more consequently, the America Wins Act introduced by Rep. J. Larson proposes a use of revenues with an estimated volume of 1.2 trillion for fiscal years 2020 to 2029 primarily for infrastructure, and a secondary use of funds for transition assistance (70$ billion) and 12.5% of revenue assigned as an energy refund to low-income households (Ye 2020: 17).

Politically, an interesting indicator for the range of support the various proposals have received is the number of their respective co-sponsors in the House and Senate. Here, virtually the only proposal with broader support among legislators is the bipartisan Deutch/Rooney proposal (Energy Innovation and Carbon Dividend Act of 2019), co-sponsored by 86 House members due to its embedding in debates held within the Climate Solutions Caucus. The only other legislative proposal coming close is the Healthy Climate and Family Security Act of 2018 (HR 4889), which received the support of 36 co-sponsors, and the America Wins Act of 2017 (H.R. 4209) with 21 co-sponsors; after its re-introduction, the latter bill proposal (H.R. 3966) won the support of only 9 co-sponsors.

All other bills surveyed here have only a single-digit number of even no co-sponsors, such as the Coons/Feinstein proposal to both the House and Senate, where just five House members (H.R. 4051) and one other Senator (S 2284) signed up as co-sponsors.

What all the proposals surveyed here have in common, however, is that none of them could be moved towards a vote in either the House or Senate, let alone be adopted as an act of legislation: Just to cover the legislative proposals with a more significant number of co-sponsors listed above, the Energy Innovation and Carbon Dividend Act was introduced to the House on 24 January 2019 and referred to the subcommittee on energy; the Healthy Climate and Family Security Act was introduced to the House on 29 January 2018 and debated in the subcommittee on the environment, and the America Wins Act of 2017 introduced to the House on 1 November 2017 with subsequent referral to several committees but no subsequent vote taken. Putting these proposals in perspective, they illustrate the wider range of existing policy alternatives in a context where carbon pricing has been introduced only in a fragmentary form and at the state level: Only some eleven US states have introduced some form of carbon pricing; moreover, pricing mechanisms in place aim mostly at raising of extraction costs of fossil resources whose costs can be exported to a wider range of consumers outside the regulating constituency, rather than at consumption where a carbon tax would create a price signal immediately visible to the members of a particular state (Rabe 2018). Against this background, the controversy on a carbon tax within Congress remains primarily discursive and relevant mainly for claiming political positions particularly within the center-left and different territorial and industrial interests represented in the House and Senate.

Finally, an initiative of major importance for defining the position of political agents towards climate change across the political spectrum is the proposal for a Green New Deal, introduced to the House as a resolution sponsored by Alexandra Ocasio-Cortez on 7 February 2019, briefly after the 2018 mid-term elections. A key to understanding this proposed piece of legislation is that it does not suggest very specific approaches or instruments for GHG reductions but adopts a very broad framing of action against climate change as a challenge requiring major political and social transformation. This vision is to be based on an expanded role of state and a fundamental re-negotiation of social relations in terms of production, consumption, and employment, but also class, gender and race relations. In this sense, the preamble of the Green New Deal proposal refers to both climate change as a cause for mass migration, lost economic output and ecological damage but also to a set of related crises concerning the overall welfare of US citizens in terms of their life expectancy, wage stagnation, income equality, and gender and racial wealth and income divides. In terms of specific demands, the proposed bill (H.R. 109) recognizing 'the duty of the Federal Government to create a Green New Deal' establishes a set of five major goals, including the achievement of net-zero GHG emissions, the creation of millions of high-wage jobs, investment in infrastructure and industry, realizing classical environmental goals of clean air and water, and the promotion of justice and equality in terms of ending oppression of indigenous peoples, communities of color as well as the poor and low-income workers. As a course of action, the bill envisages a 10-year 'national mobilization' aiming at improving resiliency against climate change-related disaster, investment in infrastructure to help achieve carbon neutrality such as smart power grids and modernization of buildings, a full transition to renewable energy supply, and a removal of GHG emissions from agriculture; beyond fields of action immediately relevant for carbon emissions, the bill calls for an agenda of transformation in economic governance by increasing public ownership and transparency, providing better training and education to 'frontline and vulnerable communities', strengthening participatory processes and improving wages and working conditions in the broadest sense including access to health care and economic security. No specific instrument of reducing GHG emissions such as a carbon tax or efficiency standards is proposed in the bill. From this brief summary, it should be clear that the Green New Deal adopts the broadest, and most politically transformative framing of any legislative proposal reviewed in this study.

Through the breadth of this approach, the Green New Deal proposal is significant particularly as a point of reference for prompting political agents to take a position towards the issue of climate change across the political spectrum, both along partisan lines but also, and perhaps more importantly, within Democrats after their resumption of the House majority in the 2018 mid-term elections. In a broader perspective, the political question raised by the introduction of the GND as a legislative proposal is how legislators in the House should position themselves towards particularly two originators of its proposed agenda: first, an intellectual community formed by mainly British activists, politicians, policy experts and entrepreneurs formed around the year 2008 to initially define the project of a Green Deal, following on the launch of the concept to the US public by Thomas Friedman in a *New York Times* article one year before (Pettifor 2020: 3); and second, a network of activist groups headed by the Sunrise Movement as a network of mostly young activists akin to the Fridays for Future movement in Europe. Its advocacy for the Green Deal agenda was made visible especially through the sit-in of Sunrise activists at the office of returning House Speaker Nancy Pelosi[26] on 13 November 2018, but also a range of publications (Prakash and Girgenti 2020; Aronoff et al. 2019, for surveys and critical assessment cp. Ajl 2021; Pettifor 2020).

The political momentum created by the Green Deal proposal is demonstrated by the fact that in spite of its slim chances for adoption, the bill introduced to the House received the support of 101 co-sponsors according to congressional records of procedure.[27] A more critical test of the support for the GND agenda by Democratic lawmakers, however, arrived through the entry of a parallel bill into the US Senate, where the bill was introduced by Senator Ed Markey. Having received very ambiguous responses from Democratic senators, Republican majority leader Mitch McConnell set up a vote on the bill on 26 March 2019, evidently with the intention of stopping the bill and provoking a split within Democratic senators. The vote resulted in a clear rejection of 0–57 votes, with all 43 Democrats voting 'present', thereby avoiding to take an explicit position on the proposal[28] and in spite of 14 senators having previously co-sponsored the bill.[29] Following on its rejection in the Senate, the proposal failed to move on further within the House,

---

[26] Reports and coverage can be retrieved from the Sunrise Movement homepage at: https://www.sunrisemovement.org/actions/pelosi-sit-in/ (last accessed: 29 August 2021).

[27] The procedure file for the House Resolution recognizing the duty of the Federal Government to create a Green New Deal can be retrieved from: https://www.congress.gov/bill/116th-congress/house-resolution/109/text (last accessed: 29 August 2021).

[28] For more detailed coverage of the vote, cp.: "Senate Blocks Green New Deal", in: *The Hill*, 27 March 2019; and "Democrats to Move on from Green New Deal", in: *The Hill*, 28 March 2019.

[29] The procedure file for the Senate resolution recognizing the duty of the Federal Government to create a Green New Deal (S. Res. 59) can be retrieved from: https://www.congress.gov/bill/116th-congress/senate-resolution/59?q=%7B%22search%22%3A%5B%22green+new+deal%22%5D%7D&s=2&r=3 (last accessed: 29 August 2021).

with no vote taken in its plenary. Here, debate on the GND therefore gained visibility mainly through its advocacy by a group of younger House Members widely known as 'the Squad',[30] but also through various hearings held on its background and ambitions. In spite of its defeat as a proposal for legislation, the GND agenda has continued to make a major impact on the debate about a political agenda to deal with climate change among Democratic policy-makers, particularly in the context of the heated competition for the nomination of a presidential candidate and campaign during the year 2020.

4.4 Civil Society Agents: Think Tanks and Advocacy Groups

Turning to civil society agents, a general feature of the US case is that interest groups and think tanks involved in the climate politics debate in Washington, DC are more closely associated with one of the main political parties and their stances towards climate change than in the European case. Against this background, many of the various legislative initiatives and related sets of agents within Congress can be associated with one or several external advocacy groups or policy experts active within a particular group or think tank. The task of the subsequent brief section is to identify those groups and institutions that have established themselves as relevant for each of the various legislative initiatives and sets of agents reviewed in the previous parts of this chapter. Based on this approach, the following review is less a survey of the most relevant environmental advocacy groups at the US federal level—particularly groups such as Friends of the Earth, the World Wildlife Fund or Sierra Club—but a more focused account of ties between legislative processes within Congress and outside groups and institutions.

First, several entities have emerged in a role of legislative watchdog and general advocacy group in terms of specific legislative progress on climate policy. In this context, the League of Conservationist Voters[31]

---

[30] By common understanding, the group of initially four and subsequently six Democratic House Members referred to with this term includes, in alphabetical order of last name, Representatives Jamaal Bowman (NY), Cori Bush (MO), Alexandra Ocasio-Cortez (NY), Ilhan Omar (MN), Ayanna Presley (MA), and Rashida Tlaib (MI).

[31] The website of the League of Conservationist Voters can be found at: https://www.lcv.orgn (last accessed: 1 September 2021).

(LCV) is recognized within the policy community as a group that monitors individual legislators within Congress and candidates for political office, assigning scores of their respective profiles as advocates for environmental legislation. Another entity that should be mentioned in this context is Climate Hawks Vote[32] (CHV), an advocacy group and political action committee (PAC) pursuing the declared goal of promoting candidates running for political office who endorse stringent political action against climate change. While not associated with a specific set of legislative proposals or group of legislators, these two groups are both clearly in favor of stringent climate action and closely associated with Democratic lawmakers in terms of political support and funding. The public endorsement of Sean Casten in the 2018 Illinois Democratic primary by CHV leader RL Miller is only one example.[33]

By comparison, several advocacy groups and research institutes can be identified that adopt a more bipartisan or politically neutral stance, often with the explicit goal of arguing for pragmatic solutions with a higher chance of receiving sufficient political support to become enacted. In this context, particularly the Citizens' Climate Lobby[34] stands out as a group that defines itself as a nonpartisan advocacy group for climate action and is closely associated with the previously mentioned, bipartisan Climate Solutions Caucus in the House of Representatives. Concerning the provision of expertise and specific policy advice, especially the Center for Climate and Energy Solutions (C2ES) stands out as a climate policy think tank that is both widely recognized in terms of its expertise and perceived as aiming to consider broader input from the business community and leading corporations before formulating policy advice to Congress. An important example for such input is the publication of the document 'Getting to Zero', a climate agenda outlining a path to carbon neutrality by 2050, presented as a result of close consultation with and contributions by major corporations including BP, Cargill, Microsoft, Pacific Gas and Electric or Toyota (C2ES 2019). Previous partnerships of the

---

[32] The website of the group can be found at: http://climatehawksvote.com (last accessed: 1 September 2021).

[33] "Politics: Uncompromising Climate Hawk Advances in Tight Illinois Primary", in: *ClimateWire*, 22 March 2018.

[34] The website of the Citizens' Climate Lobby can be found at: https://citizensclimatelobby.org (last accessed: 1 September 2021).

Center include its Business Environmental Leadership Council,[35] created in 1998 by the Pew Center on Global Climate Change, the predecessor organization of C2ES, and having grown since then to become one of the biggest groups of corporations to identify policy solutions in the US. The Center's visibility is created through its Policy Hub, providing reports about decision-making in the US Congress and market-based solutions at the US state level. Other emphases of the Center's work lie in its support for the Carbon Capture Coalition, a platform involving multiple stakeholders promoting the sequestration of carbon emissions, or its partnership with the Conference of Mayors. This profile of actions and expertise demonstrate the relatively business-friendly, pragmatic approach of C2ES as a major think tank that is not unequivocally associated with either of the two major competing parties or its more polarizing currents concerning climate change. This status sets it apart from other think tanks with a clearer association with one of the political parties, such as the Progressive Policy Institute[36] (PPI) as another of the major non-profit organizations in the climate politics field that was created by the Democratic Leadership Council. A prominent member of the institute is Paul Bledsoe, who holds a position as Strategic Adviser within PPI and previously served in the Climate Change Task Force of the White House during the Clinton Presidency.[37]

This partisan orientation, and particularly the promotion of a specific political agenda is even more present in a network of organizations associated with the promotion of the Green New Deal. The most obvious advocacy group at the level of civil society is, of course, the Sunrise Movement as both the most prominent youth organization pushing for political change and the most publicly visible group promoting the Green Deal agenda. Beyond political activism, the Green Deal is also associated with a range of policy experts and a few research entities, most notably the think tank organization New Consensus, whose President at the time of

---

[35] The website of BELC can be found on the homepage of C2ES at: https://www.c2es.org/our-work/belc/ (last accessed: 1 September 2021).

[36] The website of the PPI can be found at: http://www.progressivepolicy.org (last accessed: 1 September 2021).

[37] Cp. Bledsoe's personal website on the PPI homepage at: https://www.progressivepolicy.org/people/paul-bledsoe-2/, or, e.g., *ClimateWire* of 4 August 2020: "Campaign 2020: Why Biden's Car Plan Might Not Be a Clunker".

writing is Saikrat Chakrabarti, the former chief of staff of House Rep. and main sponsor of the Green New Deal Alexandra Ocasio-Cortez.[38]

To conclude this brief survey, at least a summary overview should be given of a set of academic and advocacy groups taking a stance against stringent climate action or, in some cases, even working to dispute the severity of climate change as a problem. A focal point for the involvement of these groups into the policy-making process at the White House was the envisaged creation of a panel tasked to produce an 'adversarial' view of climate change; launched during the Trump presidency in July 2019 and envisaged as part of the National Security Council, the project was abandoned due to conflicting opinions within the White House.[39] Three advocacy groups approached for membership in this panel include the Competitive Enterprise Institute (CEI), the Heartland Institute and the CO_2 Coalition, all of which are organizations questioning the need to act against climate change. A prominent figure in this context is Myron Ebell, who currently acts as director of the CEI's Center for Energy and Environment. His roles in coordinating initiatives opposed to action against climate change include his previous leadership for the transition team for the EPA after the 2016 election (prompting a petition signed by 57.000 persons requesting his removal from this role[40]); furthermore, it includes Ebell's leadership role within the Cooler Heads Coalition, a group of non-profit organizations questioning climate change.[41] Another actor providing a linkage between the White House and external advocacy groups is William Happer, a member of the National Security Council charged with the creation of the panel and also the founder of the CO_2 Coalition. Established as a non-profit group and seen as successor of the previous Marshall Institute, the group's mission statement is to 'educate policy-makers and the public about the essential relevance of carbon

---

[38] The website of New Consensus can be found at: https://newconsensus.com (last accessed: 1 September 2021); for additional background, see also: "People: Ocasio-Cortez's Chief of Staff Exits to Push Green New Deal", in: *ClimateWire*, 5 August 2020; and "Q&A: This Scholar Is Writing the Green New Deal Policy Book", in: *ClimateWire*, 28 June 2019.

[39] Cp. "Politics: White House Won't Review Climate Science Before Election", in: *ClimateWire*, 9 July 2019.

[40] Cp. "EPA: Green Groups Petition to Bar Ebell from Agency", in: *ClimateWire*, 15 November 2016.

[41] Cp. Ebell's personal website on the CEI homepage at: https://cei.org/experts/myron-ebell/ (last accessed: 1 September 2021).

dioxide for life on earth' and the essential role of 'abundant, reliable and reasonably priced energy' for economic growth.[42] Both groups have developed close linkages to the Trump administration and are associated with its decision to withdraw from the Paris Agreement, including through exchanges between members of a so-called beachhead team of political employees leading the transition at EPA who even questioned the participation of the US within the UN Framework Convention on Climate Change.[43]

To conclude this brief survey, a culmination for the polarization between advocacy groups and policy experts on climate change expected during the Trump presidency was reported plans by the head of the EPA, Scott Pruitt, to organize a public, deliberately adversarial debating event pitting a 'blue team' and 'red team' of experts to debate the science of climate change and suggested courses of action in front of a television audience. Although this idea was never realized mostly due to lacking support within the White House,[44] particularly the sponsorship of such an event by the leadership of an independent government agency is impressive proof of the degree of politicization that the evaluation of climate science has reached in the United States during the Trump presidency (cp. also Darwall 2017; Dunlap 2019).

4.5 Content Analysis: Framing Climate Change in US Policy Discourse

In this section we return to the main analytical focus of this study: namely, how policy initiatives and their public announcement are framed concerning the sixfold typology of climate frames, and what implications follow for the understanding of issue dimensions and political contestation. Proceeding from the primarily qualitative approach of the previous sections, the subsequent discussion presents first insights into the empirical data collected through document coding and covers the entire selection of policy documents and speeches described at the outset.

---

[42] Cp. the mission statement on the CO_2 Coalition's website: https://co2coalition.org/co2-fundamentals/ (last accessed: 1 September 2021).

[43] Cp. "EPA: Emails Show To-Do List for Tearing Down Climate Rules", in: *ClimateWire*, 4 June 2018.

[44] Cp. "EPA: Pruitt's Climate Clash Was Declared Dead. There Is a Plan B", in: *ClimateWire*, 14 March 2018.

For the executive branch, the analysis includes the previously discussed statements by both Presidents to the public, as well as programmatic documents on climate change issued by the White House and relevant government departments. For the legislative branch, the analysis covers all major proposals introduced to both chambers of Congress covering the thematic fields discussed above: namely, a set of resolutions covering the Paris Agreement from both parties, proposals for carbon pricing and resolutions about programmatic approaches to energy and climate change policy, as discussed above and introduced during the 114th to the 116th Congress (ie., from January 2015 to the general election in November 2020). A full list is included in the annex.

The methodical approach followed for running the content analysis is the same as in the previous case study on the EU. Following word frequency surveys to identify terms and word combinations relevant to the analysis, a dictionary was compiled including between 16 and 19 keywords for each of the frames across their three respective levels and 106 keywords overall. Using this dictionary for automated coding, the content analysis software coded 5844 text segments across the document selection for the United States, with slightly more weight on legislative documents (3320 coded text segments) than on documents and speeches from the executive branch (2524 segments). In both cases, greater amounts of text were reviewed and more segments were coded for the Obama administration and Democratic legislators (namely, 1741 and 2797 codes, respectively) than concerning the Trump administration and Republican members of Congress (783 and 523).

From the outset, it is evident that policy discourse on climate change in the US involves a range of variants with different emphases on the frames and issue categories under comparison. While an evaluation of these variants based on quantitative data will be presented in the subsequent comparative chapter, the task of this section is to provide a survey of the most relevant of these variants of discourse and to give insights into their respective framing and justificatory intention. The following discussion presents a survey of aggregate data but also specifies observations for subsets of discourse by four main groups of agents: namely, the two administrations of President Obama and his successor Trump; and legislators of both the Democratic and Republican party in both chambers of US Congress, with additional specification of subgroups as far as necessary. This survey seeks to establish the foundation for the subsequent comparative analysis and therefore proceeds in the three thematic steps followed already in the previous EU case study: namely, covering the structure of frames in climate change discourse, the linkages created by the respective agents between frames, and observable fault lines of political contestation and polarization within the political debate.

4.5.1 Structure of Framing: Disparate Perspectives on Climate Change

Starting with a global survey of data on the structure of frames in US climate policy discourse as shown in the Graph 4.1, particularly three forms of framing are identified: namely, a predominant economic variant of discourse that features both arguments advocating for more stringent action and opposition to climate policy; a secondary subset of discourse focusing on the material risk posed by global warming, and finally, references to terms associated with a societal frame, concerning communities, workers, citizens and local frameworks for implementation.

Perhaps the most surprising finding is that an ecological framing of policy initiatives is used with similar numerical emphases in policy discourse of both the Obama and Trump administrations. However, this involves the previously discussed tendency of the 45th President to appropriate environmental topics by stressing a commitment to clean air, water and habitats rather than references to climate change. The two remaining frames of the analytical framework are less frequent on the aggregate level but also more indicative of particular subsets of discourse. More specifically, these frames are advocated to different degrees by Republican and Democratic policy-makers: Framing climate action in terms of justice is associated almost exclusively with Congress Democrats and their proposals for carbon pricing and compensation mechanisms. Furthermore, particularly the Green Deal proposal with its emphasis on concepts of climate justice applied to disadvantaged social groups and a wider global perspective features this form of framing. By contrast, a political framing is applied in more distinctive terms particularly by Congress Republicans, where reference to the framework of UN conventions and agreements creates the foundation for raising objections against the adoption of the Paris Agreement without involvement of the Senate. This brief survey shows that the intense contestation of climate politics that characterizes the US debates evolves both through the advocacy of contrasting frames, and the related effect of highlighting different issue categories

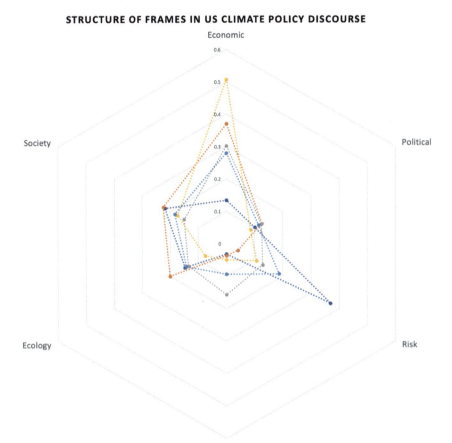

Graph 4.1 Structure of frames in US climate policy discourse

related to the appraisal of climate change as a problem, policy approaches and questions of political support and legitimacy (Table 4.1).

Comparing the four subsets of discourse promoted by Democrats and Republicans from the executive and legislative branches, major differences emerge with regard to the predominant framing of climate change. Moreover, differences emerge with regard to how coherently each agent groups adopts a coherent sort of framing across various different sorts

Table 4.1 Rank orders and cumulative percentage of frames in US policy discourse on climate change

	Obama administration	Trump administration	Legislative: Democrats	Legislative: Republicans	ALL
Economic	(4)	(1)	(1)	(1)	(1)
Political	(5)	(4)	(6)	(4)	(5)
Risk	(1)	(5)	(5)	(3)	(2)
Justice	(6)	(6)	(2)	(5)	(6)
Ecology	(3)	(3)	(4)	(6)	(4)
Society	(2)	(2)	(3)	(2)	(3)
Dominant framing (>50%)	Risk and Society	Economic and Society	Economic, Justice and Society	Economic	Economic, Risk and Society

of discourse and in relation to the respectively aligned agent between executive and Congress.

Starting with political discourse by the Obama administration, its most distinctive feature is how much it is centered on frames in the issue category of problem definition, appraising climate change as a general challenge for society. Accordingly, a risk-based framing is dominant for the entity of statements issued by the administration, particularly within the context of policy documents and reports published by the federal government and executive orders issued by the President. In combination with a societal framing referring to regions, communities and citizens particularly in terms of how these are affected by the impacts of climate change, both combined frames comprise more than half of all statements coded for the Obama administration and even over 70% of policy documents. Only public addresses and speeches made by the President towards the American and international public deviate from this pattern and adopt a primarily ecological framing. Here, the President promotes a frame urging political action by frequent mentions of carbon pollution, terms and concepts related with the environment, references to the forest and planet, and the idea of sustainability. While not entirely coherent in its framing, a common feature of this variant of discourse is its focus on climate change as a threat, making the general case for the urgency of action rather than specific policy arguments.

In comparison, the framing adopted by Democrats in Congress in legislative proposals differs by focusing on the issue category of policy evaluation and its two related frames, based on criteria of economic viability and justice. Taken together, these are the strongest frames that comprise almost half of all coded statements within legislative bills and more than half of all statements within them when combined with the society frame. In a general characterization, therefore, legislative initiatives by Democrats engage with questions of carbon pricing and reimbursement mechanism from an economic, distributive, and societal angle. Considerable variation, however, emerges within the range of proposals included in the analysis. In this context, a detail worth highlighting is the prominent emphasis on terms associated with the justice frame; these particularly relate to energy refunds and references to social security and vulnerable groups in bills proposed by House Democrats. This emphasis is strongest in the case of bills categorized as general programmatic proposals for climate policy but also present in initiatives for more specific proposals on energy policy and carbon pricing. A different framing, however, is adopted by proposals engaging with the Paris Agreement, where the primary emphasis on the frames of risk and society by the Obama administration is replicated. Policy discourse by Democrats therefore includes not one coherent but different variants of framing, with contrasting emphases on problem definition and policy evaluation.

In comparison, a more stringent and coherent framing is promoted by Republican policy-makers. Here, an economic framing of policy in combination with a societal frame, often referring to consumers, workers, and citizens, is adopted across the board. It also figures as the primary framing of statements by the Trump administration that covers over half of all coded statements. In contrast to the Obama administration, all subsets of discourse issued by the White House and federal government during the Trump presidency feature economic claims as the primary frame, including speeches, executive orders and policy documents. The only slight variation concerns the secondary frame, which covers ecological claims in executive orders and policy documents, and a societal framing in public speeches. In the highly publicized, often campaign-style public appearances by Trump during which he addressed issues of energy and environmental policy, clearly over half of all coded statements were framed in economic terms. Here, the President's speeches feature references to jobs, coal and natural gas as primary keywords of the economic frame, in addition to frequent references to society that features workers as the most frequently used keyword.

This framing is mirrored and even amplified by legislative bills proposed by Congress Republicans. Covering all documents, an economic framing is dominant and covers just over half of all coded statements, and is combined with a society frame especially in proposals on carbon pricing and energy policy. As the comparative chapter will show in more detail, many of the same terms and keywords promoted by the Trump administration are also used within these legislative bills. The only variation within this subset of documents occurs in proposals for bills covering the Paris Agreement, where a political relegates an economic framing from the primary to a secondary role in terms of its numerical frequency. References to the framework convention and UN framework are most numerous in this particular subset of documents. Particularly an ecological and justice-based framing of climate action is strongly de-emphasized, resonating with ideological principles promoted by Republicans. To conclude this survey, a review of the frames promoted in US climate policy discourse provides insights not just about variants of discourse in comparison between Republicans and Democrats, but particularly differences concerning the respective coherence of both political camps concerning their framing between the executive and legislative branches.

A final issue to address is in how far claims could be identified that directly deny the existence of climate change or question its anthropogenic causes. Particularly the rejection of climate science as a hoax or conspiracy aimed at the manipulation of the US political public is closely associated with President Trump's stance towards the issue. The propagation of such a view was checked in the data of the present case study by screening for relevant keywords (such as hoax, lie, conspiracy or China). The observation made here, however, is that this bluntest version of climate change denial is largely absent from policy documents, and also does not figure prominently in public speeches made by Trump. In this latter setting, climate change is ignored much more than denied; the only major and more extended public statement addressing the issue directly—namely, the exit announcement from the Paris Agreement—is critical of the UN framework and its efficiency rather than diagnoses of climate change.[45]

---

[45] This observation is certainly owed at least partly to the particular choice of empirical material selected here—namely, its focus on legislative and policy documents with an official character and public appearances in front of large audiences. This finding would

4.5.2 Linkages: Focused Versus Broad Approaches to Framing

As in the previous case study, this second step proceeds to the review of linkages between frames to further gain insights about the profiles of discourse promoted by agents of both parties and branches of government. As discussed in the theoretical part, we assume that frequent and exclusive linkages between two frames are indicative of a focused profile of an agent's discourse and therefore more conducive to polarized positions if different linkages occur within a policy debate. By contrast, more broadly dispersed linkages are evaluated as an indicator of more inclusive, less polarizing positions and forms of discourse.

Against this background, the US policy debate generally features relatively prominent linkages that, however, occur with different densities and variegated profiles arising from various linkages of frames across the empirical material. The central observation in this context is that particularly a linkage between a (critical) economic and societal framing emphasizing jobs, workers and communities promoted by Republicans stands out as the distinctly featured profile of discourse and contrasts with a broader and more disparate framing by Democrats. To illustrate and further specify these findings, the subsequent diagrams once again show code maps plotting the proximity of codes as measured by the frequency of their linkages. This starts with a plot covering the climate policy discourse by the Obama administration, depicted in Graph 4.2.

The code map confirms the emphasis laid by the Obama administration on the appraisal of climate change as an emerging risk and the evaluation of its impact on society. This frame is specified particularly by reference to the terms of resilience, risk, communities and health, the keywords most frequently coded within the main cluster formed by the risk and society frame. While references to paradigmatic terms of an ecological frame—addressed particularly through the terms of carbon pollution, environmental action and forests—are closest to this main cluster of terms, climate change is primarily addressed as a material threat to the security and livelihood of individuals and communities. In relation to these primary linkages, no very distinct profile of discourse can

certainly change if the material was broadened to unofficial statements and the blogosphere, but this does not take away the relevance of our current finding: Within official policy discourse, even declared opponents of action against climate change do not openly contest its existence.

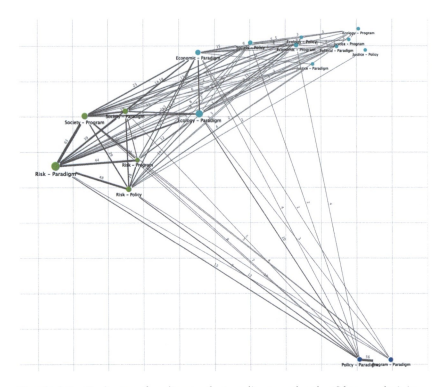

Graph 4.2 Code map for climate change discourse by the Obama administration

be discerned concerning the framing of specific policy measures: Component terms of the various other frames, particularly the economic and justice-based rationale of policy-making, emerge in a flat structure of network-like linkages with no very strong emphasis or salient linkage. In this context, it is noteworthy that particularly the political framing of climate action—as created through reference to specific action programs, initiatives or policy programs—is identified as most remote from all other frames and not integrated with reference to the other frames. As a result, the discursive framing presented here makes the case for climate action in terms of urgency and risk, but presents no very clear linkage of frames to outline the rationale for policy-making. Against this background, an interesting observation is to zoom in to the particular subset of public speeches by President Obama within the overall executive discourse of his administration, presented in the code map below (see Graph 4.3). Here, the perspective shifts more decidedly to an ecological framing of climate change, expressed in paradigmatic terms and relating this foundation to both to aspects of risk and an economic rationale for action against climate change.

The main features of the Obama administration climate discourse—namely, the disjunction between a primarily risk-based appraisal of climate change and a relatively broad, open-ended framing of policy—is to some part replicated and further diversified in the policy discourse created through legislative proposals of Congress Democrats, as demonstrated in Graph 4.4.

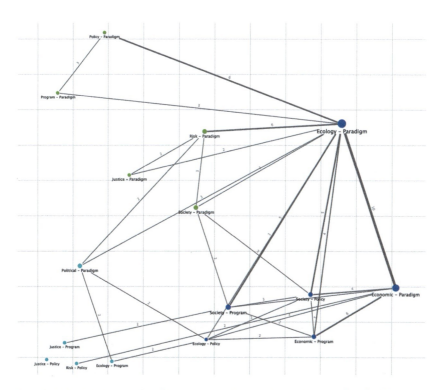

Graph 4.3 Code map for discourse on climate change in speeches by President Obama

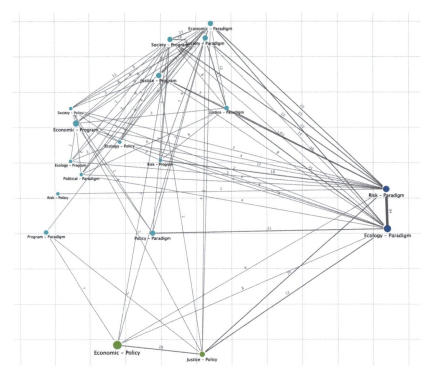

Graph 4.4 Code map for legislative proposals on climate change sponsored by Democrats

Within this subset of discourse, the only discernible stronger cluster of frames is created by a linkage between paradigmatic terms of risk and ecology, expressed particularly in preambles of legislative bills that describe climate change both as a risk to society and threat to the environment. Besides this general recognition of the urgency of climate action, an even broader and more network-like structure of framing linkages is present in legislative bills. A noteworthy aspect of policy discourse at this level, however, is the discernible emphasis on a link between the economic framing of climate policy—addressed through terms related to the broad issue of carbon pricing and trade—and keywords associated with the justice frame, particularly those stressing social security and help for vulnerable groups. While this emphasis appears intuitive for legislative proposals by Democrats, it stands in contrast with the absence of an equally clear policy framing by the Obama administration. The remainder of connections within the code map demonstrates the salience of linkages between economic arguments and references to society without, however, forming a clearly identifiable additional profile of Democrat discourse on climate action.

These observations stand in clear contrast with the more focused, clearly profiled and politically coherent discourse by the Trump administration and Republican legislators in Congress. The code map below (see Graph 4.5) shows linkages of frames in policy discourse of the Trump

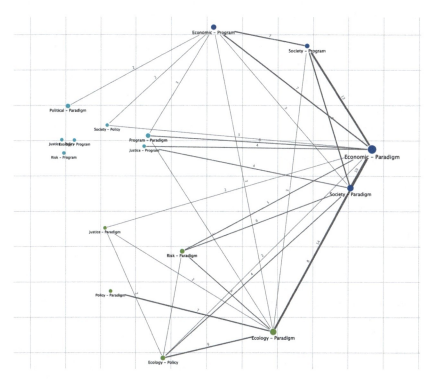

Graph 4.5 Code map of policy discourse on climate and energy policy by the Trump administration

administration, covering public speeches as well as policy programs and reports.

It is evident from this survey that the economic framing of policy-making as specified in terms of energy independence, deregulation and growth in combination with envisaged impacts of society stand out as the central and almost exclusive prominent linkage. The most relevant keywords coded within this two-point cluster are jobs, economic, coal, natural gas and growth for the economic frame; and workers, citizens, regions, city and communities for the society frame. This combination is intuitive for creating a set of terms and concepts that is clearly profiled and resonant with Republican ideological principles of deregulation and economic growth. As mentioned before, a noteworthy aspect is that references to ecological terms are relatively salient and closely attached to the main pair of frames. However, and demonstrating the previous discussion of how ecological aspects are appropriated and specified in terms of tangible, material phenomena rather than the systematic processes effected by climate change, this frame features most prominently the keywords environmental, forest, clean water and wildlife; mentions of the planet rank on fifth place with only a handful of hits in the data. A practically identical system of linkages between frames can be identified when the empirical material is reduced only to public speeches by President Trump. To summarize, it follows that while political discourse of the Trump administration about climate change is reductionist, it is relatively coherent. This aspect is further confirmed when compared with data resulting from the survey of Republican proposals in Congress (Graph 4.6).

Evidently, a caveat to be made concerning this plot is that it is based on a far smaller subset of empirical data and codings than in Democrat counterpart, as much fewer bills related to climate and energy were introduced by Republicans. However, it is striking how stringently Republican members of Congress frame legislative proposals in economic terms that are primarily linked to aspects of political action and societal impact. Within this primary and practically exclusive cluster of terms, the keywords industrial, coal, natural gas, economic and trade industry are most prominent and linked to the keywords consumer, worker, urban, city and private in the societal frame. As in the case of policy discourse of the Trump administration, these terms are coherent within each other and in relation to ideological foundations of Republican policy. Moreover,

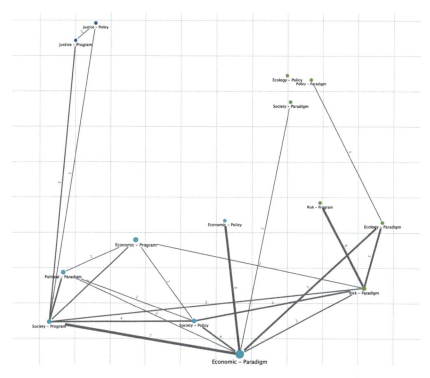

Graph 4.6 Code map of legislative proposals on climate and energy policy sponsored by Republicans

they are highly congruent between discourse of the executive branch and proposals launched within Congress.

4.5.3 Polarization: Competing Frames and Issue Categories in a Volatile Policy Debate

Political controversy in the US reaches beyond a single conflict dimension created between two political camps either recognizing or objecting to the existence of climate change, in two respects. First, while several categories of topics can be identified that create political contestation, a central finding is the co-existence of two different forms of polarization in the US debate: on the one hand, a primary dynamic of polarization resulting from a divergence of paradigms to address climate change and associated with the promotion of contrasting sets of frames in different issue categories; and on the other, a secondary dynamic of more direct contestation of contradictory arguments associated with terms proposed within the same respective frames. Combining these two related aspects, the main finding in this regard is that polarization in the US debate results less from the clash of opposed arguments but the lack of a stable set of frames established for the debate that agents involved in the debate can take up and engage with. Second, another key observation is that divisions between opposed viewpoints and arguments do not entirely run along partisan lines but also reveal discrepancies between otherwise politically aligned agents, particularly within the range of Democratic legislators in Congress proposing initiatives to promote action against climate change. The main feature of the US debate on climate change is therefore a combination of volatility and fragmentation, rather than polarization of two camps within a stable set of issue dimensions. While the comparative chapter will go into more detail to explore and evaluate these aspects in comparison to the EU case, the qualitative review of empirical material leads to the preliminary identification of the following four main categories of topics giving rise to contestation.

First, and related to the problem definition category defined in the theoretical chapter, divergent views arise with regard to the recognition of climate change as a problem and the evaluation of its scope and severity. This point obviously divides both major parties and particularly discourse by both presidential administrations compared. However, an important point to make is the asymmetrical structure of this level of debate concerning direct references to climate change. At the surface, this is already reflected in the contrasting number of references in the discourse of both administrations to the word combinations 'climate change' (118/3) and 'climate action' (65/2). Concerning the Obama administration, it was described in a previous section how the President addressed climate change in a whole range of widely publicized addresses, framing it both as an urgent environmental issue and matter of intergenerational justice. Covering policy documents issued by the White House and the federal government, however, this perspective on climate change is shifted more towards one evaluating it based on criteria of risk, particularly in relation to national security. While climate change is explicitly addressed and systematically evaluated by the US federal government during the Obama presidency, this coverage fades to practical neglect and only indirect reference by the Trump presidency, particularly through its degradation to a secondary issue in relation to the broader agenda of economic deregulation. The only notable exception of this indirect denial of climate change as an issue is marked by the publication of the Fourth Climate Assessment Report in 2018, issued by agencies of the US federal government and appraising the severity of climate change in unambiguous terms. It follows that the recognition of climate change is contested primarily by engaging with or refusing its appraisal as a problem. A related point is that the Trump administration did not go so far as to openly deny or contest its existence, at least at the level of official reports and publications.

A second fault line of debate relates more directly to the policy evaluation category and assumptions about contestation within a socio-economic left/right dimension between market freedom and state intervention. The main focal point of this set of issues is the controversy on carbon pricing, raised through proposals for legislation without a plausible perspective of realization within Congress and particularly the House of Representatives. As the previous one, this fault line is asymmetrical by being occupied almost exclusively by Democratic legislators and having no equivalent counterweight through Republican counter-proposals. The latter could only be captured by broadening the perspective to include legislative proposals covering the whole range of energy and economic policy, particularly concerning the extraction and trade of fossil fuels and deregulation of energy production.

In this context, the Green New Deal and political contestation caused by its introduction to Congress stands out as a very stringent and interventionist, but also more comprehensive proposal whose political impact cannot be simply subsumed into the previous category of socio-economic issues. In addition to advocating for a considerable expansion of state intervention and public expense, the GND also includes a strong cultural dimension by raising issues of climate and social justice in relation to questions of gender, race, as well as the rights of indigenous groups. Rather than simply introducing a proposal on raising a fee on carbon permits, an aspect not covered in the legislative proposal, the Green New Deal agenda promotes broader social change and a more inclusive society. In this function, the bill is a divisive issue for Democrats almost to the degree to which it serves as an identifier of support or objection to stringent action against climate change along partisan lines between Democrats and Republicans.

Finally, a major division in the debate is created between opposing positions on whether to endorse or object to the cooperation of the US within a global framework of action against climate change as represented by the Paris Agreement. This subset of controversy is the one where stances adopted by Democrats and Republicans can be most directly compared, as both relate to the same object of contestation: namely, the participation of the US in the provisions of the Paris Agreement. It was discussed in a previous section how Republican initiatives pushed for a de facto-repeal of the Paris Agreement by calling for full involvement of the Senate while proposals entered by Democrats during the Trump presidency advocated for continued efforts to meet requirements enshrined in the accord. The respective framing of positions taken by both sides, however, differs notably between an emphasis on sovereignty promoted within a political frame by Republicans, and a primarily ecological frame advocated by Democrats to stress the urgency of action against climate change.

This brief review of the empirical material suggests that the policy debate on climate change in the US involves more than one relevant category of contested topics and potentially resulting, longer-term issue dimensions structuring its contestation. A more systematic account of the three related features of policy discourse discussed here—its discursive structure, linkages of frames and contestation—will be presented in the comparative chapter, based on a fuller quantification of data and review. What is evident in the US case, however, is that the institutional features of its policy-making framework, particularly the shift to the administrative presidency seeking policy change through executive acts—leave strong imprints on political discourse and contestation. These can be seen to prompt divisions not just between the two main political parties but also between and within the executive and legislative branches and involved agents within the two chambers of Congress.

To conclude, comparing climate discourse between the EU and US is faced with the difficulty that a comprehensive framework for the transition to carbon neutrality as set through the European Green Deal agenda is absent in its US counterpart. This point is also mirrored in the fact that no equivalent for the set of directly comparable policy documents covering the EGD across the political spectrum—namely, the party group motions discussed in the previous section—is available for the US case. This implies that the main source of contestation in US climate policy is the format and parameters of debate, not so much the content of specific policy issues.

4.6 Conclusion: Framing as the Contested Link Between Climate Politics and Policy

In conclusion, the main observation about climate change politics in the US is its volatility and fragmentation: In spite of its involvement and continued membership in the Paris Agreement, no coherent and comprehensive policy-making framework has yet been spelled out to make an adequate contribution to limiting global warming to below two degrees Celsius. A key source of controversy within the climate debate in the US is the disconnect between the policy-making and politics of climate change: The conclusion of the Paris Agreement arrived at a time when a relatively limited and loose policy core was created mainly through the Clean Power Plan and vehicle emission standards had already been put in place; as described in previous sections, its adoption was defined by the dual conditions of the administrative presidency and contested federalism. From the outset, these conditions limited both the political legitimacy and subsequent legal applicability of envisaged measures, as challenges against their delegation to independent agencies were raised through objections ultimately adjudicated by the Supreme Court. While the transition to the Trump presidency prompted a political agenda of deregulation and rollback of provisions established by the CPP and other environmental rules, the core of the regulatory frameworks based on the Clean Air Act has proven relatively resilient not least due to their decentralized implementation at the state level. In turn, replacements such as the ACE introduced by the Trump administration arrived relatively late and equally did not go through to reach legally binding effect. Contrasting with the highly publicized clash of views on climate change by the Obama and Trump administrations, the development of specific policy has been slow and incremental, but also marked by more resilience and resulting continuity in specific provisions than suggested by the polarization between Republicans and Democrats on climate change.

The relevance of political and discursive framing, therefore, is not limited to the justificatory communication of a proposed policy package launched to enact the provisions of the Paris Agreement. In the US case, it involves the challenge of proposing a viable nexus between a far-reaching international commitment made through the accession to the Paris Agreement, and very limited domestic policies touching on issues of environmental sustainability, energy production and use, social justice, and economic competitiveness and growth. In this setting, the conceptual approach of framing is useful for highlighting the scope and rationalizing principles proposed for negotiating the evident misfit between declared ambitions at the international level and the status quo of climate-related policies at the domestic level.

Against this background, the review of executive and legislative discourse in this chapter leads to two main insights. First, public communication by presidential administrations presents very broad, programmatic views of how to rationalize the problem of climate change and what action to devise against it. The framing of climate action promoted by President Obama and his administration is comprehensive and intended to be inclusive, both towards mainstream positions of economic policy-making and security concerns in relation to public health, the protection of private assets, and migration. At the same time, it is also a very fragile discourse, particularly by failing to identify a credible political agenda to close the Paris ambition gap. By comparison, the framing established by the Trump administration is much narrower and more focused, both by concentrating almost exclusively on the domestic dimension of policy-making and adopting a much more unequivocal economic framing of growth fueled by deregulation. The main weakness of this variant of discourse is its failure to seriously engage with the dual complex of climate change and the global regime established by the Paris Agreement: While the obligations of the Paris Agreement are both overstated and misrepresented, a discourse of environmental protection, particularly in its banalized form of clean water and air, is formally adopted while ignoring rather than contesting the scientific foundations of climate change.

Second, our survey of legislative proposals addressing climate change demonstrates the diversity of concepts and variants of framing identified from the range of proposals launched by specialized committees, caucuses, informal groups working for climate advocacy and senior lawmakers. Within the spectrum of proposals supporting climate action, three currents of legislative proposals can be identified: First, initiatives to launch a program of public investment in research and infrastructure to continue efforts towards decarbonization pledged by the US through the Paris Agreement; second, more clearly market-based proposals for establishing a carbon price and linking revenue either to investment in climate action or compensatory revenue; and finally, resolutions addressing climate change as a symptom for the failure of free-market capitalism and endorsing an expansion of state intervention to promote a range of social and economic policies envisaged through the Green New

Deal agenda. It is particularly this pluralism of framing climate change and related policy proposals, and its embedding in a volatile and polarized political environment that creates an intriguing contrast to policy debates in the EU. This contrast establishes the basis of comparison between the two cases as the next step of our analysis.

References

Ahmad, Fatima, Jennifer Huang, and Bob Perciasepe. 2017. "The Paris Agreement Presents a Flexible Approach for US Climate Policy." *Climate & Carbon Law Review* 4: 283–91.

Ajl, Max. 2021. *A People's Green New Deal*. London: Pluto Press.

Andrews, Richard. 2020. *Managing the Environment, Managing Ourselves*. New Haven, CT: Yale University Press.

Aronoff, Kate, Alyssa Battistoni, Daniel Aldana Cohen, and Thea Riofrancos. 2019. *A Planet to Win: Why We Need a Green New Deal*. London and New York: Verso.

Arroyo, Vicki. 2017. "State and Local Climate Leadership in the Trumpocene." *Carbon & Climate Law Review*, no. 4: 303–13.

Atkinson, Hugh. 2018. *The Politics of Climate Change Under President Obama*. London and New York: Routledge.

Bailey, Christopher J. 2015. *US Climate Change Policy*. Transforming Environmental Politics and Policy. Farnham and Surrey Burlington, VT: Ashgate.

Bodansky, Daniel, and O'Connor, Sandra Day. 2015. "Legal Options for U.S. Acceptance of a New Climate Change Agreement." Center for Climate and Energy Solutions, Washington, DC. https://www.c2es.org/wp-content/uploads/2015/05/legal-options-us-acceptance-new-climate-change-agreement.pdf.

Brewer, Thomas L. 2015. *The United States in a Warming World: The Political Economy of Government, Business, and Public Responses to Climate Change*. Cambridge: Cambridge University Press.

Brown, George, and Benjamin K. Sovacool. 2017. "The Presidential Politics of Climate Discourse: Energy Frames, Policy, and Political Tactics from the 2016 Primaries in the United States." *Energy Policy* 111 (C): 127–36.

Bulkeley, Harriet. 2014. *Transnational Climate Change Governance*. Cambridge: Cambridge University Press.

C2ES. 2019. "Getting to Zero: A U.S. Climate Agenda." Center for Climate and Energy Solutions, Washington, DC. https://www.c2es.org/wp-content/uploads/2019/11/getting-to-zero-a-us-climate-agenda-11-13-19.pdf.

Carlarne, Cinnamon Piñon. 2010. *Climate Change Law and Policy: EU and US Approaches*. Oxford [u.a.]: Oxford University Press.

Carlson, Ann, and Dallas Burtraw, eds. 2019. *Lessons from the Clean Air Act: Building Durability and Adaptability into U.S. Climate and Energy Policy.* Cambridge: Cambridge University Press.

ClimateWire. 2017. "Congress: Climate Club: Sincere of Just Politically Convenient?" *E&E News*, 2017, Vol. 10, No. 9 edition.

———. 2018. "Congress: 2 More Republicans Join Climate Solutions Caucus." *E&E News*, 2018, Vol. 10, No. 9 edition.

———. 2019a. "Congress: Tonko Unveils 'Framework' for Climate Legislation." *E&E News*, 2019a, Vol. 10, No. 9 edition.

———. 2019b. "Politics: Bipartisan Climate Caucus Eyes a Comeback." *E&E News*, 2019b, Vol. 10, No. 9 edition.

Collomb, Jean-Daniel. 2014. "The Ideology of Climate Change Denial in the United States." *European Journal of American studies* 9 (9–1). https://doi.org/10.4000/ejas.10305.

Conlan, Timothy J. 2017. "The Changing Politics of American Federalism." *State and Local Government Review* 49 (3): 170–83. https://doi.org/10.1177/0160323X17741723.

Danish, Kyle. 2018. "Current Developments: North America." *Carbon & Climate Law Review* 1: 62–64.

Darwall, Rupert. 2017. *Green Tyranny: Exposing the Totalitarian Roots of the Climate Industrial Complex.* First American edition. New York: Encounter Books.

Dunlap, Riley E. 2019. "Partisan Polarization on the Environment Grows Under Trump." Gallup.Com, 2019. https://news.gallup.com/opinion/gallup/248294/partisan-polarization-environment-grows-trump.aspx.

Dunlap, Riley E., and Aaron M. McCright. 2011. "Organized Climate Change Denial." Edited by John S. Dryzek. *The Oxford Handbook of Climate Change and Society*, 144–60. https://doi.org/10.1093/oxfordhb/9780199566600.003.0010.

Durney, Jessica. 2017. "Defining the Paris Agreement: A Study of Executive Power and Political Commitments." *Carbon & Climate Law Review*, no. 3: 234–42.

EPA (Environmental Protection Agency). 2016. "Factsheet: The Clean Power Plan by the Numbers. Cutting Carbon Pollution from Power Plants." https://archive.epa.gov/epa/sites/production/files/2015-08/documents/fs-cpp-by-the-numbers.pdf.

Fabbrini, Sergio, ed. 2005. *Democracy and Federalism in the European Union and the United States: Exploring Post-National Governance.* London and New York: Routledge.

Fisher, Dana R., Philip Leifeld, and Yoko Iwaki. 2013. "Mapping the Ideological Networks of American Climate Politics." *Climatic Change* 116 (3): 523–45. https://doi.org/10.1007/s10584-012-0512-7.

Freeman, Jody. 2011. "The Obama Administration's National Auto Policy: Lessons from the 'Car Deal.'" *Harvard Environmental Law Review* 343 (35).
———. 2013. "Climate and Energy Policy in the Obama Administration." *Pace Environmental Law Review* 30 (1): 375.
Gehler, Michael, ed. 2005. *Towards a European Constitution: A Historical and Political Comparison with the United States*. Bd. 3. Wien: Böhlau.
Glicksman, Robert. 2017. "The Fate of the Clean Power Plan in the Trump Era." *Carbon & Climate Law Review* 11 (4): 292–302.
Guliyev, Farid. 2020. "Trump's 'America First' Energy Policy, Contingency and the Reconfiguration of the Global Energy Order." *Energy Policy*, no. 140: 1–10.
Hollibaugh, Gary E., Jr. 2016. "Rethinking the Administrative Presidency: Trust, Intellectual Capital, and Appointee-Careerist Relations in the George W. Bush Administration." *Journal of Public Administration Research and Theory* 26 (4): 818–20. https://doi.org/10.1093/jopart/muw030.
Holt, Robert T., and Leonard S. Robins. 2009. "Political Climates and the Global Climate: The First Six Months of the Obama Administration and the Congress." *Environmental Practice* 11 (3): 220–27. https://doi.org/10.1017/S1466046609990111.
Holthaus, Eric. 2015. "Buried in Obama's Climate Plan: A Promise of Business as Usual to the Fossil Fuel Industry." Slate. https://slate.com/news-and-politics/2015/08/obama-s-clean-power-plan-analysis-business-as-usual-for-the-fossil-fuel-industry.html.
Houle, David, Erick Lachapelle, and Mark Purdon. 2015. "Comparative Politics of Sub-Federal Cap-and-Trade: Implementing the Western Climate Initiative." *Global Environmental Politics* 15 (3): 49–73. https://doi.org/10.1162/GLEP_a_00311.
Inhofe, James M. 2012. *The Greatest Hoax: How the Global Warming Conspiracy Threatens Your Future*. 1st ed. Washington, DC: WND Books.
Jenkins-Smith, Hank, Daniel Nohrstedt, Christopher Weible, and Karin Ingold. 2017. "The Advocacy Coalition Framework: An Overview of the Research Program." In *Theories of the Policy Process*, edited by Christopher Weible and Paul Sabatier, 135–72. New York: Westview Press.
Jones, Michael D., and Mark K. McBeth. 2010. "A Narrative Policy Framework: Clear Enough to Be Wrong?" *Policy Studies Journal* 38 (2): 329–53. https://doi.org/10.1111/j.1541-0072.2010.00364.x.
Jotzo, Frank, Joanna Depledge, and Harald Winkler. 2018. "US and International Climate Policy Under President Trump." *Climate Policy* 18 (7): 813–17.
Karapin, Roger. 2016. *Political Opportunities for Climate Policy: California, New York, and the Federal Government*. Cambridge: Cambridge University Press.

Kincaid, Graciela, and J. Timmons Roberts. 2013. "No Talk, Some Walk: Obama Administration First-Term Rhetoric on Climate Change and US International Climate Budget Commitments." *Global Environmental Politics* 13 (4): 41–60. https://doi.org/10.1162/GLEP_a_00197.

Klein, Ezra. 2020. *Why We're Polarized*. London: Profile Books.

Konisky, David M., and Neal D. Woods. 2018. "Environmental Federalism and the Trump Presidency: A Preliminary Assessment." *Publius: The Journal of Federalism* 48 (3): 345–71. https://doi.org/10.1093/publius/pjy009.

Kramer, Ronald. 2020. "Rolling Back Climate Regulation: Trump's Assault on the Planet." *Journal of White Collar and Corporate Crime* 1 (2): 123–30.

Leggett, Jane. 2019. "Potential Implications of U.S. Withdrawal from the Paris Agreement on Climate Change." Congressional Research Service. https://sgp.fas.org/crs/misc/IF10668.pdf.

Leggett, Jane, and Richard Lattanzio. 2016. "Climate Change: Frequently Asked Questions About the 2015 Paris Agreement." Congressional Research Service. https://sgp.fas.org/crs/misc/R44609.pdf.

Mann, Michael E. 2021. *The New Climate War: The Fight to Take Back Our Planet*. New York: Public Affairs, Hachette.

Mehling, Michael. 2017. "A New Direction for US Climate Policy: Assessing the First 100 Days of Donald Trump's Presidency." *Carbon & Climate Law Review*, no. 1: 3–23.

Mehling, Michael, and Antto Vihma. 2017. "'Mourning for America'. Donald Trump's Climate Change Policy." Finnish Institute of International Affairs. https://www.fiia.fi/wp-content/uploads/2017/10/analysis8_mourning_for_america-2.pdf.

Menon, Anand, and Martin A. Schain. 2006. *Comparative Federalism: The European Union and the United States in Comparative Perspective*. Oxford and New York: Oxford University Press.

Milkoreit, Manjana. 2019. "The Paris Agreement on Climate Change—Made in USA?" *Perspectives on Politics* 17 (4): 1019–37.

Mormann, Felix. 2017. "Constitutional Challenges and Regulatory Opportunities for State Climate Policy Innovation." SSRN Scholarly Paper ID 2928840. Rochester, NY: Social Science Research Network. https://papers.ssrn.com/abstract=2928840.

Parker, Charles F., and Christer Karlsson. 2018. "The UN Climate Change Negotiations and the Role of the United States: Assessing American Leadership from Copenhagen to Paris." *Environmental Politics* 27 (3): 519–40. https://doi.org/10.1080/09644016.2018.1442388.

Pettifor, Ann. 2020. *The Case for the Green New Deal*. London: Verso.

Prakash, Varshini, and Guido Girgenti. 2020. *Winning the Green New Deal: Why We Must, How We Can*. New York: Simon & Schuster.

Rabe, Barry. 2011. "Contested Federalism and American Climate Policy." *Publius: The Journal of Federalism* 41 (3): 494–521.

———. 2018. *Can We Price Carbon?* Cambridge, MA: MIT Press.

Ramseur, Jonathan. 2019. "Market-Based Greenhouse Gas Emission Reduction Legislation: 108th Through 116th Congresses." Congressional Research Service. Washington, DC. https://fas.org/sgp/crs/misc/R45472.pdf.

Resh, William G. 2015. *Rethinking the Administrative Presidency: Trust, Intellectual Capital and Appointee-Careerist Relations in the George W. Bush Administration*. Baltimore, MD: Johns Hopkins University Press.

Richards, Mark J. 2016. "Regulating Automakers for Climate Change: US Reforms in Global Context." *Environmental Policy and Governance* 26 (6): 498–509. https://doi.org/10.1002/eet.1726.

Saad, Lydia. 2017. "Global Warming Concern at Three-Decade High in U.S." Gallup.Com. 2017. https://news.gallup.com/poll/206030/global-warming-concern-three-decade-high.aspx.

———. 2019. "Americans as Concerned as Ever About Global Warming." Gallup.Com. 2019. https://news.gallup.com/poll/248027/americans-concerned-ever-global-warming.aspx.

Sabatier, Paul, and Christopher Weible. 2007. "The Advocacy Coalition Framework. Innovation and Clarifications." In *Theories of the Policy Process*, ed. Paul Sabatier, 189–222. Westview: Westview Press.

Sbragia, Alberta M. 2008. "American Federalism and Intergovernmental Relations." In *The Oxford Handbook of Political Institutions*, edited by Sarah Binder, R. A. W. Rhodes, and Bert Rockman. Oxford and New York: Oxford University Press.

Selby, Jan. 2019. "The Trump Presidency, Climate Change, and the Prospect of a Disorderly Energy Transition." *Review of International Studies* 45 (3): 471–90.

Selin, Henrik, and Stacy D. VanDeveer. 2021. "Climate Change Politics and Policy in the United States: Forward, Reverse and Through the Looking Glass." In *Climate Governance Across the Globe: Pioneers, Leaders and Followers*, edited by Rüdiger Wurzel, Mikael Skou Andersen, and Paul Tobin, 123–41. Abingdon, OX [u.a.]: Routledge.

Shanahan, Elizabeth A., Michael D. Jones, and Mark K. McBeth. 2011. "Policy Narratives and Policy Processes." *Policy Studies Journal* 39 (3): 535–61. https://doi.org/10.1111/j.1541-0072.2011.00420.x.

Sneed, Annie. 2016. "Why Automakers Keep Beating Government Standards." Scientific American. 2016. https://www.scientificamerican.com/article/why-automakers-keep-beating-government-standards/.

Sussman, Glen, and Byron W. Daynes. 2013. *US Politics and Climate Change: Science Confronts Policy*. Boulder, CO [u.a.]: Lynne Rienner Publishers.

Thompson, Frank, Kenneth Wong, and Barry Rabe. 2020. *Trump, the Administrative Presidency, and Federalism*. Washington, DC: Brookings Institution Press.

Tomain, Joseph. 2017. *Clean Power Politics: The Democratization of Energy*. Cambridge: Cambridge University Press.

UNFCCC. 2016. "United States of America, Nationally Determined Contribution (Archived First Version)." https://unfccc.int/sites/default/files/NDC/2022-06/U.S.A.%20First%20NDC%20Submission.pdf.

———. 2021. "United States of America: Nationally Determined Contribution. Reducing Greenhouse Gases in the United States: A 2030 Emissions Target." https://unfccc.int/sites/default/files/NDC/2022-06/United%20States%20NDC%20April%2021%202021%20Final.pdf.

Vandeweerdt, Clara, Bart Kerremans, and Avery Cohn. 2016. "Climate Voting in the US Congress: The Power of Public Concern." *Environmental Politics* 25 (2): 268–88. https://doi.org/10.1080/09644016.2016.1116651.

Vezirgiannidou, Sevasti-Eleni. 2013. "Climate and Energy Policy in the United States: The Battle of Ideas." *Environmental Politics* 22 (4): 593–609. https://doi.org/10.1080/09644016.2013.806632.

Vogel, David. 1995. *Trading Up: Consumer and Environmental Regulation in a Global Economy*. Cambridge, MA [u.a.]: Harvard University Press.

Vogel, David, and Johan F. M. Swinnen, eds. 2011. *Transatlantic Regulatory Cooperation: The Shifting Roles of the EU, the US and California*. Cheltenham and Northampton, MA: Edward Elgar.

Weathers, Melinda R., and Brenden E. Kendall. 2016. "Developments in the Framing of Climate Change as a Public Health Issue in US Newspapers." *Environmental Communication* 10 (5): 593–611. https://doi.org/10.1080/17524032.2015.1050436.

Weibust, Inger, and James Meadowcroft, eds. 2014. *Multilevel Environmental Governance: Managing Water and Climate Change in Europe and North America*. Cheltenham: Edward Elgar.

White House. 2013. "Remarks by the President on Climate Change, Georgetown University." Whitehouse.Gov. 2013. https://obamawhitehouse.archives.gov/the-press-office/2013/06/25/remarks-president-climate-change.

———. 2014a. "Remarks by the President at U.N. Climate Change Summit." Whitehouse.Gov. 2014a. https://obamawhitehouse.archives.gov/the-press-office/2014a/09/23/remarks-president-un-climate-change-summit.

———. 2014b. "U.S.-China Joint Announcement on Climate Change." https://obamawhitehouse.archives.gov/the-press-office/2014b/11/11/us-china-joint-announcement-climate-change.

———. 2017. "Statement by President Trump on the Paris Climate Accord—The White House." 2017. https://trumpwhitehouse.archives.gov/briefings-statements/statement-president-trump-paris-climate-accord/.

———. 2021. "President Biden's Bipartisan Infrastructure Law." Washington, DC. https://www.whitehouse.gov/bipartisan-infrastructure-law/.

———. 2015a. "Remarks by President Obama at the First Session of COP21." Whitehouse.Gov. 2015a. https://obamawhitehouse.archives.gov/the-press-office/2015a/11/30/remarks-president-obama-first-session-cop21.

———. 2015b. "Remarks by the President in Announcing the Clean Power Plan." https://obamawhitehouse.archives.gov/the-press-office/2015b/08/03/remarks-president-announcing-clean-power-plan.

———. 2015c. "Statement by the President on the Paris Climate Agreement." Whitehouse.Gov. 2015c. https://obamawhitehouse.archives.gov/the-press-office/2015c/12/12/statement-president-paris-climate-agreement.

Ye, Jason. 2014. "Comparison of Carbon Pricing Proposals in the 113th Congress." Center for Climate and Energy Solutions, Washington, DC. https://www.c2es.org/wp-content/uploads/2014/12/113th-congress-carbon-pricing-proposals.pdf.

———. 2018. "Carbon Pricing Proposals in the 115th Congress." Center for Climate and Energy Solutions, Washington, DC. https://www.c2es.org/wp-content/uploads/2018/10/comparison-of-carbon-pricing-proposals-in-the-115th-congress.pdf.

———. 2020. "Carbon Pricing Proposals in the 116th Congress." Center for Climate and Energy Solutions, Washington, DC. https://www.c2es.org/wp-content/uploads/2020/09/carbon-pricing-proposals-in-the-116th-congress.pdf.

Zevin, Avi. 2018. "Current Developments: North America." *Carbon & Climate Law Review*, no. 3: 274–77.

———. 2019. "Current Developments: North America." *Carbon & Climate Law Review* 3: 223–27.

Zhang, Yong-Xiang, Qing-Chen Chao, Qiu-Hong Zheng, and Huang Lei. 2017. "The Withdrawal of the U.S. from the Paris Agreement and Its Impact on Global Climate Change Governance." *Advances in Climate Change Research*, no. 8: 213–19.

Zhou, Jack. 2016. "Boomerangs Versus Javelins: How Polarization Constrains Communication on Climate Change." *Environmental Politics* 25 (5): 788–811. https://doi.org/10.1080/09644016.2016.1166602.

CHAPTER 5

Comparative Analysis: Framing Climate Change Discourse in the EU and the US

The two previous case studies were presented in a mostly qualitative form, aimed at understanding key stages and issues of climate change governance in the EU and US since the conclusion of the Paris Agreement. This chapter turns towards a quantitative comparison of data from these cases and the scrutiny of comparative hypotheses. As discussed in the theoretical chapter, our analysis harnesses the concept of political space to evaluate comparative assumptions about three related aspects of framing and resulting issue dimensions: namely, the structure, linkages and contestation of frames in climate discourse. This approach was presented in detail in the previous theoretical chapter and will be briefly re-summarized in the next Sect. (5.1). The following sections go through three stages of analysis, starting by mapping the structure of discourse concerning the six climate frames and proceeding to the discussion of their linkages and contestation (5.2–5.4). Our main findings are then summarized in a discussion (5.5) and conclusion (5.6).

© The Author(s), under exclusive license to Springer Nature Switzerland AG 2022
F. Wendler, *Framing Climate Change in the EU and US After the Paris Agreement*, Palgrave Studies in European Union Politics, https://doi.org/10.1007/978-3-031-04059-7_5

5.1 Political Space of Climate Politics: Issue Categories, Linkages and Contestation

The concept of political space is generally used to capture the emergence and interrelation of several salient issue dimensions, defined as relatively stable structuring logics of political competition and conflict in a given political system (cp. Benoit and Laver 2012; Gabel and Hix 2002; Hoeglinger 2016: 23ff.; Kriesi et al. 2012: 96ff.). As discussed in the theoretical chapter, three main components are needed to unpack and explore these issue dimensions: namely, categories of related topics and issues that are raised in political debate; relevant ideological ideas or principles that are used to address these issues and their linkages to one another; and the intensity and form of their contestation between different involved political agents (cp. Albright 2010; Helbling et al. 2010; Arbour 2014). Aiming at exploring and comparing the political space of climate politics in the EU and the US, the subsequent analysis therefore seeks to evaluate three interrelated aspects of discourse about climate change: first, the *structure of framing* and resulting issue categories covering problem definitions of climate change, the evaluation of policy, and approaches to collective action, and measured both on the aggregate level and for specific subsets of the policy debate; second, *linkages between frames* and identifiable profiles of discourse resulting from these linkages for different settings and agents; and finally, the *form and intensity of contestation* between political agents as resulting from two different forms of controversy: namely, the promotion of contrasting frames to address climate change, captured here as paradigmatic polarization; and controversy arising from dissenting views within the same respective frames, considered here as discursive contestation. These two related aspects are mirrored in the literature on party politics in salience theory and mapping of party positions (Wardt 2015; Helbling and Tresch 2011; Dolezal et al. 2014; Budge 2015). These three components of issue dimensions are then to be summarized under the conceptual framework of political space. The central assumption of the comparative discussion is that the political space of climate politics is more fragmented and volatile in the US than the EU case, leading to the following three sets of hypotheses to be scrutinized in the subsequent discussion:

(1) Concerning the structure of climate frames, we evaluate the hypothesis that climate discourse is more single-dimensional in the EU by focusing on a more clearly defined and simple choice of frames and issue categories (H1a), and that the structure of framing is more coherent across different institutional settings and agents than in the US (H1b);
(2) Turning to linkages of frames in political discourse, we evaluate the assumption that climate discourse in the EU is more inclusive towards different perspectives by including broader linkages between frames (H2a) that are more coherent in a comparison between institutional settings and involved political agents (H2b);
(3) Finally, we scrutinze the assumption that contestation of climate change discourse in the US is stronger, both in the form of greater divergence between promoted frames and paradigmatic polarization (H3a), and involving stronger controversy through the advocacy of competing ideas within the same frames or discursive contestation (H3b).

As mentioned above, these three pairs of hypotheses are arranged in a sequence of analytical steps to zoom in from a global survey of climate discourse to a more specific focus on linkages and contestation of discourse between political agents.

5.2 Structure of Framing and Issue Categories of Climate Change Discourse

In order to map the structure of climate change discourse, our first step is to identify rank orders of the six climate frames as measured by the relative frequency of their occurrence in the empirical material. At this stage, the data is evaluated in relation to each individual frame and independently of the three issue categories discussed in the theoretical chapter. The table below lists the frames in descending order of their relative weight as measured through the number of times they were coded. In addition, the list specifies the cumulative percentage of the most frequently coded frames as a measurement for their combined proportional share of all coded statements, indicating the share of codes comprised in the combination of the first and second, then the first, second and third most frequent frame, and so on. This approach allows us to identify those combinations of frames covering a majority of coded statements in the empirical material; it also provides insights into the degree of concentration of discourse on only the most frequently used frames, both in comparison between and within particular subsets of the two cases compared. The table lists results for the EU and US on the aggregate level but also with regard to more specific subsets: Both surveys distinguish between executive and legislative discourse and include further specifications about subsets of discourse within these two branches. This means that data is compared between Republican versus Democratic agents in the US case and distinguises resolutions adopted by the plenary of the EP and party group motions on the European Green Deal in the EU case (Tables 5.1 and 5.2).

Contrary to our first hypothesis, the data does not confirm a more single-dimensional or selective use of frames in climate discourse of the EU. In fact, some broad similarities in the structure of framing are observed between both compared cases. A common observation for both EU and US is that particularly two frames—namely, those based on political support and justice—are relatively marginal in terms of their relative frequency; by contrast, particularly one approach of framing climate policy—namely, in terms of economic criteria—is identified as highly salient and frequently used in both cases. On a secondary level, particulary the society-based frame is also relevant for climate debates in both cases and identified as the third most relevant framing of climate change on the aggregate level.

Broadly similar structures of framing can also be identified with regard to the three main issue categories of climate change discussed at the outset. In a second step, we scrutinize a survey of the relative weight of these categories by combining the risk and ecology frame in a problem identification category, the economy and justice frame as both related to policy evaluation, and the political and society frame in the collective action category. This survey demonstrates that about a third of coded statements occurs in each of the three dimensions, indicating a relatively even spread of statements across each category with little evident difference between the EU and US debate at the aggregate level. Based on these insights, the first hypothesis concerning the overall structure of framing and relative weight of most salient frames (H1a) finds no sufficient support in the data (Tables 5.3 and 5.4).

Beyond these similarities at the aggregate level, considerable differences between the two cases emerge in a closer comparison of framing

Table 5.1 Rank order of frames with cumulative percentages in EU policy discourse on climate change

Rank order	Executive-Council	Executive-COM	EP plenary	EP motions on EGD	ALL
1st	Political (35.0)	Economic (30.4)	Society (23.6)	Ecology (33.7)	Ecology (23.8)
2nd	Risk (51.0)	Ecology (54.1)	Economic (46.9)	Economy (55.1)	Economic (47.0)
3rd	Ecology (65.1)	Society (74.8)	Ecology (65.0)	Society (71.7)	Society (66.9)
4th	Economic (77.7)	Political (86.8)	Political (82.0)	Political (86.2)	Political (83.6)
5th	Society (89.8)	Risk (95.0)	Risk (91.7)	Justice (95.5)	Risk (91.8)
6th	Justice (100)	Justice (100)	Justice (100)	Risk (100)	Justice (100)

Table 5.2 Rank order of frames with cumulative percentages in US policy discourse on climate change

Rank order	Executive-Obama	Executive-Trump	Legislative-Democrat	Legislative-Republican	ALL
1st	Risk (36.8)	Economic (37.0)	Economic (30.3)	Economic (50.7)	Economic (28.0)
2nd	Society (58.6)	Society (59.5)	Justice (45.9)	Society (68.1)	Risk (46.7)
3rd	Ecology (73.4)	Ecology (79.6)	Society (61.0)	Risk (78.8)	Society (65.0)
4th	Economic (86.8)	Political (92.2)	Ecology (74.6)	Political (87.4)	Ecology (79.3)
5th	Political (96.9)	Risk (96.3)	Risk (87.5)	Ecology (95.0)	Political (90.8)
6th	Justice (100)	Justice (100)	Political (100)	Justice (100)	Justice (100)

Table 5.3 Issue categories in climate policy discourse in the EU

	Executive-Council	Executive-COM	Legislative-EP Plenary	Legislative-EP PGMs	ALL
Problem definition	30.1	31.9	27.8	38.1	32.0
Policy evaluation	22.7	35.5	31.6	30.7	31.3
Collective action	47.1	32.7	40.6	31.1	36.6

Table 5.4 Issue categories in climate policy discourse of the US

	Executive-Obama	Executive-Trump	Legislative-Democrat	Legislative-Republican	ALL
Problem definition	51.6	24.2	26.5	18.3	33.0
Policy evaluation	16.6	40.7	45.9	55.7	37.4
Collective action	31.9	35.1	27.6	26.0	29.8

variants across different institutional settings and agents. This point involves mainly two aspects: First, emphases laid on each of the three issue categories in comparison of different legislative and executive agents; and second, the specific combinations of frames chosen within these issue dimensions, especially between Republican and Democratic policy-makers in the US case.

In the case of the EU, the combination of three dominant frames—namely, those based economic criteria, ecological principles and society—comprise about two thirds of coded statements across all subsets of discourse, with a different structure of frames adopted only by the European Council. In this context, it is not surprising that the brief conclusions adopted here, which are mostly limited to summarizing key political priorities and targets, primarily use a political framing and therefore deviate from policy discourse of other EU institutions. However, both policy documents launched by the European Commission and legislative motions and resolutions adopted by the European Parliament are relatively coherent in promoting an economic framing of climate action, combined with references to ecological principles and aspects of policy implementation at the level of society. In relation to this dominant set of frames, particularly aspects of risk and climate justice move to the background.

In comparison, greater variation of framing can be identified in the US debate. Here, only legislative proposals by Republicans within both chambers of Congress, and discourse on climate and energy by the Trump administration take a similar approach to framing climate change policy. In both cases, a strong emphasis on economic criteria is combined with frequent references to society, particulary with regard to effects of policy at the local level and impacts on workers and communities. The relative coherence of Republican discourse, however, contrasts with the more diverse forms of framing used by Democratic policy-makers. Here, a strong emphasis on questions of risk posed by climate change and its effects on society by the Obama administration contrasts with a promotion of economic and justice criteria in legislative proposals by Democrats; this latter aspect is rooted in the numerous proposals for carbon pricing and subsequent use of revenues for transition funds and against social inequality promoted by Democrats in Congress. Discourse on climate change by Republicans and Democrats therefore differs in two significant ways: First, the Republican variant relies on economic criteria and societal effects of climate policy more strongly than its Democratic counterpart; and second, its overall coherence concerning the choice of these frames is greater than policy discourse by Democrats, whose framing varies between an emphasis on risk, economic criteria, justice and ecology.

The greater degree of variation in the climate policy debate of the US is also demonstrated in a survey of the three main issue categories distinguished at the outset. Only one of these categories—namely, the one envisaging political action based on political and societal framing—shows little variation in a comparison between subsets of discourse in both cases (with a range between the lowest and highest value of 9.1 percentage points in the US and 16 percent in the EU case). Greater contrasts occur within the issue category of problem definition, contrasting discourse with very low emphasis by Republican legislators with a presence of frames of this issue category in just over half of coded statements of the Obama administration. Mirroring this variation, the policy evaluation dimension is strongly emphasized by Republican legislators particularly in comparison to the Obama administration (creating a range of 39.1 percentage points in comparison to 12.8 in the EU). This data provides support for our hypothesis that a relatively more coherent and stable framing in the EU contrasts with a more variegated and volatile discourse on climate change in the US (H1b). This prompts the question how political agents position themselves in the debate, both through linkages and the contestation of frames, as covered in the two following sections.

5.3 Linkages Between Frames: Profiles of Climate Change Discourse

The previous case study chapters have cast a light on linkages of frames as an intermediate step between the mapping of discourse and contestation between agents. Here, we move closer to a comparative assessment of their weight and density, in order to test the assumption that discourse in the US involves more clearly profiled variants of discourse that contrast more strongly in a comparison of different subsets of the policy debate.

The first analytical task is to identify what combinations of frames are most frequently found in the data, as measured through the proximity of their respective coding by the content analysis software: here, frames are identified as having a linkage to each other when they are frequently coded in overlapping text segments within a given policy document. Using the software function to calculate the relative proximity of codes and resulting clusters, the table below presents a survey of the strongest two-, three- and four-point clusters of frames for both cases and all subsets of discourse compared. The list includes a scope indicator specifying the relative proportion of statements covered by these clusters in relation to all coded statements. This means that a three-point cluster of frames with a scope indicator of 0.6 consists of three frames that taken together comprise 60 percent of all coded statements for a specific case or subset of discourse. In comparative perspective, a higher value therefore indicates a more profiled variant of discourse focused on a narrow selection of interlinked frames, whereas a lower value identifies a broader framing of discourse that includes a wider combination of frames. This scope indicator measures what has been discussed as the weight of linkages between frames: How much of a specific subset of data is covered by strongly related frames (Tables 5.5 and 5.6).

As in the first stage of analysis, a review of this data reveals some broad similarities between the EU and US. An intriguing insight is that the most frequently used frame of each subset is almost universally combined

Table 5.5 Composition, scope and density of linkages between frames in policy discourse of the EU

	Executive-EU Council	Executive-EU COM	Legislative-EP Plenary	Legislative-EP PGs	ALL in EU case study
Composition of linkage (2-, 3-, 4-point cluster)	Political Society Ecology Risk	Economic Society Ecology Political	Ecology Political Society Economic	Ecology Political Society Economic	Ecology Society Political Economic
Scope of linkages (2-, 3-, 4- point cluster)	0.45 0.60 0.76	0.47 0.70 0.85	0.38 0.59 0.80	0.47 0.65 0.86	0.42 0.60 0.82
Density of linkages (2-, 3-, 4-point cluster)	0.11 0.29 0.55	0.13 0.41 0.62	0.09 0.27 0.55	0.13 0.33 0.66	0.11 0.29 0.59

Table 5.6 Composition, scope and density of linkages between frames in policy discourse of the US

	Executive-Obama	Executive-Trump	Legislative-Democrat	Legislative-Republican	ALL in US case study
Composition of linkage (2-, 3-, 4-point cluster)	Risk Society Economic Ecology	Economic Society Ecology Political	Economic Society Justice Risk	Economic Society Political Risk	Economic Society Risk Ecology
Scope of linkages (2-, 3-, 4- point cluster)	0.53 0.70 0.88	0.56 0.76 0.91	0.45 0.62 0.73	0.67 0.75 0.86	0.47 0.62 0.78
Density of linkages (2-, 3-, 4-point cluster)	0.23 0.42 0.71	0.31 0.54 0.72	0.11 0.28 0.50	0.26 0.46 0.70	0.13 0.33 0.62

with one of the collective action frames as a secondary, related frame. While the choice of the dominant frame depends on the specific subset of discourse and relates to both the problem definition and policy evaluation categories in our data, it is almost always linked primarily with a political or societal frame to make the case for action for or against climate policy. In this context, the only outlier of this logic is the communication by the European Council, where the combination between both frames of the collective action dimension (i.e., the political and societal frame) is the most frequent; to reiterate, however, this point seems to reflect its institutional role as proclaiming and authorizing targets and steps of political action rather than rationalizing details of policy-making. On a more general level, this point indicates that the collective action frames are mostly absorbed in different variants of framing climate change within the other two categories; therefore, it does not emerge as an independent set of frames identified as distinctive for particular subsets of discourse or actor positions. By contrast, the frames that were identified as generally most relevant for defining the problem and policy categories—namely, the ecology, risk and economic frame—emerge as more independent from each other and are only rarely combined with the second frame of their respective category. These frames therefore can be identified as those that are most relevant for distinguishing profiles of discourse raised by different agents and are therefore highlighted as relevant isssue dimensions of climate politics.

Turning to comparison, the data confirms that climate debate in the US tends to be more focused on a combination of just two relatively strong frames with a wide scope for the respective policy discourse. On the aggregate level, the two most frequently related economic and societal frames comprise almost half of all coded statements. In comparison, the EU case has a lower relative share of the two most strongly associated frames relating to ecology and society. As shown in the overview, this observation holds across all the subsegments of climate change discourse compared in both case studies.

Concerning observable variation within cases, even clearer differences emerge between the EU and US case, where more outlier cases of highly selective framing and generally a greater degree of variation are identified. Scope indicators for the US stand at a higher level but also show greater degrees of variation: While the scope of the most closely associated frames varies only slightly in the EU case (between 0.38 and 0.45), a broader range of this value is observed in the US case (namely, between 0.45 and 0.67). In this context, particularly discourse of both US presidential administrations is more selectively framed, combining the risk and society framing during the Obama administration, and putting strong emphasis on economy and society frames during the Trump presidency. In a comparison of all subsets of discourse within both cases, the most strongly profiled variant of discourse is promoted by Congress Republicans. In this particular subset, the association of an economic and societal framing comprises over two thirds of all coded statements. The same observations apply to a comparison of the strongest three-frame clusters, both for the EU and for the US debate as a whole and their respective subsegments. Overall three quarters of coded statements by Republicans are covered by their three most frequently combined economic, society and political frames. This contrasts with a lower overall weight of the three most frequently linked frames in discourse of Democratic legislators (0.61), where the economic, society and justice frames are most commonly related. These observations confirm stronger and more contrasting profiles of discourse in the US than the EU policy debate, confirming our hypothesis (H2a).

While this first step informs us about rank orders of linkages between frames and helps to identify emerging issue dimensions, it does not tell us anything about the relative concentration of their linkages, or how strongly profiled primary linkages are in relation to secondary and tertiary links. In a second step, we scrutinize the density of linkages between frames, as measured by the number of linkages between two or more associated frames in relation to all linkages identified by the content analysis software. To reiterate, a linkage between two or more frames is created when a text segment was coded simultaneously with these frames. Based on this count, this approach separates the 'internal' connections within a cluster of frames (i.e., the number of times the frames involved in a cluster were coded together) in relation to all other linkages identified within the scope of analysis. The resulting ratio of internal versus all identified linkages is expressed as a value between 0 and 1. This means that higher values of this density indicator indicate a more focused and selective form of framing, while broader linkages of frames score lower values on this indicator.[1]

---

[1] One apparent contrast between this and the previous set of data points is the relative number of coded text comprised in the first and subsequent layers of clusters: Considering only the strongest two-point cluster, only a relatively small subset of coded statements is covered, whereas this figure rises very quickly with the transition to the strongest two- and three-point cluster. This effect, however, is created through the relative proportion of potential links between pairs and clusters considered here: Whereas only one possible connection can be created between two frames, this number rises exponentially when more frames are added to a cluster, creating three connections in a cluster of three and

The results confirm that primary links between frames (i.e., those that are most frequently coded in combination with each other) also tend to have greater density than other possible combinations of frames. In a comparative perspective, the survey also shows that on the aggregate level, the density of the strongest two-point clusters is slightly higher in the US (0.13) than in the EU case (0.11).

A more relevant finding in this context is, however, that the US case includes much higher peaks of linkage densities in certain segments of discourse than in any subset of discourse in the EU case. As in the previous step, data for the US includes relatively stronger degrees of variation, with a range of the density indicator between 0.13 and 0.31 for two-point clusters, as compared to 0.09 and 0.13 in the EU. In this context, particularly the framing of climate change by Republicans, both in their role as sponsors of legislative proposals in Congress and in the Trump presidential administration, reaches the highest density through the combination of an economic and societal frame. Here, the indicator reaches values of 0.31 for the Trump administration and 0.26 for Republican-sponsored legislative proposals. These values contrast with lower density scores across all EU institutions.

To summarize, evaluating the linkages between frames in climate change discourse of the EU and US leads to three main findings. First, a major commonality identified between both cases is that linkages between frames are almost universally established by combining a highly salient, dominant frame related to the problem evaluation or policy category, and one of the frames of the collective action category. Frames used in the problem identification or policy category are therefore more distinctive of different variants of discourse within the different subsets of climate discourse compared here. References to society or political frameworks, by contrast, do not appear to establish an independent issue category.

Second, the data surveyed here lends support to our hypothesis that discourse on climate change in the US is more profiled by including stronger linkages between only a few relatively salient frames (H2a). In this sense, it was demonstrated that the most closely related frames cover broader portions of text within the empirical data, and have a higher density of internal linkages than in the EU case study.

---

six in a combination of four. At the level of primary frames, a single linkage stands in comparison with fifteen other possible linkages in a distinction of six frames.

Finally, even stronger support is found for our second hypothesis expecting a greater degree of variation concerning the density of linkages of frames between different subsets of discourse in both cases compared (H2b). In this sense, the US case includes more extreme outlier values, particularly through the highly selective and dense framing of climate issues through an economic and societal frame by Congress Republicans and the Trump administration. The peak values for the weight and density of frame linkages observed here is higher than any comparable value in the EU case and also far above those observed in relation to Democratic law-makers. Linkages of frames are denser and also more asymmetrical in the US debate on climate change than in policy discourse of the EU.

5.4 Contestation of Frames and Polarization of Discourse

In this third and final step, we evaluate the contestation of climate change from a dual perspective of framing analysis: Namely, to what degree controversy emerges from the promotion of divergent variants of framing, subsequently described as paradigmatic polarization; and in how far it evolves through controversy between terms and concepts promoted within the same respective frames and labeled as discursive contestation (for a discussion of polarization as a result of issue emphasis versus discursive contestation, cp. Lefevere et al. 2019; Snow 2004; Elias et al. 2015; Arbour 2014, on emerging partisan polarization over the Green New Deal, cp. Gustafson et al. 2019).

First, we turn to evaluating polarization resulting from the advocacy of different frames and particularly their underlying paradigms. In order to identify how this form of polarization emerges within different subsets of discourse, we combine data on the relative salience of frames with an additional indicator for what is subsequently discussed as their paradigmatic weight: namely, a measurement for whether a frame is defined through terms at a very high or lower level of generality, reaching from paradigmatic to programmatic and more specific, policy-related concepts. This point integrates an aspect of the theoretical discussion positing that terms with a broader scope (i.e., paradigmatic terms) are more fundamental and carry a greater weight with regard to political contestation and polarization than more specific terms and concepts. The indicator used for the subsequent evaluation is therefore constructed in a way that combines the salience and paradigmatic weight of frames, seeking to identify what contrasts are created through different variants of framing that are both emphasized strongly and specified in relatively fundamental, ideologically defined terms.[2] This indicator, subsequently referred to as a measurement for paradigmatic salience, reaches higher values when a subset of discourse includes frequent references to the paradigmatic keywords of a particular frame, such as growth, solidarity or sovereignty. Variation in this indicator between different agents or subsets of discourse is evaluated as an instance of paradigmatic polarization: Namely, a form of divergence between variants of discourse that establish different terms with fundamental meaning in the debate, either by varying in the frequency of references to frames or by the use of either very general or more policy-specific terms. The table below presents a survey of this indicator for each of the six climate frames and various subsets of discourse throughout this analysis. The values entered into each cell are the product of values for salience and paradigmatic weight, returning an indicator increasing both with frequent uses of a frame and emphases on paradigmatic terms (Figs. 5.1 and 5.2).

On the aggregate level, the data confirms our previous findings about the most salient frames in climate discourse of both cases: Namely, an economic, ecology and societal framing in the EU case, and an economic, risk, ecology and society framing in the US case, as measured by the rank order of the paradigmatic salience indicator. Once more, this finding particularly confirms the central relevance of an economic framing in combination with a collective action frame for climate policy debates of both cases. From this point of departure, however, the data also confirms a greater variation in the US case, suggesting more divergence concerning what aspects of global warming are emphasized in paradigmatic terms in political discourse.

---

[2] This indicator is constructed from two components: on the one hand, the relative frequency of codes for a given frame as a fraction of 1 in relation to all other frames (e.g., resulting 0.2 if a particular frame has been coded 20 out of 100 times); and on the other, an indicator measuring the relative weight of paradigmatic forms of framing in relation to the program and policy level, again measured as a fraction of 1. This second indicator is created by subtracting the full relative number of policy-level references and half the relative number of program-level references from the value of 1 (e.g., returning a result of 0.6 in a case of 20 percent policy-level and 40 percent program-level framing). Calculated as the product of indicators for salience and weight, the measurement of paradigmatic salience varies between 1 and 0 and reaches higher values when applied to a discourse that makes frequent reference to paradigmatic keywords.

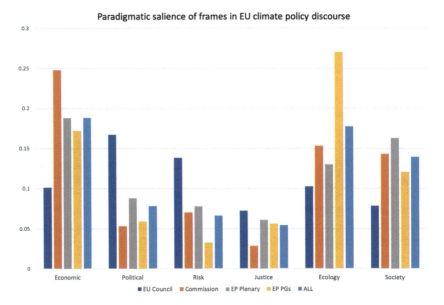

Fig. 5.1 Paradigmatic salience of frames in climate policy discourse of the EU

This finding is confirmed particularly with regard to economic frames as the most salient variant of justification across all cases. Considering the EU, especially the Commission can be identified as the discursive leader within this frame, with the EP and particularly the European Council scoring lower in terms of paradigmatic salience. However, the range of this value in the EU (0.101–0.248) is lower than in the US case, where a stronger contrast is created between the relatively low salience of economic arguments by Democratic policy-makers (0.110–0.118) and the stronger paradigmatic salience assigned to this frame by the Trump administration and Congress Republicans (0.300 and 0.364, respectively). By contrast, framing climate change in terms of risk has far higher paradigmatic salience with Democratic legislators and the Obama administration (0.120 and 0.242) than in discourse by Republican members of Congress and especially the discourse of the Trump administration (0.091 and 0.038). In terms of paradigmatic salience, a clear contrast is therefore created between a primarily economic framing by Republicans and a strong emphasis on risk by Democrats; the ecology frame is less of a distinguishing feature between both camps particularly through

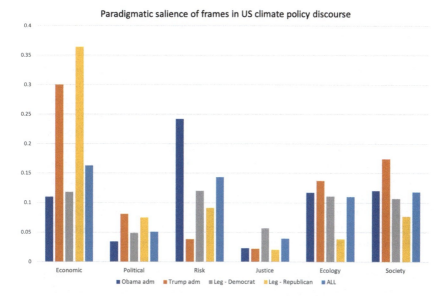

Fig. 5.2 Paradigmatic salience of frames in climate policy discourse of the US

the appropriation of environmental arguments in discourse by the Trump administration. Equally, an ecological framing does not create a clear contrast between political roles of the EU institutions, even if the salience value for EP motions on the European Green Deal create an outlier. The society frame is promoted more strongly by executive agents across the board in the US case but also does not emerge as the source of clear paradigmatic polarization between institutions or political agents in both cases. In a general survey of both cases, however, polarization between frames and their paradigmatic emphasis is observed at higher levels in the US case and particularly concerns the economic and risk-based framing of climate change.

In a second step, we now turn to a closer analysis of the main focal points of discursive polarization: How competing political agents attach different meanings to the same framing of climate change by using different key terms. To establish a first impression of how the six climate frames compared in this analysis are contested by policy-makers, the two tables below lists the five most frequent keywords coded for each of these frames, again specified for analysis on the aggregate level and subsets of debate (Tables 5.7 and 5.8).

This survey of keyword rank orders creates many qualitative insights about how different forms of framing climate change are promoted and contested in both cases. It is evident from a first glance that particularly the economic framing of climate policy in the EU diverges from the one found in the US: A relatively homogenous set of positive terms is used in the EU case promoting ideas related to investment, markets, efficiency and the circular economy; this contrasts with discourse in the US, where emphases on more critical terms such jobs, coal and natural gas are promoted by Republican policy-makers and compete with terms used by Democrats emphasizing carbon pricing within legislative proposals. Similar observations can be made in the political or ecology frame, where key terms used in the debate to promote a particular frame are relatively similar across institutional settings in the EU but differ more strongly in the US case. An important example is the contrast between Republicans' critical assessment of the UN framework of climate governance, and terms promoting climate action and cooperation from the Obama administration.

In order to go beyond the qualitative discussion of keywords and to establish a coherent quantitative foundation for comparing their similarity, a specific indicator is applied that is calculated from the smallest sum of standardized proportional frequencies of shared keywords within a given comparison of two or more lists of keyword rank orders[3]. This 'similarity indicator' can vary between 0 in the case of no overlap between the

---

[3] More specifically, the construction and evaluation of this similarity indicator proceeds in three steps. First, the absolute number of occurrences of each keyword within the five most frequent keywords of each climate frame is standardized to represent a proportion of 1 (e.g., 0.2 for a particular keyword to have been coded 40 times within a overall set of 200 most frequent keywords); second, sets of two or more lists of most frequent keywords are compared by identifying those keywords that are common in both or all lists, with a possible variation between zero and five; and finally, for each keyword shared between two or more lists, the smallest value for the occurrence of this keyword is identified from a comparison of rank order lists and summarized with other least values in case several shared keywords are found (e.g., if the keyword 'investment' is identified as common between two lists with values of 0.4 and 0.2, the smaller value is deducted as the proportion used within both subsets of discourse). Using this approach, we therefore identify the relative proportion of shared proportions of keywords that are found across two or more lists of rank order keywords, and therefore an indicator for their relative degree of similarity.

Table 5.7 Keyword rankings for six climate frames in EU policy discourse; keywords were partly abbreviated for reasons of space; full list of keywords can be found in the annex

	Executive-EU Counil	Executive-EU Com	Legislative-EP Plenary	Legislative-EP Pty Grps	ALL
Economic: Keywords	investment 18 market 18 energy effcy 9 energy market 8 cl neutral 7 ALL: 77	investment 150 market 63 energy effcy 37 industry 36 circular ecmy 33 ALL: 428	market 183 investment 176 energy effcy 102 industry 67 comptvss 46 ALL: 786	investment 145 market 104 industry 51 circular ecmy 47 climt neutral 43 ALL: 545	investment 489 market 368 energy effcy 180 industry 158 circular ecmy 107 ALL: 1836
Political: Keywords	Implement'n 57 climate action 37 cl diplomcy 29 agenda 24 counc conclsn 19 ALL: 213	clm actn 30 implementn 22 agenda 20 action plan 16 climt diplmcy 12 ALL: 169	implementn 106 climate action 99 agenda 50 climt diplmcy 49 legtive 31 ALL: 573	implementn 66 legislative 64 climate action 33 action plan 33 agenda 29 ALL: 369	implement'n 205 climate action 199 agenda 123 legislative 107 climate diplmcy 94 ALL: 1324
Risk: Keywords	security 38 risk 25 cl resilient 7 effects of cl 5 food security 4 ALL: 98	risk 45 security 20 cl resilient 8 capcty bldg 8 effects of cl 5 ALL: 115	security 120 risk 64 effects of cl 23 public health 18 impacts of cl 15 ALL: 328	risk 44 security 22 food secty 6 adptn to climt 5 climte proofing 5 ALL: 112	security 200 risk 178 effects of climt 36 public health 23 adaptn to climt 21 ALL: 653
Justice: Keywords	cl finance 18 poverty 5 gender 5 women 5 dev'ment goal 4 ALL: 62	cl finance 15 just transition 10 devpmnt goal 8 poverty 7 solidarity 5 ALL: 71	poverty 36 gender 29 just transition 26 women 26 climt fince 23 ALL: 277	just transition 69 poverty 25 gender 24 responsibility 16 energy povty 15 ALL: 238	just transition 108 poverty 73 gender 58 climt finance 56 responsibility 43 ALL: 648

(continued)

Table 5.7 (continued)

	Executive-EU Counil	Executive-EU Com	Legislative-EP Plenary	Legislative-EP Pty Grps	ALL
Ecology: Keywords	temperature 17	environmntl 72	environmntl 106	environmntl 219	environmntl 410
	sust'ble devpt 14	biodiversity 36	biodiversity 80	biodiversity 199	biodiversity 318
	environm'tl 13	zero greenhs 29	sustainbl dev 59	pollution 79	sustainbl dev 138
	water 11	land use 27	temptre 55	ecosystem 65	water 136
	glob warming 9	sustainbl dev 24	water 50	water 51	ecosystem 130
	ALL: 86	ALL: 332	ALL: 606	ALL: 857	ALL: 1881
Society: Keywords	city 19	city 52	region 216	region 86	region 359
	private 12	region 46	city 114	citizen 51	city 222
	region 11	citizen 44	local 103	local 46	local 180
	local 7	culture 33	citizen 71	culture 46	citizen 169
	civil society 6	private 31	urban 60	people 44	private 133
	ALL: 73	ALL: 288	ALL: 787	ALL: 418	ALL: 1566

five most frequent keywords of compared rank order lists, and 1 in case of a complete match between the five keywords listed and their relative frequency in the data. Based on this measurement, a value of 0.5 or higher can be taken as an indication of a very high degree of similarity between two or more lists of keywords. Further below, we present a survey of this indicator for both cases on an aggregate level and for the subsets of discourse distinguished throughout this analysis (Tables 5.9 and 5.10).

This survey of similarity indicators for keywords promoted in each of the frames generally supports, but also differentiates the observation of a greater degree of homogenity of climate discourse in the EU in comparison to the US. On an aggregate level, the indicator is significantly higher in the US than the EU for five of the six climate frames compared, with the ecology frame standing out as the notable exception. The presence of a coherent set of frequently coded keywords, considered here as a sign of relative discursive agreement between interacting agents, varies strongly between the six frames distinguished.

This systematization of data creates a distinction between frames whose discursive contestation differs clearly between the EU and US, and those where the divergence of keywords is similar. In this sense, the six frames fall into three groups: First, both the economic and political frames can be

Table 5.8 Keyword rankings for six climate frames in US policy discourse; keywords were partly abbreviated for reasons of space; full list of keywords can be found in the annex

	Executive-Obama	Executive-Trump	Legislative-Democrat	Legislative-Republican	ALL
Economic: Keywords	investment 51 economic 50 jobs 29 technology 26 energy effcy 21 ALL: 233	jobs 98 economic 53 coal 43 natural gas 33 growth 20 ALL: 290	carbon fee 163 carbon permit 97 coal 95 natural gas 76 economic 75 ALL: 848	industrial 106 coal 58 natural gas 29 economic 26 trade intensity 24 ALL: 265	coal 216 economic 204 carbon fee 163 jobs 160 natural gas 155 ALL: 1636
Political: Keywords	action plan 66 climate action 60 cooperation 19 protectn agcy 17 global leader 4 ALL: 176	great job 41 amrcn energy 38 protectn agcy 8 legislative 4 action plan 2 ALL: 99	taxable carbn 92 carbon border 49 border fee 45 protectn agcy 44 reductn target 29 ALL: 350	framewk cnvtn 19 un framewk 13 protectn agcy 6 glb efft 6 global leader 1 ALL: 45	taxable carbon 92 protectn agcy 75 action plan 68 climate action 64 carbon border 49 ALL: 670
Risk: Keywords	risk 149 resilience 119 health 72 nationl secrty 71 homeland sec 37 ALL: 641	health 15 nationl secrty 7 risk 6 resilience 1 crit infrstr 1 ALL: 32	health 178 risk 44 sea level 31 extreme wthr 30 climate assmt 15 ALL: 362	health 21 risk 17 public health 6 critical infrstrct 6 nationl secrty 3 ALL: 56	health 286 risk 216 resilience 131 nat. security 86 sea level 64 ALL: 1091

(continued)

Table 5.8 (continued)

	Executive-Obama	Executive-Trump	Legislative-Democrat	Legislative-Republican	ALL
Justice: Keywords	vulnerable 17 devlpg cntries 13 future genertns 9 poverty 6 climate fund 4 ALL: 55	social cost 10 wage 5 vulnerable 4 future genertns 4 poverty 3 ALL: 29	energy refund 97 social security 68 vulnerable 38 dividend trust 36 refund progm 35 ALL: 437	social security 12 climate fund 5 develpg cntries 5 poverty 2 wage 2 ALL: 26	energy refund 97 social security 80 vulnerable 59 poverty 45 dividend trust 36 ALL: 547
Ecology: Keywords	carbon polltn 75 environmntl 63 forest 30 planet 29 sustainable 15 ALL: 257	environmntl 94 forest 21 clean water 12 wildlife 7 planet 5 ALL: 157	environmntl 108 healthy climte 68 global warmg 52 renewbl engy 26 carbon polltn 22 ALL: 379	environmntl 19 forest 13 habitat 4 renewbl engy 2 naturl resilience 1 ALL: 40	environmntl 284 carbon polltn 98 forest 81 healthy climate 68 global warming 56 ALL: 833
Society: Keywords	regions 71 communities 70 city 66 private 53 local 46 ALL: 379	workers 56 citizen 22 region 19 city 17 communities 16 ALL: 176	communities 118 local 63 city 52 workers 43 consumer 30 ALL: 421	consumer worker urban city private ALL: 91	communities 206 city 148 local 132 worker 123 region 116 ALL: 1067

Table 5.9 Similarity of keyword rank orders in policy discourse of the EU

	Economic	Ecology	Society	Risk	Political	Justice
ALL EU	0.458	0.151	0.292	0.413	0.439	0.164
EUC-COM	0.467	0.223	0.439	0.542	0.488	0.292
EUC-EP	0.574	0.211	0.391	0.612	0.531	0.325
COM-EP	0.542	0.325	0.395	0.413	0.461	0.275

Table 5.10 Similarity of keyword rank orders in policy discourse of the US

	Economic	Ecology	Society	Risk	Political	Justice
ALL US	0.098	0.245	0.097	0.234	0.081	0
Executive: Obama v Trump	0.307	0.394	0.295	0.331	0.101	0.379
Legislative: Rep v Dem	0.290	0.335	0.297	0.497	0.126	0.156
Party: Obama v Dem	0.088	0.303	0.430	0.234	0.097	0.087
Party: Trump v Rep	0.356	0.609	0.294	0.647	0.081	0.154

identified as two forms of justification in which the most salient keywords are used more coherently on an aggregate level and across all institutional settings within the EU than the US case. In the case of these two relatively salient frames, discursive contestation is generally lower in the European setting based on similarity of terms used. Second, three other frames show some overlap of values for the indicator but still have a higher degree of similarity across subsets of discourse in the EU than the US case and are therefore identified as less discursively contested. This applies to the society and risk frames, where only a small degree of overlap of values is observed (EU range 0.292–0.439 and US 0.097–0.430 for the society frame, and EU range 0.413–0.612 and US 0.234–0.647 for the risk frame). This also applies to the justice frame, where similarity is low in both cases of the EU and US (EU range 0.164–0.325 and US

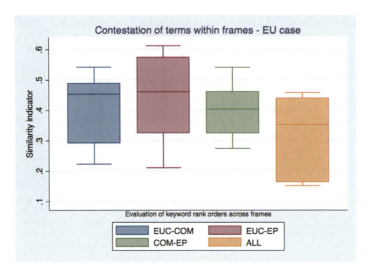

Fig. 5.3 Variation of the similarity indicator of keyword rank orders as an indicator for political contestation of climate policy discourse in the EU

range 0–0.379). Finally, the ecology frame stands out within this comparison by having a similarly diverse set of salient keywords in both cases, indicating a high degree of discursive contestation in both systems (with values ranging between 0.151–0.325 for the EU and 0.245–0.609 for the US). To put these values in perspective, it can be concluded that particularly the more coherent and salient use of an economic and political framing of climate action distinguishes EU discourse from its US counterpart; a similar observation also applies to the society and risk frames, albeit more conditionally.

Beyond comparison on the aggregate level, further insights about discursive contestation can be gained from evaluating the variation of the similarity indicator within the same frame but comparing between different institutional setting and political agents, as shown in the graphs below (Figs. 5.3 and 5.4).

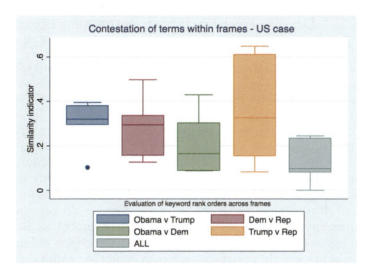

Fig. 5.4 Variation of the similarity indicator of keyword rank orders as an indicator for political contestation of climate policy discourse in the US

In this respect, the range of values for the EU case was already identified as relatively low particularly within the highly salient frames such as the economic, political and society one. Concerning the US case, however, a striking finding is the range between values indicating a relatively low and very high coherence of discourse between Republican legislators and the Trump administration within their most salient economic and society framing. This contrasts with the more divergent framing between Democratic legislators and the Obama administration, where the similarity indicator reaches some of its lowest values in the entire data set. This point adds to the previous observation that aside from contestation between Republicans and Democrats, it is also the great degree of variation in the discourse of advocates for climate action within the camp of Democratic legislators and policy-makers that contributes to the fragmentation of climate policy debate in the US case.

5.5 Discussion: Political Space and Issue Dimensions of Climate in the EU and US

Pulling together our observations about the structure, linkages and contestation of frames presented in this chapter, the following conclusions can be drawn about the political space of climate change discourse in the two cases compared.

In the case of the EU, most aspects of the previous analysis confirm the assumption of a relatively stable and coherent political space established by discourse on climate change. The issue category of collective action is identified as primary in terms of salience, receiving a slightly stronger emphasis than the problem identification and policy evaluation. Statements and claims framed within this category, however, do not emerge as an independent or strongly contested political issue dimension. Both the political and societal frame are linked frequently to claims within other issue categories and do not reach very high values in terms of paradigmatic salience or dissimilarity of terms indicating discursive contestation. The main function of these two frames is their complementary use in addition to frames both used for the appraisal of climate change as a problem and the evaluation of more specific policy. However, few indications were found of these frames as a separate or independent source of political contestation. Turning to the appraisal of climate change itself, the policy documents surveyed in the EU demonstrate a strong and relatively coherent framing in terms of ecological principles, with only marginal references to a risk frame. This ecological framing is particulary strong in case of the European Parliament and is debated with highly dissimilar terms by the EU institutions, indicating a stronger degree of discursive contestation. Considering the indicators used here, the evaluation of climate change as an ecological problem therefore emerges as the primary issue dimension in public discourse of the EU institutions. In comparison, discourse on policy evaluation is framed in very coherent economic terms emphasizing aspects of investment, market processes and efficiency. Here, the frame proposed by the EU institutions is more similar and evaluated in more coherent and recurring terms. While the economic frame is the overall most frequently used and salient one in policy discourse, the category of policy evaluation therefore emerges only as a secondary issue dimension. In comparative perspective, moreover, the data demonstrates that climate frames have broader linkages and are promoted more coherently across institutional settings in the EU.

Turning to the US, our findings confirm a strong intensity of controversy between Democrats and Republicans on climate change. Beyond this expectable point, the most relevant finding is the general lack of a coherent framing of climate action and the resulting high degree of paradigmatic polarization between both presidential administrations but also within Democrats. As in the European case, the two frames considered as part of the collective action category do not emerge as a relevant issue dimension, as this framing is most frequently linked to claims in other issue categories. However, and unlike the European case, this segment of discourse is framed in relatively coherent societal terms and neither a subject of clear paradigmatic polarization or discursive contestation. The primary issue dimension, by contrast, is discourse on policy evaluation, where an economic framing emerges as the most salient form of justification. Unlike policy discourse in the EU, however, the emphasis on this frame and also its combination with arguments framed in terms of justice differ strongly between Republican and Democrat members of Congress and both presidential administrations. Within partisan lines, Republican discourse along the executive-legislative divide is more coherent, with very high salience values on a combination of economic frames focused on jobs, growth and fossil resources. By comparison, Democratic discourse is more variegated and lacks a coherent framing: Discourse from the Obama administration emphasizes similar terms as the European debate—particular investment and efficiency—and congressional Democrats promote terms related to carbon pricing and energy resources. While discourse within dimension evolves primarily through discursive contestation, the debate on the appraisal of climate change as a problem is a clearer example of paradigmatic polarization. As demonstrated in this and the previous chapter, the Obama administration promoted a mixed framing of climate change based on risk and aspects of environmentalism, whereas congressional Democrats only partially share this frame and mostly promote an environmental frame emphasizing health and pollution aspects. While a similarity to the European case is the emergence of particularly two issue dimensions as relevant—namely, dispute on economic aspects of policy and on the broader scope and severity of climate change as a threat—both issue dimensions are more contested than in the EU case and more asymmetrical in terms of the proposed frames and underlying terms.

5.6 Conclusion: Comparative Analysis of Climate Policy Discourse in the EU and US

In conclusion, the comparative discussion of discourse about climate change in the US and the EU leads to three main findings. First, comparing the structure of frames in climate discourse at the aggregate level does not lead to the observation of evident differences with regard to relevant 'master' frames or issue categories used in the EU and US. In fact, a highly prominent use of economic frames, and a combination between one of the frames of the problem or policy evaluation dimension and a political action frame emerge as commonalities between both cases. The only major difference at the aggregate level is that the problem definition of climate change is primarily framed in terms of a risk to material assets in the US but as an ecological problem in the EU.

Second, the major difference between both cases is that climate discourse in the US involves more variation between institutional settings, legislative agents and presidential administrations that contrasts with the more coherent and homogenous EU variant of discourse about climate change. Furthermore, linkages between frames are broader in scope and denser in the US debate than in EU discourse. Particularly, those political agents most critical of action against climate change—namely, the Trump administration and Congress Republicans—stand out by creating very selective and highly emphasized linkages, particularly between an economic and a societal frame. Democrats are generally less intent on repeating the same linkages between related frames across legislative initiatives and institutional levels, resulting in variegated and more diverse forms of framing.

Finally, a comparative view on contestation leads to some intuitive findings, particularly the insight that aspects of paradigmatic polarization and discursive contestation are generally stronger in the US than in the EU debate. Beyond this general finding, however, our analysis uncovers remarkable degrees of variation concerning the contestation of different frames in a comparison between different constellations of agents. The most remarkable difference between the two cases is the existence of a salient and discursively coherent economic framing of climate policy in the EU, and its foundation within an equally salient and agreed societal frame for realizing policy. This creates the key contrast to the US, where an economic framing is highly salient but also strongly contested. Against this background, it is noteworthy that the EU struggles to establish a coherent ecological framing of climate change, while the overall definition of climate change as a problem for society is openly split between a risk and ecological framing in the US case.

References

Albright, Jeremy J. 2010. "The Multidimensional Nature of Party Competition." *Party Politics* 16 (6): 699–719. https://doi.org/10.1177/1354068809345856.

Arbour, Brian. 2014. "Issue Frame Ownership: The Partisan Roots of Campaign Rhetoric." *Political Communication* 31 (4): 604–627. https://doi.org/10.1080/10584609.2013.852639.

Benoit, Kenneth, and Michael Laver. 2012. "The Dimensionality of Political Space: Epistemological and Methodological Considerations." *European Union Politics* 13 (2): 194–218. https://doi.org/10.1177/1465116511434618.

Budge, Ian. 2015. "Issue Emphases, Saliency Theory and Issue Ownership: A Historical and Conceptual Analysis." *West European Politics* 38 (4): 761–777. https://doi.org/10.1080/01402382.2015.1039374.

Dolezal, Martin, Laurenz Ennser-Jedenastik, Wolfgang C. Müller, and Anna Katharina Winkler. 2014. "How Parties Compete for Votes: A Test of Saliency Theory." *European Journal of Political Research* 53 (1): 57–76. https://doi.org/10.1111/1475-6765.12017.

Elias, Anwen, Edina Szöcsik, and Christina Isabel Zuber. 2015. "Position, Selective Emphasis and Framing: How Parties Deal with a Second Dimension in Competition." *Party Politics* 21 (6): 839–850. https://doi.org/10.1177/1354068815597572.

Gabel, Matthew, and Simon Hix. 2002. "Defining the EU Political Space: An Empirical Study of the European Elections Manifestos, 1979–1999." *Comparative Political Studies* 35 (8): 934–964. https://doi.org/10.1177/001041402236309.

Gustafson, Abel, Seth A. Rosenthal, Matthew T. Ballew, Matthew H. Goldberg, Parrish Bergquist, John E. Kotcher, Edward W. Maibach, and Anthony Leiserowitz. 2019. "The Development of Partisan Polarization over the Green New Deal." *Nature Climate Change* 9 (12): 940–944. https://doi.org/10.1038/s41558-019-0621-7.

Helbling, Marc, Dominic Hoeglinger, and Bruno Wüest. 2010. "How Political Parties Frame European Integration." *European Journal of Political Research* 49 (4): 495–521. https://doi.org/10.1111/j.1475-6765.2009.01908.x.

Helbling, Marc, and Anke Tresch. 2011. "Measuring Party Positions and Issue Salience from Media Coverage: Discussing and Cross-Validating New Indicators." *Electoral Studies, Special Symposium: Electoral Democracy in the*

European Union 30 (1): 174–183. https://doi.org/10.1016/j.electstud. 2010.12.001.

Hoeglinger, Dominic. 2016. *Politicizing European Integration: Struggling with the Awakening Giant*. Challenges to Democracy in the 21st Century. Basingstoke: Palgrave Macmillan.

Kriesi, Hanspeter, Edgar Grande, Martin Dolezal, Marc Helbling, Dominic Hoeglinger, Swen Hutter, and Bruno Wüest. 2012. *Political Conflict in Western Europe*. Cambridge: Cambridge University Press.

Lefevere, Jonas, Julie Sevenans, Stefaan Walgrave, and Christophe Lesschaeve. 2019. "Issue Reframing by Parties: The Effect of Issue Salience and Ownership." *Party Politics* 25 (4): 507–519. https://doi.org/10.1177/135406881 7736755.

Snow, David A. 2004. "Framing Processes, Ideology, and Discursive Fields." In *The Blackwell Companion to Social Movements*, 380–412. John Wiley & Sons, Ltd. https://doi.org/10.1002/9780470999103.ch17.

van de Wardt, Marc. 2015. "Conforming to the Dominant Discourse: Framing Distance and Multiparty Competition." *West European Politics* 38 (4): 839–868. https://doi.org/10.1080/01402382.2015.1039378.

CHAPTER 6

Conclusion: Framing Climate Change in the EU and US After the Paris Agreement

The study presented in this book is completed at a time when controversy on climate change has both moved to the foreground of political debate and become more volatile through external shocks such as the COVID pandemic and the war in Ukraine, as new connections are being drawn between the challenges of economic recovery, green investment, policies covering the broad challenges of energy supply and security and the issue of climate change. Against this background, it seems likely that the politics of climate will continue to expand in scope and become more contested, as controversy on paths towards decarbonization enters the mainstream of party politics and public debate (cp. Gustafson et al. 2019, Carter et al. 2018, Carter and Little 2020, Farstad 2018). As the debate about solutions for the climate crisis is set to become more contentious, this concluding chapter seeks to set some of the approaches and findings of this book in context with the dynamic of politicization that appears to be emerging in this field (Pepermans and Maeseele 2016, Paterson 2021, Davies et al. 2021). Reflecting on both future political developments and research agendas, the following four points deserve to be pointed out.

© The Author(s), under exclusive license to Springer Nature
Switzerland AG 2022
F. Wendler, *Framing Climate Change in the EU and US After the Paris Agreement*, Palgrave Studies in European Union Politics,
https://doi.org/10.1007/978-3-031-04059-7_6

6.1 Countering the Climate Crisis: The Critical Role of Ideas and Discourse

Set in context with the extensive research literature on climate change governance, the approach of this study is based on two main premises: first, that a key problem for acting against climate change lies in the question of political action and discursive justification rather than technical feasibility or economic affordability, serious as these latter two material challenges may be for actual political debates (for a comprehensive discussion of this point, cp. Stammer et al. 2021); and second, that the foremost challenge for overcoming hurdles to collective action is rooted in prevalent ideas about climate change and their promotion through discourse aimed at the justification of political action in the context of a global climate regime that increasingly relies on voluntary and ideas-based cooperation (cp. Aykut et al. 2017; 2021, Meckling and Allan 2020). This point is not to deny that institutions, and particularly their role for structuring access to venues of decision-making and resulting influence on agenda-setting and veto points, matter; nor does it deny the importance of how individuals and social groups define their interests and promote them through mechanisms of interest representation and electoral participation. By focusing on discourse and its constitutive role for creating issue dimensions and patterns of polarization concerning action against the emergent climate crisis, however, our focus highlights the mediating link between two elements: policy beliefs formed on the basis of ideas about climate change and promoted by political agents on the one hand, and the negotiation of broader policy packages between groups of agents within given institutional settings, on the other.

In outlining the rationale of this study, we have argued that climate change is a particularly relevant field for exploring the structure of ideas and policy beliefs, for two major reasons: First, due to the slow, diffuse and systemic effects caused by global warming, efforts of intellectual abstraction and subsequent discursive justification are inevitable to reflect on climate and its effects, and to make the case for action. Grasping climate change as a problem for society, in this sense, is impossible without recourse to abstracting concepts and assumptions. The question of how and why to act against climate change is therefore essentially a contest of ideas, understood here as a summary term for both normative principles of action and causal assumptions, scenarios and projections. The plausibility of this assumption seems to be corroborated on a very fundamental level by the fact that the material effects of climate change and vulnerability of societies in relation to them are no plausible factor for explaining divergent political responses to global warming. Second, in terms of political action, the temporal and institutional boundaries of climate policy are flexible and open to a range of different interpretations. These can reach from relatively narrow perspectives on a specific source of carbon pollution in a regional context and limited time frame to much wider, global and intergenerational perspectives. In this context, it appears that the urgency assigned to climate action and emphases laid on questions of ethical principles and justice depend on the choice of these temporal and political boundaries of action, gaining urgency and contentiousness when the time and geographical range is expanded (cp. Slawinski et al. 2017; Aykut 2016). This highlights the critical role of framing: What issue dimensions and ideological conflicts are activated by raising the issue of climate politics appears to depend to a great degree on what timeframe and political conception are associated with it.

In conceptual and methodological terms, exploring the ways in which climate change is addressed has to strike a balance between inductive observation of the myriad ways through which climate is reflected in discourse, and deductive categorization based on a pre-defined typology of frames and issue dimensions. A further difficulty is the multi-layered structure of this thematic field, as climate change invites controversy about problem definitions as well as policy solutions and frameworks of action. Recognizing this complexity through the distinction of issue categories, this study has sought to propose a typology of frames that is both able to capture the diversity of perspectives on climate change and is useable for comparative tests of hypotheses. On an empirical level, these hypotheses are applied to a comparison of two entities with far-reaching similarities but strongly contrasting forms of discourse, political controversy and policy responses to the problem of climate change: namely, the EU and US since the adoption of the Paris Agreement.

6.2 Climate Politics in the EU and US: Discourse as the Link Between Ideas, Agents and Institutions

Considering the relevance of the EU and US as agents of global climate policy, it is striking how few direct comparisons have been drawn in the literature between both entities in terms of their progress in climate policy-making. The question remains: What explains the different responses of both systems to this global challenge, given their similarities in terms of economic development, vulnerability to threats posed by climate change, institutional setup as multi-level systems with a strong division between executive and bicameral legislative institutions, multiple veto points, and not too distant individual perceptions of climate change? While this study has no complete answer to this question, it seeks to contribute to approaches in the research literature focusing on links between political agency and institutional features of both entities: particularly, those approaches highlighting differences in access to agenda-setting, and the form of interactions in the horizontal and vertical division of powers, as epitomized for the US by the concepts of the administrative presidency and contested federalism, and for the EU through varieties of multi-level governance.

While institutional approaches open relevant pathways towards explaining the variation of policy output of both systems, they do not provide a full explanation without a more complete account of the policy solutions advocated by political agents and their underlying ideas and policy beliefs. Based on the observation that policy-making is more stringent, more consistently implemented and more coherent as part of an overall policy-making framework in the EU than in the US, this study has sought to explore this underlying structure of ideas as expressed through discourse: Assuming that ideas at different levels of generality—namely, those defining paradigmatic beliefs, programmatic visions and policy-specific concepts—tie political agents to proposed policy options leads to the rationale of exploring these layers of ideas as promulgated through discourse and evaluated through the approach of framing analysis. The main heuristic applied here to systematize the link between ideas and different policy options as well as their contestation is the concept of political space, used to explore and relate three aspects of political discourse: first, what categories of related issues and evaluating ideological principles are highlighted, as derived in this study from the structure of framing; second, what observations can be made about discursive positions of agents as observed from linkages of frames and their relation to one another; and finally, how contestation evolves from the dual effect of competing advocacy for divergent frames and discursive contestation within the same frames. While the inductive approach used to explore the political space of climate in the case studies and comparative analysis does not deliver position data based on a pre-defined grid of issue dimensions, the main rationale pursued here is to define the underlying criteria and dimensions of such a grid to be applied in future stages of research.

The present study has proceeded in two steps, through the reconstruction of policy-making developments in the case studies, and their evaluation as the political space of climate politics in two contrasting settings as highlighted in the comparative chapter. This survey demonstrates the link between institutional features of both systems, political discourse about climate change and resulting policy outputs: Guided by the scrutiny of three sets of comparative hypotheses, the EU and US emerge as entities setting different frameworks for climate discourse in terms of issue categories, linkages of frames and contestation.

The EU creates a stable political space for the negotiation of the current agenda established by the European Green Deal, establishing a highly salient but coherent framing based on an economic issue dimension emphasizing the ideas of investment, efficiency and a circular economy. The main field of contestation is the appraisal of climate change as a threat to the intactness of ecosystems, where particularly the European Parliament emerges as a discursive leader with strong environmental framing, creating a contrast particularly to the discourse of the European Council. In this context, it is remarkable that a justice frame was identified only in a small subset of discourse by the EU institutions but not as one of the most salient forms of framing. Assuming that questions of climate justice are politically charged by raising questions of responsibility, distributive injustice and compensation, the remarkably low presence of this frame is a factor further reducing the contentiousness of EU policy proposals. However, it is evident that aspects in this category will continue to be raised by Member States most critical of the current EU climate policy agenda and be further promoted particularly by civil society movements. Furthermore, it is clear that this aspect of climate governance creates an incomplete and potentially incoherent aspect of the EU's ambition of presenting itself as a leader in global climate policy, particularly in relation to emerging economies and countries most vulnerable to climate change.

In contrast, the political space of climate discourse in the US is characterized by volatility and fragmentation: Both the case study and comparative discussion identify a political space in which approaches to framing climate change differ not just between presidential administrations and the two major parties but also between the numerous legislative proposals launched within Congress by a range of caucuses and groups of legislators that promote competing concepts of climate action. The range of policy-making options identified at this level reaches beyond the one found in the EU, ranging from a diversity of moderate to more stringent proposals for carbon pricing to the transformative agenda envisaged by the Green New Deal. The resulting volatility of the legislative debate contrasts with policy development that is based almost exclusively on forms of executive action and characterized not so much by sharp reversals than by relative continuity resulting from policy-making blockade. Concerning debate about the severity and consequences of climate change, the rejection of climate science as a hoax is mostly absent in spite of the close association commonly drawn between the Trump administration and organized climate denial. What is observable, however, is an intensive controversy about the adherence of the US to the Paris Agreement, in terms of the legality of its adoption without consent by the Senate and the questioning of its fairness particularly in President Trump's announcement to withdraw. The rejection of the UN framework for climate governance by Republicans contrasts with several initiatives by Democrats deploring the decision to withdraw and seeking to enact legislation requiring the federal government to implement policies in compliance with its content. Contrary to the European case, climate justice is more clearly present as a framing of climate action, reaching from the emphasis of racial, gender and indigenous aspects of climate injustice in the Green New Deal to a whole range of proposals by Congress Democrats to combine carbon pricing with social compensation and support mechanisms. Three main issue dimensions can be identified, including intense debate on policy evaluation emerging from disputes on the economic framing of climate policy and questions of justice; polarization created by competing stances towards multilateralism and cooperation within the global climate regime; and finally, a third issue dimension created by the asymmetrical debate on problem definitions of climate change, raised as a risk and ecology issue by Democrats and largely sidelined within Republican discourse on energy independence and economic growth. Climate politics in the US, therefore, does not evolve from a dualism of two ideological coherent camps represented by the two major parties that either believe or reject the reality of climate change. Instead, it evolves in a political space that is wider but also more fragmented and polarized than in the European case. The fragmented structure of climate ideas and discourse establishes the missing link between agents and the institutional framework of the US political system, adding to the explanation why policy-makers have been unable to adopt a comprehensive package of climate policy reforms to date.

6.3 Framing Climate Change in Post-Pandemic Times: Mainstreaming and Policy Linkages

Looking forward, particularly the onset of the COVID-19 pandemic and its impact on economic development and public spending have set a new context for the further development of climate policy. While concerns have been raised that the economic downturn caused by the pandemic will create a dynamic pushing environmental concerns aside in favor of priorities focused on economic growth, the political effects of the pandemic appear more ambiguous and difficult to oversee at the time of writing (cp. Elliott et al. 2020; Lahcen et al. 2020; Sovacool et al. 2020). A political effect of the pandemic that seems very likely at this point, however, is that global efforts to manage a recovery from the economic recession will further increase the relevance of policy linkages between climate and economics, highlighting how action against climate change is framed in conjunction with and as a part of recovery programs.

A likely result of the current dynamic is the mainstreaming of climate action and its central target of carbon neutrality, particularly through its inclusion into economic stimulus packages and investment programs (Mukanjari and Sterner 2020; Barbier 2020); in this regard, an open question is whether such measures will be sufficient or a distraction for efforts to manage the energy transition required for achieving decarbonization (Andrijevic et al. 2020). As the economic impact of the global pandemic has prompted an expansion of public investment into the renewal of infrastructure, programs supporting ongoing transitions in forms of working and mobility, and compensatory payments to those groups hit hardest by the Covid-related downturn, introducing a green or climate conditionality has become a common theme for policies on both sides of the Atlantic. For the European Union, a whole range of initiatives stand out in this context: Introducing conditionality criteria on climate-friendly investment and technology in the recovery funds assigned to Member States through the NextGeneration program, emphasizing green priorities for fiscal and economic governance within the European Semester, and promoting climate targets into the strategy review announced by the European Central Bank are only the most important components of this mainstreaming (Ekerbout et al. 2020; Meles et al.

2020). In the case of the United States, the ambitions for more stringent climate action announced by the Biden administration are pursued (and contested) primarily in the context of bills promoting an expansion of spending on infrastructure and social security, rather than through a relaunch of proposals for a federal cap-and-trade system or a resurrection of ambitions promoted through the Clean Power Plan.

This suggests that climate action is promoted not primarily in its own right, but as a catalyst and component of broader economic and technological renewal. The defining motto of this approach is to 'Build Back Better', as promoted in both the US and United Kingdom as a launching pad for an expanded role of the state, and as a new approach to framing economic recovery and growth. It follows from these observations that the framing of climate change, global public health and economic recovery may become more connected and interdependent. The potential variants of framing climate action in a post-crisis recovery include all of the various frames covered in this study: In a context of recovery led by public investment, an economic framing of climate-friendly investment as a step towards technological modernization and competitiveness is likely to be adopted; at the same time, it is evident that many of the social, intergenerational and global forms of injustice emphasized by the climate movement are reiterated in the evaluation of the Covid pandemic and its highly asymmetrical impact on social groups and world regions. Equally, the global spread of a virus most likely originating from a lack of safety standards and sustainable practices in the field of meat production and consumption is almost certain to be taken up as proof for the vulnerability of societies in relation to various forms of globalized risk, and as a demonstration that the transition to more ecologically sustainable forms of living and consumption is imperative.

In this sense, it is possible that the Covid pandemic strengthens an awareness of global systemic risks created by climate change (cp. Howarth et al. 2020; Herrero and Thornton 2020; Klenert et al. 2020). It is also unsurprising that comparisons have been drawn in public debate between the Covid pandemic and climate change, even though the threats posed by a global virus pandemic and climate change are rather dissimilar: Both are not identical in terms of time frames, the visibility of harmful effects and mitigation measures, direct links between agency and mitigation effects, and certainly with regard to the difference in the sheer scope of both problems. However, the pandemic has worked as a catalyst for intense debate about the rationales, limitations and failures of political cooperation on a global level concerning the distribution of vaccines, trade and free movement, with a potential impact on climate discourse framed in political and societal terms. These controversies set into sharp relief the antagonism between calls for better multilateral cooperation and the nationalistic framing of the Covid pandemic as a matter of national survival and case for protectionism. How this aspect of post-crisis politics will affect action against climate change is an open question.

As these observations suggest, the post-pandemic phase of investment programs and economic recovery is far from certain to bring advances for climate policy. What they highlight, however, is that broader and more numerous links are established between climate policy and a wider agenda of economic, technological and societal modernization. Particularly in policy documents of the European Union, aiming at a 'green and digital' revision of policies has become a catchword of this unfolding agenda. This suggests that in the context of post-crisis recovery, mitigating climate change is no longer considered a subset of policies under the heading of environmental governance, but envisaged in broader terms of economic development, technological competitiveness, and social cohesion. This underlines the critical importance of framing: what principles and policy paradigms are applied to rationalize the case for climate action, and what priority is assigned to environmental issues in relation to other, potentially competing policy goals.

A further consequence of mainstreaming is the adoption of climate change as an issue of primary importance by virtually all political parties across the ideological spectrum, at least in a European setting. The relatively progressive stance taken by UK Prime Minister Boris Johnson at least on the level of public announcements and appeals to act against climate change, or the recognition of climate change as an issue of essential importance by all parties considered as potential partners in a future governing coalition during the German federal election in the fall of 2021 are cases in point. These examples illustrate that political parties of the moderate center agree on the importance of achieving climate neutrality until mid-century, but continue to propose radically different approaches towards resulting policies. The divergent approaches at this level cover the issue dimensions discussed throughout this analysis, particularly the balance between state and markets, perceptions of risk and ecological sustainability, and the recognition of international frameworks to coordinate actions to reduce carbon emissions. Ultimately, a key question is whether climate change becomes absorbed in existing issue dimension of political competition—particularly the socio-economic left/right dimension between state intervention and market freedom—or whether it creates a dynamic to shift and re-organize current political issues and patterns of polarization.

Finally, the variable boundaries of climate governance and the shifts that can occur in its linkages to related policy fields through exogenous shocks are dramatically highlighted by the events unfolding in Ukraine since February 2022. The full implications of the military aggression unleashed by Russia and resulting security and humanitarian crisis cannot be assessed at the time of writing. However, it is already evident that from both a Western European and North American perspective, energy policy is affected in significant ways by the unfolding war with potentially far-reaching implications for the entire complex of global climate change governance. This is clear from the way in which controversies on the calibration of energy production, consumption and prices, but also on decisions concerning the security and independence of the energy supplies of EU Member States and the US have moved center stage and are increasingly re-framed through criteria of military and geopolitical security in debates responding to the crisis. As this book goes to press, it is too early to tell what this means for the future progress of climate governance: It is an open question whether agendas aiming at a full decarbonization of the economy will become crowded out by a shift of political attention and public spending on military and related security issues such as border control and migration crisis management; or whether the current development towards a limitation or even a cutoff of fossil fuel supplies from Russia and resulting price spikes on gas and oil will work as a kickstart to boost the transition to more energy efficiency and renewables in the US and European Union. A likely outcome of the present security crisis in Europe, however, is that arguments framed in terms of military risk and security will gain in importance in the debate about the future of climate and energy policies.

6.4 Future Research Agendas: Politicization and Policy-Making on Climate Change

Turning to future research agendas and considering the points discussed above, a topic of major relevance for the future of climate politics is a dynamic highlighted as politicization at the outset of this chapter. After its rise particularly in research about European and global governance, the term is now commonly used in political science for an expansion of public controversy on governance processes in terms of their visibility and scope of involved agents, in combination with an increased contentiousness of claims and arguments raised in public discourse (Zürn 2019; Schimmelfennig 2020, Börzel and Risse 2018; Hutter et al. 2016; Statham and Trenz 2013). While politicization has been recognized as an important dynamic for the future development of climate change governance, the research literature on this topic is still emerging and mostly focused on the question whether an increase of political conflict and mechanisms of democratic politics is 'good' or 'bad' for further progress of policies aiming at carbon neutrality (Pepermans and Maeseele 2016; Willis 2020; Davies et al. 2021; Blühdorn and Deflorian 2021; Hulme 2019). Empirical accounts of this dynamic, however, remain relatively scarce and mostly cover developments at the international level and within local and particularly urban settings (Paterson 2021; Bulkeley 2016; Castro 2021; Ciplet et al. 2015), while broader comparative accounts covering parties, media, elections and representative institutions are only starting to emerge (Carter and Little 2020; Tosun and Peters 2021; Gustafson et al. 2019; Chinn et al. 2020; Bernauer 2013).

Climate change appears as a particular important example to investigate one of the core puzzles of the literature on politicization cited above: namely, the increasing tension between dynamics and targets of governance processes at the trans-, supra- and international level on the one hand, and the continued relevance of processes of representation, contestation and accountability within democratic institutions primarily at the national level, on the other. Focusing particularly on parliamentary institutions and their interactions with executives in the respective political systems of the EU and US, this study has sought to contribute to emerging research about the link between policy-making and issue dimensions and contestation of climate change policy in this regard.

Within the context of this research agenda, a limitation of the present study arguably is that it has focused on framing and policy discourse exclusively within highly institutionalized, legislative and executive policymaking settings. A relevant task for future research in this sense is to expand this perspective to include civil society agents and organizations, political parties in their role during election campaigns, and contributions to public debate about climate change from a wider range of scientists, experts, advocacy groups and citizens. Future research particularly needs to engage with questions covering how claims raised by civil society protest and movements such as Fridays for Future impact processes of policy-making within the institutional settings investigated in this present study (cp. Zabern and Tulloch 2021; Boulianne et al. 2020; Corry and Reiner 2021; Haunss and Sommer 2020; Ciplet 2014). Potential questions raised from this perspective include exploring interactions between settings, and the role of gatekeepers and mediating agents promoting the transfer of messages from civil society into political institutions. On a more general level, the effect of politicization on policy-making is a highly relevant research question beyond the issue of climate change: Similar research agendas covering trade, security or migration and looking into the effect of increased contestation on governance beyond the nation-state have not yet established definitive findings, but are engaged in a vital research debate on explanations for the varied effects of politicization on supra- and transnational governance.

Future findings of research in this field matter both academically and politically. Concerning the interrelation between the politics and policy dimensions of climate governance, the stakes could not be higher: Engaging with ideas about climate change will be of key importance, both for academics seeking to explore perspectives for political agendas stringent enough to abate its most severe consequences; and for each individual seeking to come to terms with a problem whose recognition is an intellectual and ethical challenge as much as the realization of an increasingly present part of our future.

References

Andrijevic, Marina, Carl-Friedrich. Schleussner, Matthew J. Gidden, David L. McCollum, and Joeri Rogelj. 2020. "COVID-19 Recovery Funds Dwarf Clean Energy Investment Needs." *Science* 370 (6514): 298–300. https://doi.org/10.1126/science.abc9697.

Aykut, Stefan C. 2016. "Taking a Wider View on Climate Governance: Moving beyond the 'Iceberg', the 'Elephant', and the 'Forest.'" *Wires Climate Change* 7 (3): 318–328. https://doi.org/10.1002/wcc.391.

Aykut, Stefan C., Jean Foyer, and Edouard Morena. 2017. *Globalising the Climate: COP21 and the Climatisation of Global Debates*. Abingdon: Routledge.

Aykut, Stefan C., Edouard Morena, and Jean Foyer. 2021. "'Incantatory' Governance: Global Climate Politics' Performative Turn and Its Wider Significance for Global Politics." *International Politics* 58 (4): 519–540. https://doi.org/10.1057/s41311-020-00250-8.

Barbier, Edward B. 2020. "Greening the Post-Pandemic Recovery in the G20." *Environmental and Resource Economics* 76 (4): 685–703. https://doi.org/10.1007/s10640-020-00437-w.

Bernauer, Thomas. 2013. "Climate Change Politics." *Annual Review of Political Science* 16 (1): 421–448. https://doi.org/10.1146/annurev-polisci-062011-154926.

Blühdorn, Ingolfur, and Michael Deflorian. 2021. "Politicisation beyond Post-Politics: New Social Activism and the Reconfiguration of Political Discourse." *Social Movement Studies* 20 (3): 259–275. https://doi.org/10.1080/14742837.2021.1872375.

Börzel, Tanja A., and Thomas Risse. 2018. "From the Euro to the Schengen Crises: European Integration Theories, Politicization, and Identity Politics." *Journal of European Public Policy* 25 (1): 83–108. https://doi.org/10.1080/13501763.2017.1310281.

Boulianne, Shelley, Mireille Lalancette, and David Ilkiw. 2020. "'School Strike 4 Climate': Social Media and the International Youth Protest on Climate Change." *Media and Communication* 8 (2): 208–18. https://doi.org/10.17645/mac.v8i2.2768.

Bulkeley, Harriet, Matthew Paterson, and Johannes Stripple. 2016. *Towards a Cultural Politics of Climate Change: Devices, Desires, and Dissent*. Cambridge: Cambridge University Press. https://doi.org/10.1017/CBO9781316694473. Accessed March 17, 2022.

Carter, Neil, Robert Ladrech, Conor Little, and Vasiliki Tsagkroni. 2018. "Political Parties and Climate Policy: A New Approach to Measuring Parties' Climate Policy Preferences." *Party Politics* 24 (6): 731–42.

Carter, Neil, and Conor Little. 2020. "Party Competition on Climate Policy: The Roles of Interest Groups, Ideology and Challenger Parties in the UK and Ireland." *International Political Science Review*. https://doi.org/10.1177/0192512120972582.

Castro, Paula. 2021. "National Interests and Coalition Positions on Climate Change: A Text-Based Analysis." *International Political Science Review* 42 (1): 95–113. https://doi.org/10.1177/0192512120953530.

Chinn, Sedona, P. Sol Hart, and Stuart Soroka. 2020. "Politicization and Polarization in Climate Change News Content, 1985–2017." *Science Communication* 42 (1): 112–129. https://doi.org/10.1177/1075547019900290.

Ciplet, David. 2014. "Contesting Climate Injustice: Transnational Advocacy Network Struggles for Rights in UN Climate Politics." *Global Environmental Politics* 14 (4): 75–96.

Ciplet, David, J. Timmons Roberts, and MIzan Khan. 2015. *Power in a Warming World : The New Global Politics of Climate Change and the*

Remaking of Environmental Inequality. Cambridge, Massachusetts: The MIT Press.

Corry, Olaf, and David Reiner. 2021. "Protests and Policies: How Radical Social Movement Activists Engage with Climate Policy Dilemmas." *Sociology* 55 (1): 197–217. https://doi.org/10.1177/0038038520943107.

Davies, Anna R., Vanesa Castán Broto, and Stephan Hügel. 2021. "Editorial: Is There a New Climate Politics?" *Politics and Governance* 9 (2): 1–7. https://doi.org/10.17645/pag.v9i2.4341.

Ekerbout, Milan, Christian Egenhofer, Jorge Nunez Ferrer, Mihnea Catuti, Irina Kustova, and Vasileos Rizos. 2020. "The European Green Deal after Corona: Implications for EU Climate Policy." *CEPS Policy INsight*.

Elliott, Robert J. R., Ingmar Schumacher, and Cees Withagen. 2020. "Suggestions for a Covid-19 Post-Pandemic Research Agenda in Environmental Economics." *Environmental and Resource Economics* 76 (4): 1187–1213. https://doi.org/10.1007/s10640-020-00478-1.

Farstad, Fay M. 2018. "What Explains Variation in Parties' Climate Change Salience?" *Party Politics* 24 (6): 698–707.

Gustafson, Abel, Seth A. Rosenthal, Matthew T. Ballew, Matthew H. Goldberg, Parrish Bergquist, John E. Kotcher, Edward W. Maibach, and Anthony Leiserowitz. 2019. "The Development of Partisan Polarization over the Green New Deal." *Nature Climate Change* 9 (12): 940–944. https://doi.org/10.1038/s41558-019-0621-7.

Haunss, Sebastian, and Moritz Sommer, eds. 2020. *Fridays for Future—Die Jugend Gegen Den Klimawandel*. Bielefeld: Transcript Verlag.

Herrero, Mario, and Philip Thornton. 2020. "What Can COVID-19 Teach Us about Responding to Climate Change?" *The Lancet. Planetary Health* 4 (5): e174. https://doi.org/10.1016/S2542-5196(20)30085-1.

Howarth, Candice, Peter Bryant, Adam Corner, Sam Fankhauser, Andy Gouldson, Lorraine Whitmarsh, and Rebecca Willis. 2020. "Building a Social Mandate for Climate Action: Lessons from COVID-19." *Environmental and Resource Economics* 76 (4): 1107–1115. https://doi.org/10.1007/s10640-020-00446-9.

Hulme, Mike. 2019. "Climate Emergency Politics Is Dangerous." *Issues in Science and Technology*, 2019. https://issues.org/climate-emergency-politics-is-dangerous/.

Hutter, Swen, Edgar Grande, and Hanspeter Kriesi, eds. 2016. *Politicising Europe: Integration and Mass Politics*. Cambridge: Cambridge University Press.

Klenert, David, Franziska Funke, Linus Mattauch, and Brian O'Callaghan. 2020. "Five Lessons from COVID-19 for Advancing Climate Change Mitigation." *Environmental and Resource Economics* 76 (4): 751–778. https://doi.org/10.1007/s10640-020-00453-w.

Lahcen, B., J. Brusselaers, K. Vrancken, Y. Dams, C. Da Silva Paes, J. Eyckmans, and S. Rousseau. 2020. "Green Recovery Policies for the COVID-19 Crisis: Modelling the Impact on the Economy and Greenhouse Gas Emissions." *Environmental and Resource Economics* 76 (4): 731–750. https://doi.org/10.1007/s10640-020-00454-9.

Meckling, Jonas, and Bentley B. Allan. 2020. "The Evolution of Ideas in Global Climate Policy." *Nature Climate Change* 10 (5): 434–438.

Meles, Tensay Hadush, Lisa Ryan, and Joe Wheatley. 2020. "COVID-19 and EU Climate Targets: Can We Now Go Further?" *Environmental and Resource Economics* 76 (4): 779–787. https://doi.org/10.1007/s10640-020-00476-3.

Mukanjari, Samson, and Thomas Sterner. 2020. "Charting a 'Green Path' for Recovery from COVID-19." *Environmental and Resource Economics* 76 (4): 825–853. https://doi.org/10.1007/s10640-020-00479-0.

Paterson, Matthew. 2021. *In Search of Climate Politics*. Cambridge: Cambridge University Press.

Pepermans, Yves, and Pieter Maeseele. 2016. "The Politicization of Climate Change: Problem or Solution?" *Wires Climate Change* 7 (4): 478–485. https://doi.org/10.1002/wcc.405.

Schimmelfennig, Frank. 2020. "Politicisation Management in the European Union." *Journal of European Public Policy* 27 (3): 342–361. https://doi.org/10.1080/13501763.2020.1712458.

Slawinski, Natalie, Jonatan Pinkse, Timo Busch, and Subhabrata Bobby Banerjee. 2017. "The Role of Short-Termism and Uncertainty Avoidance in Organizational Inaction on Climate Change: A Multi-Level Framework." *Business & Society* 56 (2): 253–282. https://doi.org/10.1177/0007650315576136.

Sovacool, Benjamin K., Dylan Furszyfer Del. Rio, and Steve Griffiths. 2020. "Contextualizing the Covid-19 Pandemic for a Carbon-Constrained World: Insights for Sustainability Transitions, Energy Justice, and Research Methodology." *Energy Research & Social Science* 68: 101701. https://doi.org/10.1016/j.erss.2020.101701.

Stammer, Detlef, Anita Engels, Jochem Marotzke, Eduardo Gresse, Christopher Hedemann, and Jan Petzold. 2021. *Hamburg Climate Futures Outlook: Assessing the Plausibility of Deep Decarbonization by 2050*. https://doi.org/10.25592/uhhfdm.9104.

Statham, Paul, and Hans-Jörg Trenz. 2013. *The Politicization of Europe: Contesting the Constitution in the Mass Media*. 8. London [u.a.]: Routledge.

Tosun, Jale, B. Guy, and Peters. 2021. "The Politics of Climate Change: Domestic and International Responses to a Global Challenge." *International Political Science Review* 42 (1): 3–15. https://doi.org/10.1177/0192512120975659.

von Zabern, Lena, and Christopher D. Tulloch. 2021. "Rebel with a Cause: The Framing of Climate Change and Intergenerational Justice in the German Press." *Media, Culture & Society* 43 (1): 23–47. https://doi.org/10.1177/0163443720960923.

Willis, Rebecca. 2020. *Too Hot to Handle? The Democratic Challenge of Climate Change*. Bristol: Bristol University Press.

Zürn, Michael. 2019. "Politicization Compared: At National, European, and Global Levels." *Journal of European Public Policy* 26 (7): 977–995. https://doi.org/10.1080/13501763.2019.1619188.

Annex: List of Documents Coded for the Empirical Analysis

European Union

European Council Conclusions

European Council. "Conclusions European Council 12 December 2019." General Secretariat of the Council, EUCO 29/19, December 12, 2019. https://www.consilium.europa.eu/media/41768/12-euco-final-conclusions-en.pdf.

———. "Conclusions European Council 22/23 June 2017." General Secretariat of the Council EUCO 8/17, June 23, 2017. https://www.consilium.europa.eu/media/23985/22-23-euco-final-conclusions.pdf.

———. "Conclusions European Council 23/24 October 2014." General Secretariat of the Council EUCO 169/14, October 24, 2014. https://www.consilium.europa.eu/media/24561/145397.pdf.

———. "Conclusions on Climate Diplomacy 26 February 2018." General Secretariat of the Council 6125/18, February 26, 2018. https://data.consilium.europa.eu/doc/document/ST-6125-2018-INIT/en/pdf.

———. "Conclusions on European Climate Diplomacy after COP 21, 15 February 2016." General Secretariat of the Council 6061/16, February 15, 2016. https://data.consilium.europa.eu/doc/document/ST-6061-2016-INIT/en/pdf.

———. "Council Conclusions on Paris Agreement and Preparations for the UNFCCC Meetings (Bonn, 6-17 November 2017)." General Secretariat of the Council, Press Office, October 13, 2017. https://www.consilium.europa.eu/en/press/press-releases/2017/10/13/conclusions-paris-agreement-and-unfccc-meetings/pdf.

———. "Preparations for the UNFCCC Meetings in Katowice (2 - 14 December 2018)." General Secretariat of the Council 12901/18, October 9, 2018. https://www.consilium.europa.eu/media/36619/st12901-en18.pdf.

———. "Preparations for the United Nations Framework Convention on Climate Change Meetings in Marrakech (7 - 18 November 2016)." General Secretariat of the Council 12807/16, September 30, 2016. https://data.consilium.europa.eu/doc/document/ST-12807-2016-INIT/en/pdf.

European Commission Documents

EU Commission. "A Clean Planet for All. A European Strategic Long-Term Vision for a Prosperous, Modern, Competitive and Climate Neutral Economy." Brussels, COM(2018) 773 final, November 28, 2018. https://eur-lex.europa.eu/legal-content/EN/TXT/PDF/?uri=CELEX:52018DC0773&from=EN.

———. "Accelerating Europe's Transition to a Low-Carbon Economy." Brussels, COM(2016) 500 final, July 20, 2016. https://eur-lex.europa.eu/legal-content/EN/TXT/PDF/?uri=CELEX:52016DC0500&from=EN.

———. "Energy Union Package. The Paris Protocol—A Blueprint for Tackling Global Climate Change beyond 2020." Brussels, COM(2015) 81 final, February 25, 2015. https://eur-lex.europa.eu/resource.html?uri=cellar:e27fdb4d-bdce-11e4-bbe1-01aa75ed71a1.0003.03/DOC_1&format=PDF.

———. "The European Green Deal." Brussels, COM(2019) 640 final, November 12, 2019. https://eur-lex.europa.eu/resource.html?uri=cellar:b828d165-1c22-11ea-8c1f-01aa75ed71a1.0002.02/DOC_1&format=PDF.

———. "The Road from Paris: Assessing the Implications of the Paris Agreement and Accompanying the Proposal for a Council Decision on the Signing, on Behalf of the European Union, of the Paris Agreement Adopted under the United Nations Framework Convention on Climate Change." Brussels, COM(2016) 110 final, February 3, 2016. https://eur-lex.europa.eu/legal-content/EN/TXT/PDF/?uri=CELEX:52016DC0110&from=EN.

European Parliament Plenary Resolutions

European Parliament. "Climate and Environmental Emergency (2019/2930(RSP))." Brussels P9_TA(2019)0078, November 28, 2019. https://www.europarl.europa.eu/doceo/document/TA-9-2019-0078_EN.pdf.

———. "Climate Change—A European Strategic Long-Term Vision for a Prosperous, Modern, Competitive and Climate Neutral Economy in Accordance with the Paris Agreement (2019/2582(RSP))." Brussels, P8_TA(2019)0217, March 14, 2019. https://www.europarl.europa.eu/doceo/document/TA-8-2019-0217_EN.html.

———. "Climate Diplomacy (2017/2272(INI))." Brussels, P8_TA(2018)0280, July 3, 2018. https://www.europarl.europa.eu/doceo/document/TA-8-2018-0280_EN.pdf.

———. "The European Green Deal—European Parliament Resolution (2019/2956(RSP))." Brussels, P9_TA(2020)0005, January 15, 2020. https://www.europarl.europa.eu/doceo/document/TA-9-2020-0005_EN.html.

———. "The Role of EU Regions and Cities in Implementing the COP 21 Paris Agreement on Climate Change (2017/2006(INI))." Brussels P8_TA(2018)0068, March 13, 2018. https://www.europarl.europa.eu/doceo/document/TA-8-2018-0068_EN.pdf.

———. "Towards a European Energy Union (2015/2113(INI))." Brussels P8_TA(2015)0444, December 15, 2015. https://www.europarl.europa.eu/doceo/document/TA-8-2015-0444_EN.pdf.

―――. "Towards a New International Climate Agreement in Paris (2015/2112(INI))." Brussels, P8_TA(2015)0359, October 14, 2015. http://www.europarl.europa.eu/sides/getDoc.do?pubRef=-//EP//TEXT+TA+P8-TA-2015-0359+0+DOC+XML+V0//EN.

―――. "UN Climate Change Conference (COP25)—Thursday, 28 November 2019 (2019/2712(RSP))." Brussels, P9_TA(2019)0079, November 28, 2019. https://www.europarl.europa.eu/doceo/document/TA-9-2019-0079_EN.html.

―――. "UN Climate Change Conference in Bonn, Germany (COP23) (2017/2620(RSP))." Brussels, P8_TA(2017)0380, October 4, 2017. http://www.europarl.europa.eu/sides/getDoc.do?pubRef=-//EP//TEXT+TA+P8-TA-2017-0380+0+DOC+XML+V0//EN.

―――. "UN Climate Change Conference in Katowice, Poland (COP24) (2018/2598(RSP))." Brussels, P8_TA-PROV(2018)0430, October 25, 2018. http://www.europarl.europa.eu/sides/getDoc.do?pubRef=-//EP//TEXT+TA+P8-TA-2018-0430+0+DOC+XML+V0//EN.

―――. "UN Climate Change Conference in Marrakesh, Morocco (COP22) (2016/2814(RSP))." Brussels, P8_TA(2016)0383, October 6, 2016. http://www.europarl.europa.eu/sides/getDoc.do?pubRef=-//EP//TEXT+TA+P8-TA-2016-0383+0+DOC+XML+V0//EN.

EP Party Group Motions on the European Green Deal

European Parliament. "Joint Motion for a Resolution on the European Green Deal on Behalf of the PPE, S &D, Renew and the Verts/ALE Group," January 14, 2020. https://www.europarl.europa.eu/doceo/document/RC-9-2020-0040_EN.html.

―――. "Motion for a Resolution on the European Green Deal on Behalf of the ECR Group, 10 January 2020 (2019/2956(RSP))." Brussels, B9-0041/2020, January 10, 2020. https://www.europarl.europa.eu/doceo/document/B-9-2020-0041_EN.html.

―――. "Motion for a Resolution on the European Green Deal on Behalf of the GUE / NGL Group, 10 January 2020 (2019/2956(RSP))." Brussels B9-0044/2020/REV, January 10,

2020. https://www.europarl.europa.eu/doceo/document/B-9-2020-0044_EN.html.

———. "Motion for a Resolution on the European Green Deal on Behalf of the ID Group, 10 January 2020," 2020. https://www.europarl.europa.eu/doceo/document/B-9-2020-0046_EN.html.

———. "Motion for a Resolution on the European Green Deal on Behalf of the PPE Group, 10 January 2020," 2020. https://www.europarl.europa.eu/doceo/document/B-9-2020-0042_EN.html.

———. "Motion for a Resolution on the European Green Deal on Behalf of the Renew Group, 10 January 2020," 2020. https://www.europarl.europa.eu/doceo/document/B-9-2020-0043_EN.html.

———. "Motion for a Resolution on the European Green Deal on Behalf of the S & D Group, 10 January 2020," 2020. https://www.europarl.europa.eu/doceo/document/B-9-2020-0045_EN.html.

———. "Motion for a Resolution on the European Green Deal on Behalf of the Verts / ALE Group, 10 January 2020," 2020. https://www.europarl.europa.eu/doceo/document/B-9-2020-0040_EN.html.

UNITED STATES

Executive Discourse—Policy Programs and Executive Orders

Obama Administration

White House. "Executive Order—Preparing the United States for the Impacts of Climate Change," November 1, 2013. https://obamawhitehouse.archives.gov/the-press-office/2013/11/01/executive-order-prEPAring-united-states-impacts-climate-change.

———. "Presidential Memorandum—Climate Change and National Security," September 21, 2016. https://obamawhitehouse.archives.gov/the-press-office/2016/09/21/presidential-memorandum-climate-change-and-national-security.

———. "Presidential Memorandum—Power Sector Carbon Pollution Standards," June 25, 2013. https://obamawhitehouse.archives.gov/the-press-office/2013/06/25/Presidential-memorandum-power-sector-carbon-pollution-standards.

———. "The National Security Implications of a Changing Climate." Executive Office of the President, Washington, DC, May 2015. https://obamawhitehouse.archives.gov/sites/default/files/docs/National_Security_Implications_of_Changing_Climate_Final_051915.pdf.

———. "The President's Climate Action Plan." Executive Office of the President, Washington DC, 2013. https://obamawhitehouse.archives.gov/sites/default/files/image/president27sclimateactionplan.pdf.

Department of Homeland Security. "Climate Action Plan." DHS, Washington DC, September 2013. https://www.dhs.gov/sites/default/files/publications/DHS%20Climate%20Action%20Plan.pdf.

Trump Administration
White House. "A Better Way to Ensure Clean, Reliable Energy, by Acting EPA Administrator Andrew Wheeler," August 21, 2018. https://trumpwhitehouse.archives.gov/articles/better-way-ensure-clean-reliable-energy/?utm_source=twitter&utm_medium=social&utm_campaign=wh.

———. "Executive Order on Promoting Energy Infrastructure and Economic Growth," April 10, 2019. https://www.federalregister.gov/documents/2019/04/15/2019-07656/promoting-energy-infrastructure-and-economic-growth.

———. "Executive Order: Reducing Regulation and Controlling Regulatory Costs." Federal Register Vol. 82, No. 22, January 30, 2017. https://www.federalregister.gov/documents/2017/02/03/2017-02451/reducing-regulation-and-controlling-regulatory-costs.

———. "Executive Order Regarding Efficient Federal Operations," May 17, 2018. https://trumpwhitehouse.archives.gov/presidential-actions/executive-order-regarding-efficient-federal-operations/.

———. "Presidential Executive Order on Promoting Energy Independence and Economic Growth," March 28, 2017. https://trumpwhitehouse.archives.gov/presidential-actions/presidential-executive-order-promoting-energy-independence-economic-growth/.

Executive Discourse—Presidential Speeches and Announcements

Obama Administration
White House. "Remarks by National Security Advisor Susan E. Rice on Climate Change and National Security at Stanford University." Office of the Press Secretary, October 12, 2015. https://obamawhitehouse.archives.gov/the-press-office/2015/10/12/remarks-national-security-advisor-susan-e-rice-climate-change-and.

———. "Remarks by President Obama at the First Session of COP21, Le Bourget, Paris, France." Office of the Press Secretary,

November 30, 2015. https://obamawhitehouse.archives.gov/the-press-office/2015/11/30/remarks-president-obama-first-session-cop21.

———. "Remarks by the President at U.N. Climate Change Summit, United Nations Headquarters, New York." Office of the Press Secretary, September 23, 2014. https://obamawhitehouse.archives.gov/the-press-office/2014/09/23/remarks-president-un-climate-change-summit.

———. "Remarks by the President on Climate Change at Georgetown University." Office of the Press Secretary, June 25, 2013. https://obamawhitehouse.archives.gov/the-press-office/2013/06/25/remarks-president-climate-change.

———. "Remarks by the President on Energy and Climate Change, Department of Energy, Washington, DC." Office of the Press Secretary, March 19, 2015. https://obamawhitehouse.archives.gov/the-press-office/2015/03/19/remarks-president-energy-and-climate-change.

———. "Statement by the President on the Paris Climate Agreement." Office of the Press Secretary, December 12, 2015. https://obamawhitehouse.archives.gov/the-press-office/2015/12/12/statement-president-paris-climate-agreement.

———. "U.S.-China Joint Presidential Statement on Climate Change." Office of the Press Secretary, September 25, 2015. https://obamawhitehouse.archives.gov/the-press-office/2015/09/25/us-china-joint-presidential-statement-climate-change.

———. "Weekly Address: Confronting the Growing Threat of Climate Change." Office of the Press Secretary, June 29, 2013. https://obamawhitehouse.archives.gov/the-press-office/2013/06/29/weekly-address-confronting-growing-threat-climate-change.

———. "Weekly Address: Meeting the Global Threat of Climate Change." Office of the Press Secretary, August 29, 2015. https://obamawhitehouse.archives.gov/the-press-office/2015/08/29/weekly-address-meeting-global-threat-climate-change.

Trump Administration

White House. "Remarks by President Trump at Signing of Executive Order to Create Energy Independence, Environmental Protection Agency Headquarters, Washington, D.C.," March 28, 2017. https://trumpwhitehouse.archives.gov/briefings-statements/remarks-president-trump-signing-executive-order-create-energy-independence/.

———. "Remarks by President Trump at the Unleashing American Energy Event, US Department of Energy, Washington, D.C.," June 29, 2017. https://trumpwhitehouse.archives.gov/briefings-statements/remarks-president-trump-unleashing-american-energy-event/.

———. "Remarks by President Trump on American Energy and Manufacturing | Monaca, PA," August 13, 2019. https://trumpwhitehouse.archives.gov/briefings-statements/remarks-president-trump-american-energy-manufacturing-monaco-pa/.

———. "Remarks by President Trump on America's Environmental Leadership, East Room," July 8, 2019. https://trumpwhitehouse.archives.gov/briefings-statements/remarks-president-trump-americas-environmental-leadership/.

———. "Remarks by President Trump on Environmental Accomplishments for the People of Florida | Jupiter, FL," September 8, 2020. https://trumpwhitehouse.archives.gov/briefings-statements/remarks-president-trump-environmental-accomplishments-people-florida-jupiter-fl/.

———. "Remarks by President Trump on Proposed National Environmental Policy Act Regulations," January 9, 2020. https://trumpwhitehouse.archives.gov/briefings-statements/remarks-president-trump-proposed-national-environmental-policy-act-regulations/.

———. "Remarks by President Trump on Renewable Energy," June 11, 2019. https://trumpwhitehouse.archives.gov/briefings-statements/remarks-president-trump-renewable-energy/.

———. "Remarks by President Trump on Restoring Energy Dominance in the Permian Basin | Midland, TX," July 29, 2020. https://trumpwhitehouse.archives.gov/briefings-statements/remarks-president-trump-restoring-energy-dominance-permian-basin-midland-tx/.

———. "Statement by President Trump on the Paris Climate Accord," June 1, 2017. https://trumpwhitehouse.archives.gov/briefings-statements/statement-president-trump-paris-climate-accord/.

Legislative Discourse—House Resolutions

Democrat-Sponsored Bills and Resolutions

114th Congress, H.R. 972. "To Amend the Internal Revenue Code of 1986 to Reduce Greenhouse Gas Emissions by Requiring a Federal Emission Permit for the Sale or Use of Covered Substances and to Return Funds to the American People." lead sponsor Mr. McDermott, February 13, 2015. https://www.congress.gov/bill/114th-congress/house-bill/972?q=%7B%22search%22%3A%5B%22114th+congress%2C+H.R.+972%22%2C%22114th%22%2C%22congress%2C%22%2C%22H.R.%22%2C%22972%22%5D%7D&s=7&r=15.

114th Congress, H.R. 1027. "To Cap the Emissions of Greenhouse Gases through a Requirement to Purchase Carbon Permits, to Distribute the Proceeds of Such Purchases to Eligible Individuals, and for Other Purposes." lead sponsor Mr. van Hollen, February 24, 2015. https://www.congress.gov/bill/114th-congress/house-bill/1027?q=%7B%22search%22%3A%5B%22H.R.+1027%2C+114th+congress%22%2C%22H.R.%22%2C%221027%22%2C%22114th%22%2C%22congress%22%5D%7D&r=21&s=6.

114th Congress, H.R. 4283. "To Amend the Internal Revenue Code of 1986 to Impose a Tax on Coal, Oil, and Natural Gas, and for Other Purposes." lead sponsor Mr. McNerney, December 17, 2015. https://www.congress.gov/bill/114th-congress/house-bill/4283?q=%7B%22search%22%3A%5B%22114th+congress%2C+H.R.+4283%22%2C%22114th%22%2C%22congress%2C%22%2C%22H.R.%22%2C%224283%22%5D%7D&s=8&r=2.

115th Congress, H.Con.Res. 137. "Expressing the Sense of Congress That the United States Is Committed to Ensuring a Safe and Healthy Climate for Future Generations, and to Cre- Ating Solutions for Restoring the Climate." lead sponsor Mr. Raskin, September 25, 2018. https://www.congress.gov/bill/115th-congress/house-concurrent-resolution/137?q=%7B%22search%22%3A%5B%22115th+congress%2C+H.Con.Res.+137%22%2C%22115th%22%2C%22congress%2C%22%2C%22H.Con.Res.%22%2C%22137%22%5D%7D&s=9&r=5.

115th Congress, H.R. 2014. "To Amend the Internal Revenue Code of 1986 to Impose an Excise Tax on Greenhouse Gas Emissions." lead sponsor Mr. Delaney, April 6, 2017. https://www.congress.gov/bill/115th-congress/house-bill/2014/text.

115th Congress, H.R. 2958. "To Reduce Greenhouse Gas Emissions and Protect the Climate." lead sponsor Mr. Ted Lieu of California, June 20, 2017. https://www.congress.gov/bill/115th-congress/house-bill/2958?r=82&s=1.

115th Congress, H.R. 4209. "To Rebuild the Nation's Infrastructure, Provide a Consumer Rebate to the American People, Assist Coal Country, Reduce Harmful Pollution, and for Other Purposes." lead sponsor Mr. Larson of Connecticut, November 1, 2017. https://www.congress.gov/bill/115th-congress/house-bill/4209.

115th Congress, H.R. 7173. "To Create a Carbon Dividend Trust Fund for the American People in Order to Encourage Market-Driven Innovation of Clean Energy Technologies and Market Efficiencies Which Will Reduce Harmful Pollution and Leave a Healthier, More Stable, and More Prosperous Nation for Future Generations." lead sponsor Mr. Deutch, November 27, 2018. https://www.congress.gov/bill/115th-congress/house-bill/7173.

115th Congress, H.R. 7220. "To Require the Secretary of State to Publish a Quarterly Assessment Regarding the Paris Agreement, and for Other Purposes." lead sponsor Mr. McEachin, December 6, 2018. https://www.congress.gov/bill/115th-congress/house-bill/7220?s=1&r=2.

115th Congress, H.Res. 85. "Expressing the Commitment of the House of Representatives to Continue to Support Pledges Made by the United States in the Paris Agreement." lead sponsor Mr. Krishnamoorthi, February 2, 2017. https://www.congress.gov/bill/115th-congress/house-resolution/85?r=48.

115th Congress, H.Res. 390. "Expressing Strong Disapproval of the President's Announcement to Withdraw the United States from the Paris Agreement." lead sponsor Mr. Schneider, June 16, 2017. https://www.congress.gov/bill/115th-congress/house-resolution/390.

115th Congress, H.Res. 660. "Recognizing the 2d Anniversary of the Adoption of the International Paris Agreement on Climate Change." lead sponsor Mr. Lowenthal, December 12, 2017. https://www.congress.gov/bill/115th-congress/house-resolution/660?r=87&s=1.

116th Congress, H.Con. Res. 15. "Expressing the Commitment of the Congress to the Paris Agreement." lead sponsor Mr. Huffman, February 8, 2019. https://www.congress.gov/bill/116th-congress/house-concurrent-resolution/15?r=5&s=1.

116th Congress, H.Con.Res. 35. "Expressing the Sense of Congress That the United States Is Committed to Ensuring a Safe and Healthy Climate for Future Generations, and to Cre- Ating Solutions for Restoring the Climate." lead sponsor Mr. Raskin, April 22, 2019. https://www.congress.gov/bill/116th-congress/house-concurrent-resolution/35?q=%7B%22search%22%3A%5B%22isPrivateBill%3A%5C%22Y%5C%22%22%5D%7D&r=9&s=1.

116th Congress, H.R. 9. "To Direct the President to Develop a Plan for the United States to Meet Its Nationally Determined Contribution under the Paris Agreement, and for Other Purposes." lead sponsor Mrs. Castor, May 6, 2019. https://www.congress.gov/bill/116th-congress/house-bill/9?q=%7B%22search%22%3A%5B%22S.+692%22%5D%7D.

116th Congress, H.R. 330. "To Reduce Greenhouse Gas Emissions and Protect the Climate." lead sponsor Mr. Ted Lieu of California, January 8, 2019. https://www.congress.gov/bill/116th-congress/house-bill/330.

116th Congress, H.R. 763. "To Create a Carbon Dividend Trust Fund for the American People in Order to Encourage Market-Driven Innovation of Clean Energy Technologies and Market Efficiencies Which Will Reduce Harmful Pollution and Leave a Healthier, More Stable, and More Prosperous Nation for Future Generations." lead sponsor Mr. Deutch, January 24, 2019. https://www.congress.gov/bill/116th-congress/house-bill/763.

116th Congress, H.R. 1960. "To Cap the Emissions of Greenhouse Gases Through a Requirement to Purchase Carbon Permits, to Distribute the Proceeds of Such Purchases to Eligible Individuals, and for Other Purposes." lead sponsor Mr. Beyer, March 28, 2019. https://www.congress.gov/bill/116th-congress/house-bill/1960/text.

116th Congress, H.R. 3966. "To Amend the Internal Revenue Code of 1986 to Reduce Social Security Payroll Taxes and to Reduce the Reliance of the United States Economy on Carbon-Based Energy Sources, and for Other Purposes." lead sponsor Mr. Lipinski, July 25, 2019. https://www.congress.gov/bill/116th-congress/house-bill/3966.

116th Congress, H.R. 4142. "To Rebuild the Nation's Infrastructure, Provide a Consumer Rebate to the American People, Assist Coal Country, Reduce Harmful Pollution, and for Other Purposes." lead sponsor Mr. Larson of Connecticut, August 2, 2019. https://www.congress.gov/bill/116th-congress/house-bill/4142.

116th Congress, H.R. 4986. "To Authorize Appropriations for Climate Financing, and for Other Purposes." lead sponsor Mr. Espaillat, November 5, 2019. https://www.congress.gov/bill/116th-congress/house-bill/4986?r=66&s=1.

116th Congress, H.R. 5457. "To Amend the Internal Revenue Code of 1986 to Impose an Excise Tax on Fuel Based on the Carbon Content of Such Fuel, and for Other Purposes." lead sponsor Mr. Sean Patrick Maloney of New York, December 17, 2019. https://www.congress.gov/bill/116th-congress/house-bill/5457.

116th Congress, H.R. 8175. "To Amend the Internal Revenue Code of 1986 to Impose a Tax on Fossil Fuels and to Use the Revenues for Economic Benefit." lead sponsor Mr. McNerney, September 4, 2020. https://www.congress.gov/bill/116th-congress/house-bill/8175.

116th Congress, H.Res. 109. "Recognizing the Duty of the Federal Government to Create a Green New Deal." lead sponsor Ms. Ocasio-Cortez, February 7, 2019. https://www.congress.gov/bill/116th-congress/house-resolution/109.

116th Congress, H.Res. 367. "Recognizing That Climate Change Most Severely Impacts Vulnerable and Dis- Advantaged Communities in the United States and around the World, and That It Is the Responsibility of the United States Government to Work with Its Global Partners to Promote Environmental Justice and Cli- Mate Justice." lead sponsor Mr. Espaillat, May 9, 2019. https://www.congress.gov/bill/116th-congress/house-resolution/367?s=1&r=30.

116th Congress, H.Res. 743. "Expressing Strong Disapproval of the President's Formal Notification to the United Nations of His Intent to Withdraw the United States from the Paris Agreement." lead sponsor Mr. Schneider, December 5, 2019. https://www.congress.gov/bill/116th-congress/house-resolution/743?s=1&r=42.

116th Congress, H.Res. 762. "Recognizing the 4th Anniversary of the Adoption of the International Paris Agreement on Climate Change." lead sponsor Mr. Lowenthal, December 12, 2019. https://www.congress.gov/bill/116th-congress/house-resolution/762?r=16&s=1.

Republican-Sponsored Bills and Resolutions
114th Congress, H.Con.Res. 97. "Expressing the Sense of Congress That the President Should Submit to the Senate for Advice and Consent the Climate Change Agreement Proposed for Adoption at the Twenty-First

Session of the Conference of the Parties to the United Nations Framework Convention on Climate Change, to Be Held in Paris, France from November 30 to December 11, 2015." lead sponsor Mr. Kelly of Pennsylvania, November 19, 2015. https://www.congress.gov/bill/114th-congress/house-concurrent-resolution/97.

114th Congress, H.Con.Res. 105. "Expressing the Sense of Congress Regarding the '"Paris Agreement"' Announced on December 12, 2015, at the 21st Session of the United Nations Framework Convention on Climate Change." lead sponsor Mr. McKinley, December 18, 2015. https://www.congress.gov/bill/114th-congress/house-concurrent-resolution/105?s=1&r=18.

114th Congress, H.Res. 218. "Expressing the Sense of the House of Representatives Regarding the Conditions for the United States Becoming a Signatory to Any International Agreement on Greenhouse Gas Emissions under the United Nations Framework Convention on Climate Change." lead sponsor Mr. Sensenbrenner, April 21, 2015. https://www.congress.gov/bill/114th-congress/house-resolution/218.

114th Congress, H.Res. 544. "Expressing the Sense of the House of Representatives That the President Should Submit Any Binding and Universal Agreement on Climate Change Adopted at the Conference of the Parties ('"COP21"') of the United Nations Framework Convention on Climate Change to the Senate as a Treaty under Article II, Section 2, Clause 2 of the Constitution." lead sponsor Mr. Yoho, December 1, 2015. https://www.congress.gov/bill/114th-congress/house-resolution/544?s=1&r=9.

115th Congress, H.Con.Res. 55. "Expressing the Sense of Congress That the United States Should Withdraw from the Paris Agreement, Adopted in December 2015." lead sponsor Mr. McKinley, May 18, 2017. https://www.congress.gov/bill/115th-congress/house-concurrent-resolution/55?r=30&s=1.

115th Congress, H.R. 6463. "To Amend the Internal Revenue Code of 1986 to Eliminate Certain Fuel Excise Taxes and Impose a Tax on Greenhouse Gas Emissions to Provide Revenue for Maintaining and Building American Infrastructure, and for Other Purposes." lead sponsor Mr. Curbelo, July 23, 2019. https://www.congress.gov/bill/115th-congress/house-bill/6463.

116th Congress, H.R. 4058. "To Amend the Internal Revenue Code of 1986 to Impose a Tax on Greenhouse Gas Emissions, Accordingly Reduce Tax Rates on Payroll, and for Other Purposes." lead sponsor Mr. Rooney, July 25, 2019. https://www.congress.gov/bill/116th-congress/house-bill/4058?r=7&s=1.

116th Congress, H.R. 4520. "To Amend the Internal Revenue Code of 1986 to Eliminate Certain Fuel Excise Taxes and Impose a Tax on Greenhouse Gas Emissions to Provide Revenue for Maintaining and Building American Infrastructure, and for Other Purposes." lead sponsor Mr. Fitzpatrick, September 26, 2019. https://www.congress.gov/bill/116th-congress/house-bill/4520?r=12&s=1.

116th Congress, H.Res. 676. "Expressing the Sense of the House of Representatives That the United States Should Formally Withdraw from the Paris Agreement." lead sponsor Mr. Arrington, November 1, 2019. https://www.congress.gov/bill/116th-congress/house-resolution/676?r=93&s=1.

Legislative Discourse—Senate Resolutions

Democrat-Sponsored Bills and Resolutions
114th Congress, S. 1548. "To Amend the Internal Revenue Code of 1986 to Provide for Carbon Dioxide and Other Greenhouse Gas Emission Fees, Reduce the Rate of the Corporate Income Tax, Provide Tax Credits to Workers, Deliver Additional Benefits to Retired and Disabled Americans, and for Other Purposes." lead sponsor Mr. Whitehouse, June 10, 2015. https://www.congress.gov/bill/114th-congress/senate-bill/1548?s=1&r=61.

114th Congress, S. 2399. "To Provide for Emissions Reductions, and for Other Purposes." lead sponsor Mr. Sanders, December 10, 2015. https://www.congress.gov/bill/114th-congress/senate-bill/2399.

115th Congress, S.Res. 155. "Expressing the Sense of the Senate That the United States Should Work in Cooperation with the International Community and Continue to Exercise Global Leadership to Address the Causes and Effects of Climate Change, and for Other Purposes." lead sponsor Mr. Cardin, May 4, 2017. https://www.congress.gov/bill/115th-congress/senate-resolution/155?s=1&r=36.

115th Congress, S.Res. 342. "Expressing the Sense of the Senate That States, Cities, Tribal Nations, Busi- Nesses, and Institutions of Higher Education in the United States Should Work towards Achieving the Goals of the Paris Agreement." lead sponsor Mr. Markey, November 16, 2017. https://www.congress.gov/bill/115th-congress/senate-resolution/342.

116th Congress, S. 1128. "To Amend the Internal Revenue Code of 1986 to Provide for Carbon Dioxide and Other Greenhouse Gas Emission Fees, Provide Tax Credits to Workers, Deliver Additional Benefits to

Retired and Disabled Americans, and for Other Purposes." lead sponsor Mr. Whitehouse, April 10, 2019. https://www.congress.gov/bill/116th-congress/senate-bill/1128?s=1&r=68.

116th Congress, S. 1743. "To Direct the President to Develop a Plan for the United States to Meet Its Nationally Determined Contribution under the Paris Agreement, and for Other Purposes." lead sponsor Mrs. Shaheen, June 5, 2019. https://www.congress.gov/bill/116th-congress/senate-bill/1743.

116th Congress, S. 4484. "To Amend the Internal Revenue Code of 1986 to Establish a Carbon Fee to Reduce Greenhouse Gas Emissions, and for Other Purposes." lead sponsor Mr. Durbin, August 6, 2020. https://www.congress.gov/bill/116th-congress/senate-bill/4484?q=%7B%22search%22%3A%5B%22%5B2020-09-15+TO+2020-09-15%5D%22%5D%7D&r=7&s=1.

116th Congress, S. Res. 59. "Recognizing the Duty of the Federal Government to Create a Green New Deal." lead sponsor Mr. Markey, February 7, 2019. https://www.congress.gov/bill/116th-congress/senate-resolution/59?s=1&r=8.

116th Congress, S.Res. 404. "Expressing the Sense of the Senate That the United States Should Work in Cooperation with the International Community and Continue to Exercise Global Leadership to Address the Causes and Effects of Climate Change, and for Other Purposes." lead sponsor Mr. Cardin, October 31, 2019. https://www.congress.gov/bill/116th-congress/senate-resolution/404.

116th Congress, S.Res. 449. "Expressing the Sense of the Senate That the Nation, States, Cities, Tribal Nations, and Businesses, Institutions of Higher Education, and Other Insti- Tutions in the United States Should Work toward Achieving the Goals of the Paris Agreement." lead sponsor Mr. Markey, December 10, 2019. https://www.congress.gov/bill/116th-congress/senate-resolution/449?r=32&s=1.

Republican-Sponsored Bills and Resolutions
114th Congress, S.Con.Res. 25. "Expressing the Sense of Congress That the President Should Submit the Paris Climate Change Agreement to the Senate for Its Advice and Consent." lead sponsor Mr. Lee, November 19, 2015. https://www.congress.gov/bill/114th-congress/senate-concurrent-resolution/25.

114th Congress, S.Res. 290. "Expressing the Sense of the Senate That Any Protocol to, or Other Agreement Regarding, the United Nations Framework Convention on Climate Change of 1992, Negotiated at the 2015 United Nations Climate Change Con- Ference in Paris Will Be

Considered a Treaty Requiring the Advice and Consent of the Senate." lead sponsor Mr. Paul, October 20, 2015. https://www.congress.gov/bill/114th-congress/senate-resolution/290.

114th Congress, S.Res. 329. "Expressing the Sense of the Senate Regarding an Agreement Reached at the United Nations Climate Change Conference Held in Paris in December 2015." lead sponsor Mr. Inhofe, December 7, 2015. https://www.congress.gov/bill/114th-congress/senate-resolution/329.

115th Congress, S. Con. Res. 17. "Expressing the Sense of Congress That the United States Should Withdraw from the Paris Agreement, Adopted in December 2015." lead sponsor Mr. Paul, May 22, 2017. https://www.congress.gov/bill/115th-congress/senate-concurrent-resolution/17.

Dictionary of keywords used for coding EU policy documents

	Paradigmatic terms	*Programmatic terms*	*Policy terms*
Economic	Climate neutral Economic growth Neutral economy Green growth Industry Investment Market carbon economy	Energy efficiency Circular economy Energy market Energy System Resource efficiency competitiveness	Emission trade Carbon price Trade system Cost effective Supply chain Business model digitalisation
Political	Global Climate Third country Internt'l ccooperation Climate ambition Ambitious climate UN Climate Global leader Framework convention	Climate action Climate diplomacy Carbon leakage Climate objective Climate target agenda border adjustment implementation	Action Plan Council conclusion Legislative Determined Contr Impact assessment
Risk	Climate resilient Security Risk Flood Effects of climate Impacts of climate Climate impact Climate disaster Extreme weather	Public health Regional stability Refugee migratory Food security International security	Adaptation action Adaptation to climate Resil't infrastructure Risk management Risk assessment Capacity building Climate proofing Preparedness

(continued)

ANNEX: LIST OF DOCUMENTS CODED FOR THE EMPIRICAL ... 249

(continued)

	Paradigmatic terms	*Programmatic terms*	*Policy terms*
Justice	Climate justice Responsibility Future generations Gender Women Solidarity Human right Most vulnerable Least developed	Just transition Inclusive transition Developed country Climate finance Socially sustainable Social impact Social cohesion	Development goal Energy poverty Transition mech'sm Transition fund Social protection Social security Green Climate Fund
Ecology	Global warming Species Pollution Environmental Biodiversity Ecosystem planet temperature	Sustainable dev.mt Zero greenhouse Environm'tl protection Animal welfare Decarbonisation Green transition Ecological transition	Clean energy Farm to fork Deforestation Land use Water habitat
Society	Civil Society Non state actor Citizen Culture Identity Local People Community sovereignty Tradition	City Region Private Urban	Voluntary Flexible Quality of life Daily life lifestyle sharing economy

Dictionary of keywords used for coding US policy documents

	Paradigmatic terms	*Programmatic terms*	*Policy terms*
Economic	Growth Economic Jobs Industrial Investment Market-based	Energy efficiency Coal Natural gas Technology Energy resource Carbon economy	Cap and trade Carbon permit Emission permit Carbon fee Equivalency fee Carbon dividend Trade intensity

(continued)

(continued)

	Paradigmatic terms	Programmatic terms	Policy terms
Political	Great job Frankework convent'n Nations framework Global effort Global leader Cooperation	Climate action Carbon border Border fee American energy Reduction target	Taxable carbon Action plan Determined Contr Legislative Protection Agency
Risk	National security Extreme weather Sea level Health Heat wave Risk Migration Global threat	Homeland security Climate assessmt Climate impact Critical infrastrctre Public health	Change adaptation Clim preparedness Resilience Risk assessment Risk management
Justice	Climate justice injustice Future generations Gender Vulnerable Solidarity	Social Security Social Cost Poverty Line Wage Developing countries Climate finance	Refund program Dividend Trust Climate Trust Climate fund Energy refund
Ecology	Global warming Healthy Climate Environmental Carbon pollution Natural Resource Biodiversity Ecosystem Planet	Zero emission Net-zero Decarbonization Sustainable	Clean energy Clean water Forest Habitat Wildlife Natural conservtn
Society	Communities Citizen Worker American people Indigenous people Tribal Civil society Way of life	City Urban Region Local Municipal	Voluntary Private Consumer Flexible Corporate social

Index

A

Administrative presidency, 122, 123, 126, 127, 129, 137, 176, 177, 220

Advocacy, 7, 8, 18, 36, 82, 85, 90, 91, 145, 148, 150, 155–160, 178
  and discourse, 4, 20, 21, 35, 36, 120, 121, 136, 137, 162, 189, 200, 220, 227
  and framing analysis, 220

Advocacy Coalition Framework (ACF), 137

Affordable Clean Energy Act (ACE), 120, 126, 128, 129, 177

Agenda-setting, 8, 16, 18, 66, 70, 71, 76, 81–83, 101, 218, 220

Alarmism, 41

America Wins Act, 151–153

Annex I countries, 123

Anthropocene, 3, 21, 37

Appropriation of environmentalism, 203

Aronoff, Kate, 155

Article 111 (d), 127

Attitudes towards climate change, 8

Attribution science, 2

Automated coding, 54, 94, 161

Aykut, Stefan, 21, 22, 69, 218, 219

B

Bäckstrand, Karin, 1, 7

Barrasso, John, 149

Bicameralism, 6, 122, 220

Biden, Joseph
  2020 campaign pledges, 6, 134
  infrastructure and social security bill 2021, 224
  re-joinder to Paris Agreement, 6

Biedenkopf, Katja, 8, 22, 73, 87

Biodiversity, 40, 47, 80, 93, 95, 106, 206

Bledsoe, Paul, 158

Blockade of decision-making, 222

Blue vs Red debate, 160

Boykoff, Max, 21

Brewer, Thomas, 7, 15, 16, 119, 123, 124
Build Back Better, 132, 224
Bulkeley, Harriet, 22, 125, 227
Burns, Charlotte, 82
Byrd/Hagel resolution, 123

C
C40, 125
California, 7, 11, 14, 125, 130, 132–134
Cap and trade, 144, 148, 151
Carbon border adjustment mechanism, 74, 81
Carbon capture and storage, 158
Carbon leakage, 74, 87
Carbon neutrality, 6, 10, 18, 65, 72, 84, 154, 157, 176, 223, 227
Carbon pollution, 127, 139, 164, 167, 219
Carbon pricing, 5, 7, 120, 135, 145, 146, 148, 151–153, 161, 162, 165, 166, 170, 175, 194, 204, 213, 222
Carlarne, Cinnamon, 7, 8, 119
Case study, 21, 23, 44, 55, 70, 92, 93, 121, 122, 161, 162, 166, 167, 195, 196, 199, 221
Castor, Kathy, 151
Center for Climate and Energy Solutions (C2ES), 151, 157, 158
Central and Eastern European Countries, 15
Chakrabarti, Saikrat, 159
China, 69, 81, 139, 141, 166
Circular economy, 78, 80, 93, 204, 221
Cities, 43, 97, 98, 125, 172, 206
Citizens, 46, 85, 97, 98, 103, 107, 154, 162, 164, 165, 172
Citizens' Climate Lobby, 146, 157
Claims-making, 44

Clean Air Act, 124, 127, 130, 131, 140, 177
Clean Power Plan (CPP), 119, 124, 126–129, 140, 177, 224
Climate Action Network (CAN), 91
Climate Action Now Act, 150
Climate capitalism, 45
Climate change
    and observation bias, 2, 14, 36, 44, 90, 95, 100, 105, 107, 121, 141, 161, 166, 168, 171, 174, 177, 190, 197, 224
    attribution, 2
    definition, 1, 3, 5, 40, 43, 164, 188, 214, 222
    ideational dimension, 2
    use of term, 58
Climate denial, 5, 22, 107, 222
Climate diplomacy, 71–73, 75, 87, 88, 93, 94
Climate emergency, 89, 94
Climate Futures Outlook, 218
Climate Hawks, 157
Climate hysteria, 41
Climate Impact Lab, 13
Climate justice, 41, 47, 94, 103, 109, 139, 143, 152, 162, 194, 221, 222
Climate neutrality, 68, 72–75, 78, 79, 82, 84, 89, 225
Climate Policy Index, 14
Climate resilience, 167
Climate skepticism, 48, 106, 142
Climate Solutions Caucus, 146, 147, 151, 152, 157
Climate targets, 70, 88, 107, 223
    longer-term to 2050, 9, 68, 74
    mid-term to 2030, 9, 10, 93
ClimateWire, 147, 148, 159, 160
Clusters of frames, 108, 195
CO_2 Coalition, 159, 160
Code, 99, 161, 167, 189, 195, 201

Code map, 99–104, 167–171, 173
Collective action category, 38, 190, 213
Comparative federalism, 15
Comparative politics, 24, 35, 53, 58, 109, 188
Competitive Enterprise Institute (CEI), 159
Complexity, 92, 135, 219
Conciliation, 17
Conditionality of recovery funds, 223
Conference of the Parties (COP), 69, 71, 75
  COP 21, 87, 138
Congress. *See* Senate and House of Representatives
Consensus system, 17
Contestation, 2, 4–7, 10, 19, 23, 24, 35, 48–52, 55–58, 66, 85, 92, 95, 97, 104, 108, 122, 125, 133, 135, 160, 162, 173–176, 187–189, 195, 200, 206, 209–214, 220, 221, 227, 228
Contested federalism, 122, 123, 126–129, 177, 220
Cooler Heads Coalition, 159
Co-sponsors of legislation, 152, 153, 155
Covid-19
  and climate change, 223–225
  recovery measures, 223

D
Daviter, Falk, 36, 70
Decarbonization, 10, 76, 119, 125, 128, 178, 217, 223, 226
Delbeke, Jos, 7, 67, 68
Delegated acts, 84, 122
Deliberation, 22
  in the European Parliament, 23
  in global climate governance, 20

Democratization of climate governance, 20, 23, 90
Department of Energy, 140
Deutch, Ted, 146, 151, 152
'Devil shift', 137
Dictionary, 54, 55, 94, 95, 161
Dictionary-based coding, 54
Directorate-General Climate (DG), 18
Discourse
  critical approaches, 109
  definition, 194, 196
  in discursive institutionalism, 47, 54
  variants of justification, 39
Distributive justice, 39
Division of powers, 15–17, 220
Dryzek, John, 1–4, 21, 23, 37, 90

E
Ebell, Myron, 159
Ecological framing, 41, 42, 106, 162, 164, 169, 203, 212, 215
Ecology, 46, 47, 170, 190, 194, 197, 201, 202, 204, 206, 210, 222
Eco-Modernism, 45
Economic framing, 101, 102, 105, 106, 109, 165, 166, 170, 172, 178, 194, 201, 202, 204, 213, 214, 222, 224
Economic interests, 8, 11
Efficiency, 2, 38, 45, 47, 48, 67, 70, 78, 80, 85, 94, 125, 129–131, 133, 134, 136, 138, 149, 154, 166, 204, 212, 213, 221, 226
Effort sharing regulation, 15, 70
Emission trading, 8, 10, 11, 16, 22, 45, 70, 85–87, 125, 136, 151
Emission trading system (ETS), 10, 67
Energy independence, 140, 142, 172, 222

Energy policy, 11, 136, 140, 142, 145, 146, 165, 166, 171, 173, 226
Entman, Robert, 36
ENVI, 19, 83, 85
Environmental Protection Agency (EPA), 18, 120, 124, 127–133, 135, 147, 159, 160
Ethical reasoning, 40
EU and US
  as agents of global climate governance, 5, 7, 87, 88, 121, 125
  as multi-level systems, 6, 8, 15, 17, 122, 220
  case studies, 7, 8, 21, 22, 24, 54, 59, 109, 135, 187, 197
  climate policy output, 5, 221
  direct comparison, 7, 23, 105, 219
  institutional similarities, 6, 15, 17, 20, 122
  rationales of comparison, 5
EU climate and energy package, 70, 76, 85
EU climate law, 65, 70, 82–85, 107
EU Member States, 7, 12–15, 67, 70, 71, 73, 83–85, 87, 88, 221, 226
European Central Bank, 223
European Climate Pact, 81, 90
European Commission, 16, 18, 67, 71, 72, 81, 93, 94, 101, 193
European Conservatives and Reformists (ECR), 93, 105, 106
European Council (EC), 16, 53, 67, 71, 72, 74–76, 81, 92–94, 193, 197, 202, 221
European Environmental Bureau (EEB), 91
European Green Deal (EGD), 5, 6, 9, 53, 59, 65, 66, 68, 70, 72, 74, 75, 77, 79, 80, 82, 89, 92–95, 98, 103–105, 107, 108, 176, 190, 203, 221
European Investment Bank (EIB), 73, 81
European Parliament (EP)
  committees, 17, 19, 83, 85
  and global climate agreements, 87
  leadership, 16
  party groups, 19, 53, 83, 85, 86, 89, 93–96, 98, 103–105, 108, 190
  policy record, 68
  resolutions, 53, 82, 87–90, 92, 93, 95, 98, 102–105, 108, 190, 193
European People's Party (EPP), 86, 93, 105, 106
European Semester, 79, 81, 223
Eurosceptic groups, 86
Executive action, 7, 11, 120, 126, 127, 131, 132, 135, 222
Executive agreement, 123
Executive institutions, 16, 81
Experimentation, 22
Expertise, 18, 20, 22, 157, 158
Extraction tax, 135
Extreme weather, 2, 11, 37, 43, 47, 106

F
Falkner, Robert, 4
Farm to fork, 80, 93
Federalism, 129
Feinstein, Dianne, 151–153
Filibuster, 17
Fossil fuels, 3, 15, 129
  extraction and use, 136, 142, 175
Fourth Climate Assessment Report, 175
Fracking, 136
Fragmentation, 58, 125, 136, 174, 177

of policy-making, 5
of political discourse, 221
Frames
  operationalization, 53, 55–57, 107
  scope, 37, 47, 100, 178, 195–198, 213, 214
  typology, 5, 35, 37–39, 41, 43, 44, 46, 47, 67, 160, 219
Framing analysis, 51, 58, 66, 67, 87, 138, 200, 220
Freedom, 42, 43, 86, 143, 175, 226
Fridays for Future, 41, 91, 155, 228
Friedman, Thomas, 155
Friends of the Earth (FoE), 91, 156

G
Gaetz, Matt, 147
Gender, 97, 102, 105, 109, 153, 154, 175, 222
Generation, 127, 129
German federal election 2021, 225
'Getting to Zero' proposal, 157
Glasgow/COP 22, 68, 75, 88, 121
Global Adaptation Index, 12, 14
Global governance, 3, 6, 21, 39, 227
Globalized multi-level governance, 6, 71
Green Climate Fund, 68, 123, 150
Green conditionality, 81
Green growth, 45
Greenhouse gas (GHG), 5, 9, 10, 23, 66–68, 72, 76, 78, 79, 81–85, 89, 90, 106, 119, 122–124, 126, 129, 135–137, 144, 148, 151, 153, 154
  link with climate change, 84, 106
  reduction targets, 15, 67, 83, 86, 122, 126
Green New Deal
  activists, 42, 154, 155
  conceptual origins, 154, 158
  resolution in Congress, 120
Green party group, 106
Greenpeace, 91
Guteland, Jytte, 83

H
Habitat, 40, 80, 136, 142, 162
Handbooks of climate governance, 7
Healthy Family and Climate Securities Act, 151–153
Heartland Institute, 159
Helbling, Marc, 36, 188
Hoax, 42, 107, 120, 149, 166, 222
Homeland Security, 143
House Committees, 145
House of Representatives, 17, 18, 20, 120, 144, 146–148, 157, 175
Hulme, Mike, 3, 40, 43, 227
Hypotheses
  application to comparative analysis, 24, 35, 48, 51, 53, 58, 59, 187, 221
  discussion, 52, 55, 58, 188
  overview, 53, 55
  presentation and discussion, 55

I
Ideas of climate change, 1–4, 8, 20, 21, 23, 24, 36, 37, 41, 99, 218
Identity, 20, 40, 42, 107, 109
Identity & Democracy group (ID), 86, 93, 105–107
Ideology, 4, 20, 24, 39, 44, 49, 50, 58, 104, 108, 120, 139, 166, 172, 188, 219, 220, 222, 225
Inhofe, James, 42, 44, 128, 149
Institutions, 7, 9, 13, 16, 18–20, 23, 24, 39, 42, 43, 48, 53, 66, 67, 71, 81–84, 86–92, 94, 95, 97–100, 103, 107–109, 145,

156, 193, 199, 203, 212, 218, 220, 221, 227, 228
Instrumental rationality, 37, 47
Inter-coder reliability, 54
Interest groups, 156
Intergenerational justice, 174
Interim (2030) targets, 10, 83
Intra-frame contestation, 48, 50, 200, 203–211
Investment, 12, 58, 66, 73, 79, 81, 94, 95, 97, 99, 108, 109, 129, 132, 138, 144, 145, 154, 178, 204, 205, 212, 213, 221, 223–225
IPCC, 44, 77
Issue category, 24, 35–39, 42–46, 48–52, 57, 58, 161, 162, 164, 174, 188–190, 193, 194, 199, 212–214, 219, 221
Issue dimension, 4, 22, 23, 38, 46, 49, 52, 53, 57, 58, 86, 87, 160, 174, 176, 187, 188, 193, 198, 212, 213, 218–222, 225, 227
ITRE, 19, 83, 85

J

Jahn, Detlef, 8, 16, 18
Jamieson, Dale, 2
Johnson, Boris, 225
Jordan, Andrew, 22, 45, 109
Justice frame, 41, 97, 106, 165, 170, 190, 198, 209, 221
Justification, 1, 5, 36, 39, 40, 42–44, 46–48, 50, 54, 57, 58, 65, 95, 96, 100, 101, 106, 120, 202, 209, 213, 218
Justificatory ideas, 37

K

Karapin, Roger, 7, 14, 15, 119, 136
Kerry, John, 18

Keystone XL, 136
Klimapaket/climate policy package, 46
Kriesi, Hanspeter, 42, 49, 188
Kyoto Protocol, 8, 68, 76, 82, 124
  ratification in US, 6, 123

L

Lakoff, George, 35
Leadership
  in conceptual terms, 3
  of European Parliament, 16
  by US in environmental policy, 3
League of Conservations Voters (LCV), 156
Left/right politics, 108, 175, 226
Leggett, Jane, 124
Legislative initiative, 132, 156, 165, 214
Legislative politics, 18
Lifestyles, 3, 78
Lijphart, Arend, 17
Linkages of frames
  in comparative perspective, 195, 199, 212
  in conceptual terms, 188
  in EU policy discourse, 51, 92, 108
  in US policy discourse, 167
  measurement, 52, 55, 56
  scope and density, 196
Lövbrand, Eva, 1, 7, 21, 49

M

Mainstreaming, 72, 73, 75, 81, 88, 223, 225
Mann, Michael, 120
Markey/Waxman bill, 16, 144
Markey, Ed, 148, 155
Marshall, George, 21
Marshall Institute, 159
Material factors, 8, 11, 43
MaxQDA, 54

McCarthy, Gina, 18
McConnell, Mitch, 155
Meckling, Jonas, 8, 22, 35, 218
Media frames, 21
Merkel, Angela, 46
Middle Ages warm period, 44
Mid-term election, 148, 149, 151, 153, 154
Migration, 3, 106, 154, 178, 226, 228
Mildenberger, Matto, 7
Milkoreit, Manjana, 122, 123, 125
Moral reasoning, 40
Multilateralism, 75, 143, 222
Multi-level governance, 6, 23, 71, 129, 220

N
Nationalism, 43, 143
Narrative Policy Framework (NPF), 137
Narratives, 21, 41
National Climate Action Program, 139
National Climate Assessment Report, 143
Nationalist right parties, 22, 42
Nationally Determined Contribution (NDC), 9, 10, 75, 124, 151
National Security Council (NSA), 143, 159
Nature, 40, 41, 57, 121
Net-zero targets, 9, 10, 77
New Consensus Project, 158, 159
Newell, Peter, 36, 45
New York state, 7, 14
NextGenerationEU, 223
Non-state actor zone for climate action (NAZCA), 125
Normative rationality, 37, 47

O
Obama, Barack
  address to Georgetown University, 139
  climate policy record, 147
  speeches to climate summit, 138
Oberthür, Sebastian, 4, 7, 68, 71
O'Brien, Karen, 3, 40
Ocasio-Cortez, Alexandra, 149, 153, 156, 159
Okereke, Chukwumerije, 3, 23, 41
One Planet for All communication, 77, 93
Ordinary Legislative Procedure (OLP), 17, 83
Ostrom, Elinor, 22
Otto, Friederike, 2

P
Paradigm, 47, 80, 103, 174, 200, 225
Paradigmatic salience, 57, 201–203, 212
Paris Agreement
  ratification in EU, 6
  ratification in US, 6, 123, 150
  resolutions in House and Senate, 150
  withdrawal and re-joinder of US, 6, 121
Parliamentary systems, 16, 17
Pettifor, Ann, 155
Phase IV, 67, 85
Planet, 139, 164, 172, 208
Polarization, 5, 7, 24, 40, 49–53, 57, 58, 86, 122, 139, 160, 162, 173, 174, 177, 188, 189, 200, 201, 203, 213, 214, 218, 222, 226
Policy beliefs, 1, 22, 218, 220
Policy change, 4, 22, 38, 39, 47, 176
Policy continuity, 66
Policy cycle, 45, 66, 67, 70, 71, 76, 82

Policy evaluation category, 38, 175
Policy paradigms, 47, 225
Political frame, 45, 100, 105, 176, 198, 206
Political parties
  and issue dimensions, 22, 49, 58, 86, 176
  and polarization, 6, 49, 58, 226
  and positions on climate change, 20–22, 105, 153, 154
Political space, 1, 4, 5, 24, 35, 48, 49, 51, 54, 57, 58, 86, 109, 187, 188, 212, 220–222
Politicization, 160, 217, 226–228
Politics v policy, 23, 177, 228
Polycentric, 4, 22, 23
Popovski, Vesselin, 4, 22, 68
Position data, 220
Prakash, Varshini, 155
Presidentialism, 7, 10, 16, 18, 53, 68, 121, 122, 127, 137, 139, 140, 150, 156, 174, 178, 197, 199, 213, 214, 221
Problem definition category, 37, 174
Progressive Policy Institute (PPI), 158
Pruitt, Scott, 128, 135, 160

Q
Qualified majority voting, 17
Qualitative approach, 160
Quantitative content analysis, 67

R
Rabe, Barry, 7, 119, 122, 123, 136, 144, 153
Rank order
  of frames, 98, 164, 189, 191, 192
  of keywords, 54, 57, 95, 204, 210, 211
  of linkages between frames, 198
Rapporteur, 19, 20, 83

Ratification, 6, 123, 150
Recovery programs, 223
Regional Greenhouse Gas Initiative (RGGI), 11, 125
Renewable energy, 16, 70, 75, 78, 129, 154
Renew group, 105
Resources, 12, 40, 43, 73, 88, 136, 153, 213
  economic, 1, 45
  political, 45
Risk frame, 43, 209, 210, 212
Road Map from Paris, 76, 93
Rooney, Francis, 146, 151, 152

S
Salience
  as aspect of polarization, 57, 214
  paradigmatic salience, 57, 103, 200–203, 212
Scenarios, 77, 78, 218
Schmidt, Vivien, 35, 39, 47, 54
Scope
  of climate frames, 46, 201
  of framing linkages, 198
  of political action, 38, 143
Sea level rise, 138, 140
Securitization, 20
Select Committee on the Climate Crisis, 19, 151
Senate and House of Representatives, 18, 144, 146
Senate Committees, 128, 145
Senate of the United States, 17, 44, 123, 124, 128, 146, 155
Sierra Club, 156
Similarity indicator, 58, 204, 206, 210, 211
Similarity of keyword rank orders, 209
Socialists and Democrats (S&D), 83, 86, 105

Social security, 152, 165, 170, 208, 224
Society frame, 42, 46, 165–167, 172, 190, 197, 203, 209
Spending targets, 81
Sponsor, 121, 159
Squad, 156
Stakeholder consultation, 90
State vs market, 73, 226
Stern Report, 44
Structure of framing
  comparative hypotheses, 51, 188
  in comparative perspective, 15, 22, 23, 58, 122, 195, 199, 212
  in conceptual terms, 92, 219
  in EU policy discourse, 51, 92, 96, 97, 107
  in US policy discourse, 160, 161, 163
Sunrise Movement, 155, 158
Supranationalism, 6, 9, 16, 39, 86
Supreme Court, 126–128, 140, 177
Sustainability, 45, 106–108, 120, 164, 177, 225
Sustainable Energy and Environment Coalition (SEEC), 147

T
Thunberg, Greta, 69, 91, 92
Timmermans, Frans, 69
Tonko, Paul, 147, 148
Transnational governance, 43
Trilogue, 83, 85
Trump, Donald
  policy record, 128–129, 131–132, 136
  public appearances, 142, 165
  withdrawal from Paris Agreement, 41, 72, 141, 150, 160
Two degrees target, 122, 136, 177

U
Uncertainty, 4, 130, 143
UN framework, 150, 166, 204, 222
UN Framework Convention on Climate Change (UNFCCC), 72, 124, 160
US states
  and federal government, 11, 53, 130, 133, 135, 143, 154, 165, 174, 222
  Climate Policy Index, 14
  vulnerability, 12–14, 220, 224

V
Vehicle emission standards, 132, 134, 177
Veto points, 16, 17, 47, 218, 220
Voluntary standards, 133
von der Leyen, Ursula, 6, 65
Vulnerability, 11–14, 219, 220, 224

W
Wehling, Elisabeth, 35
Wheeler, Andrew, 128
White House, 10, 18, 69, 127, 137–141, 144, 158–161, 165, 174
Whitehouse, Sheldon, 148, 151
Wicked problem, 2
Withdrawal of US from Paris Agreement, 41, 121, 150, 151
Workers, 142, 154, 162, 165, 167, 172, 194, 208
World Wildlife Fund (WWF), 91, 156

Z
Zero-carbon pledge, 130
Zürn, Michael, 6, 71, 227

Printed by Printforce, the Netherlands